Sceptical Histo

M000308727

'The analysis of the complexities of feminist (post-colonial) scholarship is well worth the price of purchase . . . [S]tudents and teachers alike will find this book an invaluable introduction to the nature of history as it is understood and contested today.'

Alun Munslow, *University of Chichester*

'One of the great virtues of the book is that it uses examples from historical writing worldwide, examining global subjects . . . [T]he book is clearly written and full of insights about a wide range of historical topics. It is a welcome handbook for both teachers and students, even for advanced historians who want to know more about postmodern theory.'

Bonnie Smith, *Rutgers University*

Sceptical History familiarises readers with the postmodern critique of history whilst also focusing upon the question of how to practise postmodernist feminist (sceptical) history.

A highly original work, this book considers major themes including cultural, class and sexual identity and 'difference', weaving them into debates on the nature and methods of history. In so doing it arrives at new ways of doing 'history and theory' that do not exclude feminist approaches nor attention to non-Western history.

Hélène Bowen Raddeker's arguments extend beyond the postmodernist critique of history to other aspects of postmodernist thinking, including the post-colonial challenge to humanism and eurocentric metanarratives of progress. Using a wide range of historical and cultural examples, she draws extensively on feminist scholarship and historiography.

Sceptical History provides an accessible guide to some of the most complex theories current today.

Hélène Bowen Raddeker is Senior Lecturer in the School of History, University of New South Wales, Sydney. The author of *Treacherous Women of Imperial Japan* (Routledge, 1997), she has published in Asian Studies, Feminist Studies and other journals in Australia, Europe and the USA.

Sceptical History

Feminist and postmodern approaches in practice

Hélène Bowen Raddeker

Routledge
Taylor & Francis Group

LONDON AND NEW YORK

First published 2007
by Routledge
2 Park Square, Milton Park, Abingdon, Oxon OX14 4RN

Simultaneously published in the USA and Canada
by Routledge
270 Madison Ave, New York, NY 10016

Routledge is an imprint of the Taylor & Francis Group, an informa business

© 2007 Hélène Bowen Raddeker

Typeset in Baskerville and Gill Sans by
Florence Production Ltd, Stoodleigh, Devon
Printed and bound in Great Britain by
Antony Rowe Ltd, Chippenham, Wiltshire

British Library Cataloguing in Publication Data
A catalogue record for this book is available
from the British Library

Library of Congress Cataloging in Publication Data
Raddeker, Hélène Bowen, 1952–
    Sceptical history: feminist and postmodern approaches in practice/
    Hélène Bowen Raddeker
        p. cm.
    Includes bibliographical references.
    1. History – philosophy. 2. Postmodernism. 3. Feminism
    I. Title.
    D16.9.R26 2007
    901 – dc22

                                                        2006032202

ISBN10: 0–415–34115–9 (hbk)
ISBN10: 0–415–34114–0 (pbk)
ISBN10: 0–203–47916–5 (ebk)

ISBN13: 978–0–415–34115–8 (hbk)
ISBN13: 978–0–415–34114–1 (pbk)
ISBN13: 978–0–203–47916–2 (ebk)

For Sasuke

Contents

Preliminaries

This book is not only for professional historians, those wanting to familiarize themselves more with critical theory; or, more precisely, with its application in History. Given the book's focus upon inter-disciplinary feminist scholarship to an extent that is unusual in works of history theory, it should be of interest to postgraduates and teachers in women's or gender studies, as well. Yet the reader-ship I particularly had in mind when embarking on the project was undergraduate students of History: history majors and research students not yet at the higher, graduate levels.

Essentially, the book is about practising postmodernist ('sceptical') history. There are many works available on history theory, for example critiques of conventional empiricist[1] history by those who are broadly termed 'postmodernists', or by others who are sceptical of the discipline's traditional methods, claims and beliefs. Yet comparatively few authors spend much time reflecting upon how, in an age widely deemed to be one of 'suspicion', historians might go about translating this scepticism into practice. Speaking from experience, I wonder whether this is because in some ways the question of practice can be more difficult to deal with than 'high' theory. The reference to 'suspicion', in any case, is to radical doubt about traditional certainties. British philosopher, Hilary Lawson, has noted that Friedrich Nietzsche (1844–1900), Martin Heidegger (1889–1976) and Jacques Derrida (1930–2004), three of the great philosophers now commonly associated with 'postmodernism', all tended to speak in 'grand apocalyptic' terms about the end of the era of Enlightenment-derived, modernist certainties about Know-ledge, Truth and Reason.[2] Another 'great', the historian, Michel Foucault (1926–84), may be added to the list as well. There has been some variation, however, between whether these and other similar thinkers saw this new era of suspicion as about to dawn or already with us.

'Postmodernism' is an umbrella term that covers others that are interrelated and more specific, such as 'poststructuralism', 'deconstruction' and the 'linguistic turn'. These will be discussed (or, in the case of deconstruction, discussed further) in Chapter 1. Readers may have come across the term 'postmodernism', however, in a wide variety of contexts – the arts, including music, fashion, architecture, literature, as well as in the social sciences – and it is a term that carries a range of meanings. Jean-François Lyotard (philosopher/ literary theorist, 1924–98), in an often reprinted work entitled *The Postmodern Condition* that was first published in French in 1979,[3] described this condition as characterized by the failure of the traditional grand narratives ('metanarratives') of Enlightenment-derived modernism. From a widespread suspicion of its transcendental (fixed or absolute) meanings, realities, knowledge, facts and truth, as well as Reason or rationalism, postmodern doubt has been extended to how modernist metanarratives sought 'to explain and justify human history and progress', as history theorist and self-described epistemological sceptic, Alun Munslow, puts it.[4] Indeed, modernists invariably took progress, at least in 'the West', for granted. Postmodernism therefore encourages 'relativism', 'tentative beliefs' and 'playfulness'[5] even in scholarship; while challenging the certitude and authority of traditional conceptual norms and hierarchies. Epistemology, it should be noted, is the study of, or theories concerning, the grounds, nature and production of knowledge(s): it is concerned with how knowledges come to be, what characterizes them, how they function. Hence, with respect to history, an epistemological sceptic is one who questions the basic principles of history as a 'knowledge'; who, as we will see in Chapter 1, may even question its status as a distinct or independent knowledge.

By way of explaining how the book came to be, I would like to begin with a brief chronological narrative about my own background: my experience as a tertiary student and then a lecturer in History. The irony of my beginning in such a manner will not be lost on some readers. In my defence, let me first admit that for an historian I have a poor memory, especially when it comes to dates, even more especially dates that should be of significance in my own life-story. A better defence might be to claim that my memory is not so atypical for an historian, to the extent that it is essentially selective, but my point is that I cannot be fully confident that what

I recall of the 'late 1980s' was not in fact of the early 1980s. Nor can I be certain that my narrative of those times is not coloured by hindsight. And there is also another risk involved. Perhaps I will make too much of my own experience (or my memory now of it) and resort to indefensible generalities. In reality, the picture I paint of my past/the past may not be representative of Australian universities, much less of others in the Anglophone world. Yet, all this is the stuff of narrative, the stuff of 'History', isn't it? Arguably, it is the stuff of traditional empiricist history, and I would not want to begin by unthinkingly practising that. Hence, I should acknowledge first that what follows in this short narrative preamble is only one possible story of my academic life. Second, though it does seem to me to be a 'true' record of changes that have occurred in the discipline since I was an undergraduate student, I lay no claim to its being a definitive account of the recent history of History. Some historians will doubtless relate to the experiences I 'remember' or to my perceptions of the ways in which academic history has been transformed since the 1970s. Others, however, may not find them true to their own experiences and perceptions.

Before proceeding, I would like to be able to dispense with the capital letter I sometimes feel I must use for the word 'History'. 'History' is what we in the present make of the 'past'. It is now often emphasized that the two terms should not be conflated, for they are not the same thing. Though above I capitalized the word at times to indicate that it signifies the 'discipline' (or formal academic study of the past) as I might capitalize 'Sociology' or 'Media Studies', henceforth 'history' will refer to (academic or popular, written and other) *interpretations or representations of the past*. That is, I try to avoid the popular usage of the word 'history' to mean merely the passage of time before now, or the sum total of, say, a country's traditions, experience, or course of development, as in the construction: 'Ireland's history reveals an intimate connection between superior liquor and resistance to British rule.' Actually, contrary to what was meant, the speaker of such a sentence would be quite right to use the term history here since the cause(s) of such resistance is a matter of interpretation and the superiority of Irish whiskey or stout a matter of personal taste.

But, to begin my narrative, the usual entry point into a story is not at its beginning but rather in the present. This is one aspect of the 'stuff of narrative/history' I alluded to earlier with my reference to hindsight (and will also be discussing at length in Chapter 2).

Above I also noted that I embarked on the writing of this book with a target readership in mind that included undergraduate students. That may have been primarily because of my belief that students need to be introduced to history theory early in their tertiary career, but student demand was also a factor. In recent years, since around the turn of the century, I have encountered at the university where I teach (The University of New South Wales, in Sydney) a growing number of first-year students keen to *further* their study of 'historiography'. 'Historiography', it should be noted, can be used literally to mean 'history writing' – the sum total of history writing on a particular area of the world as in 'the historiography of India' – but can also signify a particular paradigm or approach to history, as in Marxist, feminist or postmodernist historiography. Otherwise, it means the philosophy of history as a whole or history theory and methodology which is the sense in which these students meant it and I will use it, unless one of the other meanings is specified.

The fact that even the odd high school student is developing some acquaintance with historiography strikes me as quite a contrast with the 1970s. I began my study of history at a university in Melbourne in 1975 (La Trobe University) in a department that was very large, comprising a range of different sorts of historians, and known for its radicalism. Yet what I recall of those early years is that students of history at university were rarely encouraged to reflect upon competing styles of history, unless with respect to different ideo-logical approaches; or the differences between traditional political or intellectual histories on the one hand and the newer style of social history on the other. Social history had been practised for some decades but was really popularized from the 1960s. At first social history was mostly produced by male leftist (Marxist and other) historians, but with the advent of Second Wave Feminism women soon became more visible in the academy, and many feminist historians aligned themselves with this 'History from below'. 'Queens and battles' was not in their view much of an advance on the 'kings and battles' focus of conventional political history; nor did they accept that the foci of social history would remain restricted to the male 'masses'.

My memory of the 1980s is that by the latter part of the decade developments in the department suggested that a tertiary education in history was beginning to get more complex. It seemed more intellectually challenging and more stimulating. (The trend, if that it was, may have begun earlier, but between 1983 and 1986 when

I was a research student in Japan, I was absent from the department.) I doubt that this perception was only due to my being a History postgraduate by 1986. Now, for example, differences were being drawn, not so often between histories by conservatives versus histories by radicals such as Marxist and/or feminists, or not only along political lines but in terms of other differences as well. Though historians had long borrowed from other disciplines for theoretical and methodological inspiration, for example social historians and sociology, now the term 'interdisciplinary' seemed to be more in vogue. My department was a hotbed of 'Ethnographic History', which was influenced by new developments in both anthropology and literary theory. This was a style of history that was more than usually theorized or 'reflective' about the assumptions and procedures both of conventional (especially linear narrative or chronological) history *and its own practices* (i.e. reflexively). Certainly in some of its expressions, it was already quite a sceptical form of history at a time when 'postmodernist' epistemological scepticism was just on the rise.

Greg Dening's name first springs to mind in connection with ethnographic history, which has otherwise been termed the 'new cultural' history, or sometimes 'semiotic' history (because of its common 'structuralist' focus on 'sign' systems in language, culture, ritual and so on). Dening was the leader of the widely known 'Melbourne Group/School' of Ethnographic History and its most radical proponent and practitioner. By that time he was no longer at La Trobe, but rather at Melbourne University. (His style of history will be discussed in Chapter 2.) By now, another ethnographic historian from my Alma Mater, La Trobe, Inga Clendinnen, is at least as widely known and respected for her award-winning works on the history of the Maya and Aztecs.[6]

My general point about the 1980s (that I'm currently in danger of losing sight of) was that already by midway through the decade students were being encouraged by more teachers of history to 'reflect' critically upon the nature of history production or upon 'epistemology': i.e. the grounds, methods, etc. of history as a knowledge. At the beginning of the twenty-first century, tertiary students can expect to become acquainted with a confusing array of terms used to preface or accompany the word 'history', indicating different styles or approaches within the discipline. To name just some that gained in popularity in or since the 1980s, apart from the above-mentioned ethnographic history (aligned with what others might term the 'new cultural' or 'semiotic' history, or even 'history of mentalities'), we can add gender history and then the history of sexualities, and of course the 'postist' histories: postmodernist, poststructuralist, postcolonial. Still, I wonder whether for most tertiary students this acquaintance with historiography will develop into an intimacy.

In Australia, despite the fact that there may be increasing numbers of high schools where history theory is being taught, even a university major in history will not necessarily involve a good education in historiography. Though different institutions may vary considerably in this respect, whether students are or are not familiarized with it is often the luck of the draw, dependent upon the particular history courses they do and the teachers they encounter.[7] Yet I doubt that Australia is particularly remiss in this. In 2005, during a short stay in the United States where I was giving a paper at the famous Berkshire conference of women's history, I asked a publisher's representative at a bookstall for the history theory list. The said publisher, Routledge, handles an unusually large number of works on historiography and thus includes a section on this in its normal history catalogues (at least those circulated in Britain, Australia and New Zealand). Much to my surprise, however, I was told that such a list was not available because there is little interest in such texts in the United States.

That notwithstanding, since the 1990s there have been many texts available in English, which are focussed upon historiography and often highly critical of the traditional claims, assumptions and methods of the discipline. Among the single-authored texts by well-known history theorists (Hayden White, Joan Wallach Scott, Dominick LaCapra, Alun Munslow, Keith Jenkins, to name only some of the more radical ones), those by Jenkins have targeted students in particular as a readership. Examples are his very popular *Re-Thinking History* of 1991, and its sequel, *Refiguring History*, published in 2003.[8] In addition, 'Reader'-type works and books of collected essays on history and theory have been appearing in print more often than hitherto, sporting titles such as the following: *The Postmodern History Reader, The Routledge Companion to Historical Studies, The Nature of History Reader, Experiments in Rethinking History, The Feminist History Reader* and *Practicing History: New Directions in Historical Writing after the Linguistic Turn*.[9] In the 'old days', interested students could expect to be pointed in the direction of only a few such works, for example Geoffrey E. Elton's *The Practice of History* or the very popular and repeatedly reprinted *What is History?* by E. H. Carr (1892–1982).[10] Carr, an historian of Bolshevik Russia, was one of a few historians who in some ways helped to carve out a path to the critique of empiricism that forms a large part of sceptical history; another was R. G. Collingwood (1889–1943).[11]

If I may risk a generalization, although the overall trend in past years is for history research works to be becoming increasingly theorized, history teaching in the academy may be lagging far behind. Although we might expect undergraduate teaching never to keep pace equally with research in the discipline, I wonder whether more than ever before there is a disjunction between teaching practice and theory that is fairly broadly adhered to (at least 'in principle') – for example, concerning scepticism toward history's traditional status as an unproblematic 'knowledge' able to access past realities or 'facts' and impart them with 'objectivity'. Are such doubts imparted in lectures to students, one wonders, or do we still put forward our 'knowledge' of the 'facts' of the past in an overly confident, authoritative manner, in the omniscient voice of the professional historian? One wonders what is so wrong with 'speculation', much more of which goes on in history than is usually acknowledged, if it is *educated* 'guesswork'. The past is gone, some of it long gone, and surely part of the fascination of studying it is wonderment at its distance and thus strangeness, the impossibility of our truly knowing it.

Personally, I would like to see an end put to at least one sort of history taught in tertiary institutions: the type that encourages some students in the belief that a history course will be an 'easy option'. Their expectation is that it will not involve theory, at least not as explicitly as in other disciplines or interdisciplinary studies. Surely, theory is not something that should be put aside, relegated to courses designed for advanced students so that, suddenly, at 'honours' or fourth-year level, research students discover that there is (and has long been) such a thing as history theory. Admittedly, this expectation is suggestive of practical constraints that may affect how much history lecturers 'talk theory', or position themselves in the classroom in relation to radical critiques of history such as postmodernism.

If the academic environment is such that, due to insufficient government funding and a resultant 'marketization' of higher education, lecturers/professors face pressures to prioritize quantity over quality, they may be loathe to offer courses in critical history. Too many students may see these to be unusually 'hard'. That is, if one must attract the highest possible number of students and keep them entertained, prioritizing popularity over pedagogic principles, the quality of higher education is likely to suffer for it. To offer a practical example, if, in the mind of many students, history is an exercise merely in building up a store of knowledge of what really happened in the past, s/he may take the view that reflecting upon the nature of the discipline 'takes the fun out of History' (a view I have encountered more than once). On the other hand, one danger with a teacher's being 'subjective' (obviously positioned or, more generally, disinclined to effect/affect objectivity) or too 'relativist' is that, in offering up more than one reasonable interpretation without offering a judgement on 'the' true one, the sceptical historian could be taken merely to be lacking in knowledge about his/her subject: not an 'expert'. Academics are expected to speak with authority about their own interpretations, as if they are the last word on the subject at hand. Convention has it that one's object should be to convince others not of the mere plausibility of an interpretation – a reasonable one based upon educated guesses, as I said – but of its correctness or 'truth'.

My commitment to an education in historiography as important for tertiary students is probably both a reflection of the times and the product of my background. I was never more appreciative of my own education in historiography than when I was first appointed as a lecturer (in 1990) and began to mount my own courses in history. At first, they were on Japanese history, my speciality, and later also on world women's and gender history and the history of feminism. On occasion, I have also taught advanced courses on history and interdisciplinary theory and method; and from 2006 a 'prehonours' one on writing feminist histories. But, the way I see it, it is not just that theory is 'important', for I fail to comprehend how history can be studied without due attention to it. The two are not separable. Admittedly, even some professional historians have a strange way of speaking of 'history' versus 'theory', as if histories were not always the product of different theoretical (and political) paradigms in the human sciences,which in turn inform a consensus in the discipline about acceptable historical practice. Who was it that observed that those who imagine that they do not 'do theory' just unconsciously regurgitate someone else's, or something to that effect? The same goes for 'politics'. To my mind, the question is rather one of history as 'praxis' (theorized practice) versus a naïveté about the possibility of unpositioned (untheorized and, by extension, impartial, disinterested, objective) knowledge – if not on the part of the historian, at least with respect to the impression given to students.

Other history lecturers may relate to my experience, perceptions and opinions, or they may not, but my personal narrative should help explain why I would want to write a history theory text that is accessible to students. What it does not explain, however, is why it would be one focussed particularly upon so-called postmodernism (or postmodern-style scepticism) and history. The reason is that 'postmodern history' features the strongest contrasts with traditional historiography. It may not be the most recent trend or fad in history circles in different places, but it is still the most radical. In the last chapter I will consider one trend, but even that, the 'practical turn' in history,[12] represents a partial acceptance of postmodernist theory and a partial turn *back* from principles associated with its 'linguistic turn'.

With postmodernist thinking becoming topical, particularly since the late 1980s, and widely contested even in the media, we would expect it to have its champions and opponents among historians, too. Postmodernism is commonly misunderstood and, misunderstood or not, can elicit defensiveness or even hostility in traditionalists. What is the point of history, they ask, if one can no longer speak of 'the truth' with respect to the past? That is a good question. But, apart from the likelihood that a postmodernist (specifically, a 'deconstructionist') would be the first to recognize that to say 'There is no truth' is itself a truth statement (i.e. reflexively paradoxical), it is more the 'the' in the above formula re *the* truth of the past that would be cause for concern. 'Deconstruction' will be discussed in detail in Chapter 1 in connection with 'self-reflexivity'. Briefly, however, it is a style of critique associated with Jacques Derrida that involves more than merely pointing out the inconsistencies in arguments, and can be applied to any text including the critic's own, thereby 'self-reflexively' turning one's own text or argument back on itself. This, indeed, is what Derrida typically did. Hilary Lawson, author of *Reflexivity: The Postmodern Predicament*, which I cited on p. 1, defines deconstruction as:

> reading a text so closely that the conceptual distinctions, on which the text relies, are shown to fail on account of the inconsistent and paradoxical employment of these very concepts within the text as a whole. Thus the text is seen to fall by its

own criteria – the standards or definitions which the text sets up are used reflexively to unsettle and shatter the original distinctions.[13]

Postmodernists often contest the underlying implication of many works of mainstream history, that there is only one possible 'true story' of something or someone in the past, a story with one particular storyline, plot and central meaning. Further, they challenge the common suggestion that *the* story was actually out there in reality, so the historian has simply to 'find' and retell it (or find traces of it in surviving documents or other texts). The term usually used is 'reconstruct': the reconstruction of a story from the past or of past realities. We can already see why traditionalists have typically seen postmodernism as spelling the death or even 'killing'[14] of history, since 'reconstructionist' history is still common even in the academy.[15] It is difficult to say whether it is still dominant, since that rather depends on where and how far and wide one looks. However, this is history based upon traditional notions of recovery. As American political scientist, Michael Gibbons, once observed, the hermeneutics (interpretative theory) of 'recovery' stemmed largely from nineteenth-century theology: the exegesis of scripture as containing only one possible meaning since it represented the 'Word of God'. Translated into secular parlance, it represents an insistence that the aim of interpretation is the recovery of the original/true meaning of 'a political or social practice' (or, still today, a text), and the recovery also of 'the ideas, beliefs and [importantly] intentions of authors and actors'.[16] From ethnographic to postmodernist historians, those critical of the certainties of histories of reconstruction or recovery have also been suspicious of 'intentionality' – the notion that we can confidently know the intentions or motives of authors or historical actors ('get into their heads').

Those sympathetic to postmodern ideas would be unlikely to mourn the end of history *at least as it has been known by the mainstream*. Even where they stop short of accepting some of the more radically sceptical propositions, such sympathizers see traditional history to be too flawed in its theoretical and methodological foundations to continue its dominance of the field. They therefore recommend a thorough 'rethinking' of the discipline. This alone might suggest that traditionalists who warn of the death of history are not paranoid – are not expressing entirely unreasonable fears. One can only imagine their reactions to serious discussions, such as can be found in the final part of *The Nature of History Reader*, not just of whether history is dead, or at death's door, but of whether that is a good thing.[17] Keith Jenkins, who co-edited that work with Alun Munslow, has also suggested in his work *Refiguring History* that if postmodernism does spell the end of modernist history, it might be no great loss, given its 'passé' nature in contrast to the 'rich acts of the imagination' of a number of non-historian theorists who have reflected critically upon the nature of history. Nevertheless, Jenkins then ventured the hope that his book might 'breathe what fresh air can be breathed in an "old discipline"' through its advocacy of 'critical disobedience' to mainstream history's professional norms of theory and practice.[18]

I don't know that I would go so far as to describe the state of professional academic history as even 'somewhat' moribund. This Jenkins does, even if he grudgingly concedes that it 'still displays the *appearance* [my emphasis] of occasional vitality'. Perhaps I am more convinced that epistemological scepticism has impacted upon history's mainstream; that many historians do accept the justice of some 'postmodernist' criticisms, even if only at the level of principle without (yet?) following through in their writing or teaching practices. Time will tell whether, compared with other academic disciplines, history really is at death's door or languishing, or whether it takes time for those historians who are open to change to find ways of working productively with such critiques. As I will show in Chapter 1 and elsewhere, consistently putting sceptical principles into practice is no easy task.

My first object in the book is to demonstrate why the epistemological critique of mainstream history that has been gaining in popular acceptance for some time has been so effective. If it were not influential, it would be hard to explain the defensiveness and hostility with which it has been greeted by some in the discipline; to understand why, if reconstructionist history were still so secure, traditionalists would bother trying to refute postmodernism and often in a rather unscholarly, vituperative manner.[19] This, too, I find a little strange – not the abuse, that is, but rather the frequent implication that 'postmodern' scepticism and relativism is a *new* threat to the discipline. Central aspects of the critiques of history that are associated with postmodernism actually extend back to the nineteenth century in Europe, even further if we accept the proposition put in the 2006 work *Is History Fiction?* (by Australian scholars, Ann Curthoys and John Docker) that there have been two main streams of history in the so-called West: the conventional empiricist or positivist style described above (and defended by historians such as Keith Windshuttle or Geoffrey Elton); and another more sceptical, relativist and polyphonic (competing accounts) form that can be traced back to Herodotus.[20] Similarly, if our focus were not limited to the so-called West, important elements of 'postmodern' (*sic*) critiques of history or, more broadly, of discourses that purport to be 'Knowledge(s)' of the world would hardly appear to be new or radical. (I shall be discussing an example of this in Chapter 4: the parallels between Buddhist and postmodern concepts of the Self.) Nevertheless, without a doubt the closing decades of the last century saw the foundations of the traditional knowledge of history being more obviously and more widely shaken. This is due to the increasing popular acceptance of critiques from a growing number of influential philosophers and theorists, not excluding theorists specifically of history who have been 'multiplying' at what for some is doubtless an alarmingly rapid rate.

In this book I begin each chapter by explaining such critiques, first through the preliminary discussion in Chapter 1 of the critique of history that is now regarded as 'postmodern'. Here I begin by paying particular attention to one of those influential theorists, Roland Barthes (1915–80). In subsequent chapters I both discuss further what I take to be central problems with conventional history writing, and also reflect upon how we might deal with them. The three problem areas I have selected for particular scrutiny in the chapters that follow – teleology and presentism, 'difference' and processes of differentiation, and identity or subjectivity – may appear to be somewhat arbitrary, but they derive from my focus upon theory *and practice*. Works of history theory now abound in which other problem areas – say, conventional history's adherence to facticity and objectivity, or its interpretative recourse to the conventional plot structures seen in 'serious' literature, the conduct of the law, fairy tales and so on – are discussed at length, usually just in abstract terms. A concern with practice, however, leads one in the direction (also) of different sorts of works for inspiration, for example, feminist interdisciplinary scholarship. Thus, in this book I pay as much attention to works of history theory as to other scholarship that has a bearing upon a radical, 'sceptical' practice of history.

Since the 1980s, feminist scholarship has increasingly featured a central concern with constructs of difference – perceived differences based on gender, sexuality, race/ethnicity, culture/nation, peoples' different relations to colonialism and neo-colonialism, and more. 'Difference' is often considered in connection with questions of human identity or subjectivity. Feminist and queer scholars usually focus their attention upon issues of gender and/or sexuality, though not so often these days in isolation from other markers of difference. I will be drawing substantially upon feminist works, especially in Chapters 4 and 5 where I consider theory on difference/differentiation and identity/subjectivity and its application to works of history. Postmodernist feminists, not least the well-known American historian and theorist, Joan Wallach Scott, have made insightful contributions to debates or topics I shall be discussing in other chapters, too.

I will expand in subsequent chapters upon themes I discuss in a preliminary way in Chapter 1, both with respect to the postmodern critique of conventional history and to what I prefer to call a sceptical practice of history. Chapter 2, 'Reinventing the wheel: the present-past nexus', deals with teleology in history and debates in the discipline over presentism. 'Teleology' is a term that can be used to signify predetermined ends to 'history' (the notion that human development has always been heading towards some end or has arrived at one); or to mean backwards causation whereby representations of the past (as, for example, causing the present) are determined in the first instance by present contexts, perceptions and/or concerns ('presentism'). Unconscious teleology or presentism is a problem particularly in linear narrative or chronological history, but is not confined to it. Since the issue of teleology is related to causation in history, the chapter will include discussion of Foucault's often-cited alternative of emphasizing ruptures, breaks or discontinuities in developments or processes in the past rather than continuities. On the other hand, to the extent that the sceptic would insist that we cannot be other than 'present-minded' in our interpretations of the past, my focus upon teleology/presentism must necessarily include consideration of other issues raised earlier in connection with traditional reconstructionist history (its belief that it can recover past realities/true stories from the past: i.e. its realism or facticity and objectivity or disinterestedness).

A central question addressed in this chapter is how we are to marry a critique of teleology/presentism in conventional history, to a sceptical position that accepts the inevitable present-mindedness of our own representations of the past. There would seem to be a reflexive paradox involved in critiquing presentism in others, albeit others who fail to recognize or acknowledge it, whilst going so far as to recommend it in the political sense of treating the practice of history as an instrument of power: for example, the empowerment of marginalized groups. Finally, I end the chapter with a consideration of some examples of experimental history writing that incorporate a self-reflexive awareness of the 'ever-present' nature of representations of the past.

Chapter 3, 'Negotiating "difference"', is structured around the problem of dealing with 'difference' in works of history. Above I indicated that both cultural difference and differences of gender, class, race/ethnicity, sexuality, etc. are at issue here. However, the chapter addresses the distinction that must be made between a postmodern sort of focus upon *differentiation* – the social construction of hierarchized differences where negative values are attributed to woman, queer, non-white, Muslim, the 'Third World', and so on – and merely a greater *recognition* of difference. The latter assumes that differences are necessarily real. We might think of the example of what is termed postcolonial theory or scholarship where one often encounters the demand that differences of race/ethnicity, colour, religion or culture be acknowledged and respected. Such arguments, as we shall see, are often premised upon quite justified critiques of 'Western' humanist universalism, or the tendency in humanism to treat anything Western (and, feminists have added, male) as normative – *'the'* human subject as at least implicitly Anglo-European, white, male, heterosexual and privileged in terms of class, wealth or social position. Yet, on the postmodernist side of postcolonial scholarship, or feminist theory, or queer theory, we also often find a suspicion of a common *naturalization of difference*, its treatment as 'natural' and thus fixed rather than discursively or politically produced and subject to change over time.

In this chapter I shall consider other problems associated with difference approaches. For example, we need to remember that new intellectual trends are often strongly reactive. There are dangers involved in overreacting against humanist universalist models and norms, thereby either overemphasizing difference or emphasizing difference to the exclusion of similarities. First, whether it be in hegemonic discourses of eurocentrism or in discourses that resist them, an unthinking embracement of 'difference' can lead to an essentialization of the 'Other'. Overemphasizing difference in the area of culture can also lead us to exoticize the 'Other', losing sight of areas in which people may have similar experiences and problems, needs and desires. We do not have to adhere to meta-narratives or metahistories, universalist visions of global historical development, to recognize that capitalism, for example, affects many peoples around the world similarly; or that some repressive gender/sexual norms and practices extend widely beyond national boundaries. Some feminist scholars have also noted a tendency in the 'difference fad' for it to be celebrated, while the conditions that produce differences and inequalities go unnoticed. Finally, even epistemological sceptics may fall prey to ascribing a problematic homogeneity to the past, assuming in line with a linear 'progress' model that (modernist) past thinking and political movements were always less 'enlightened, sophisticated, and theoretically self-conscious' than we (in 'post-modernity') are now[21] – less subject to and aware of difference, perhaps, as well as being less liberal or more authoritarian. Even self-titled 'difference' theorists, that is, may fail to account for heterogeneity in the past.

In Chapter 4, 'The "positioned" subject', I will first elaborate on postmodernist critiques of the essentialism and teleology that inhere in modernist (humanist and individualist) constructs of identity. At base, the epistemological problems with such constructs are much the same, whether we happen to be speaking of individual, or group, or ethnic/cultural/national identity, but the focus in this chapter is particularly upon individual identity. A related issue is the foundational status in traditionalist history of the analytical concept of 'experience', which is tied to its central goals of the recovery of past realities, truth and scholarly objectivity. Roland Barthes is famous both for his scepticism concerning such claims on the part of historians, and for his critique of the centred (essentialist) Self or 'Subject' of humanism, so I begin this chapter once again with an elucidation of his views.

The postmodernist rejection of modernist identity has elicited heated defences from its advocates, for whom claiming an identity as a woman, or gay/lesbian, or black has proven its political usefulness. Marginalized groups cannot so easily dispense with identity politics, they warn. But, the question is whether one need represent oneself as essentially this *or* that rather than this *and* that – and at times something else, too – the latter in recognition of the multiple, complex and also changing nature of subjectivity, in order to practise effective resistance to oppressive norms and practices. Some have put forward the concept of a strategic, shifting 'positionality' as at least equally useful, politically. With respect to history, the question is how we speak of the historical actors we happen to be researching or discussing. Where they are clearly modernist, do we, for example, take as given the singular, centred and fixed identities that they claimed derived from the 'truth' of their experience? Or do we suspend the classic biographical concern with subjects' truthfulness by enquiring into the positionalities they *performed*, asking in what context and to what ends subjects *spoke to* the truth of their experience and formation of their identities?

In my 'conclusion' to the book, I intend to try to redress a little my inevitable lapses and oversights. Apart from addressing the question of whether this book has proved to be as self-reflexive as I believe it should be, there I shall also reflect upon other problems, difficulties and paradoxes I encountered while writing it. Ultimately, I leave it up to my readers to decide whether I managed to 'iron' out the wrinkles and bumps or whether, like with a good linen shirt, they really need to be. Extending the simile a little further, one might ask whether they *can* be, since such wrinkles and bumps have a way of soon recurring.

Finally, to return to the beginning of this chapter, there I expressed the hope that this book will make a contribution to the comparatively slim body of work that concentrates on the *practice* of (postmodernist and feminist, 'sceptical') history. One cannot, however, concentrate on that alone. Readers need to understand why an increasing number of sceptics have come to see conventional history as flawed at the level of its foundations, and sought radical alternatives. To help facilitate that understanding, I shall try to adhere to a style of expression that is in line with my belief that theory need not be incomprehensible to the uninitiated, whether they be academics or students or people outside the so-called 'halls of higher learning'. Thus, I try to remember to offer practical historiographical and other examples where necessary to illustrate theoretical points, and also to minimize my use of 'jargon'. That being said, I do insist that so-called theoretical jargon, when its meaning is understood, can offer more precision and, thereby, clarity. I leave the suspicion of technical language to others: for example, the conventional narrative historians, who amidst their attacks upon either postmodernism or theory per se, have demanded (what American literary historian, Katherine Kearns, has referred to critically as 'manly') 'plain language' in history. Her critique of such demands for 'the plain language of truth' includes discussion of rejections of figurative language as well, as if, as Nietzsche put it, truth were not 'always . . . a mobile army of metaphors'.[22] Kearns offers an incisive and playful reading of the gendered implications of the contempt for theory (as encouraging 'unmanly doubt' and effeminate obfuscation and frivolity) witnessed in traditionalists such as the British historian and 'defender of the faith', Geoffrey Elton. Her point is that works such as Elton's *Return to Essentials* (1991) represent a call to arms against postmodern 'effeminacies': doubt, irony, indecisiveness, deconstruction, inconclusiveness, playfulness and so on. On the other hand, another scholar, F. R. Ankersmit, whose works on postmodern historiography have been becoming very influential, has suggested that 'only metaphors "refute" metaphors'.[23]

If the period since the 1980s has witnessed an increasingly sceptical turn in history about foundational premises of the discipline, my question is: If there is no going back, which way forward? I do not claim that the sort of history I recommend here will be any less a pastiche of old and new than any other 'postist' discourse. Nor do I come bearing ready solutions to the inevitable difficulties and paradoxes that attend the writing of any sort of history, to say nothing of postmodern history. Despite predictions that postmodernism spells history's demise, my concern is nevertheless with what practitioners of history can *do* – short of throwing up their hands in despair or burying their heads in the proverbial sand – when they find postmodernist critiques of history persuasive, and seek to work creatively with them in their own representations of the past. Among those practitioners I of course include students, particularly those who are embarking upon or will soon be conducting higher research in history, and perhaps facing some of the problems, quandaries and paradoxes I address in this book. It is to future research students that I dedicate the book. I must also express my indebtedness to those students who, in years past, have encouraged my habit of talking theory, even in connection with a 'scholarly' field where it is still widely held not to exist.

Otherwise, while on the subject of debts, I could not fail to acknowledge those who helped a few years ago to bring me 'up to speed' with contemporary feminist, queer and related theory. This was when, suddenly, as convenor-administrator of my university's Women's and Gender Studies programme (mid-2001 to 2005), I was called upon to teach outside my usual area of expertise, mounting courses in feminism's history and feminist scholarship at the introductory and advanced levels. Those to whom I must express my thanks are Ingrid Nonjongo Tufvesson, Rodney Hughes, Gemma Edgar, Kate Bower and Ana Carden-Coyne. But for Ana, who was a lecturer, all were then honours or postgraduate students.

Chapter 1

History, postmodern critique and alternative visions

I

> I read it [history] a little as a duty, but it tells me nothing that does not either vex or weary me. The quarrels of popes and kings, with wars or pestilences, in every page; the men all so good for nothing, and hardly any women at all – it is very tiresome: and yet I often think it odd that it should be so dull, for a great deal of it must be invention. The speeches that are put into the heroes' mouths, their thoughts and designs – the chief of all this must be invention, and invention is what delights me in other books.
>
> (Jane Austen, *Northanger Abbey*)[1]

I hope readers will bear with me whilst I begin with a clarification of central terms. First, I have indicated that the phrase 'postmodern history' denotes histories by authors who take seriously, critiques of the discipline associated with the twentieth-century 'linguistic turn' in the human sciences. In this broad usage it encompasses 'deconstructionist' or 'poststructuralist' approaches to history. The inspirations for the linguistic turn came from a number of directions, initially from structural linguistics, which began in 1916 with the posthumous publication of Ferdinand de Saussure's (1857–1913) *Course in General Linguistics*.[2] He proposed a model of language in which 'words are "signs" defined in their differentiation from other words, and not because of any natural link with the real world of objects/things'.[3] As Alun Munslow explains in his *Deconstructing History*, signs are made up of signifier (the word or concept) and signified (the thing referred to); and the relationship between them is not naturally but linguistically (socially, culturally) constituted. Structuralists and the poststructuralists who followed them have opposed the empiricist assumption of 'referentiality', arguing that the connection between a real thing or phenomenon (signified or referent) and a word that 'refers' to it and signifies its meaning is arbitrary. Words refer to other words (self-referentiality), often through opposed hierarchical meanings: 'freedom' has no meaning without 'despotism' or oppression. To give another example, we might ask whether the 'event' so often spoken of in histories is really that outside discourse? An occurrence can be styled as such only in opposition to 'non-events', occurrences deemed too insignificant (unmeaningful) by an historian to qualify as an event.

It has been observed that what unites the various forms of 'pre- and poststructuralisms' is their shared reliance upon:

> a language-model epistemology, which views language not as a reflection of the world it captures in words, but as constitutive of that world, that is, as 'generative' rather than 'mimetic'. Despite considerable differences among the polemicists and practitioners of poststructuralism, all begin from the premise that language is somehow anterior to the world it shapes; that what we experience as 'reality' is but a socially (i.e. linguistically) constructed artifact or 'effect' of the particular language systems we inhabit.[4]

This emphasis by Gabrielle Spiegel (medievalist and history theorist) on language as 'prior to' our *experience or, rather, perceptions* of the world or material reality seems accurate enough, but her observation about linguistic determination of the world itself is off the mark. From structuralism to poststructuralism, the concern has rather been with the habit historians and others have of confusing the two: that is, language and reality.

In his argument for a postmodern historiography, the narrative theorist Frank R. Ankersmit noted that historians have been in the habit of speaking of historical language 'as if it were part of reality itself and vice versa'. 'Thus, Marx spoke of the *contradiction* between the production forces and production relations as if he were discussing *statements* about reality instead of *aspects* of this reality.'[5] Ankersmit also cites Nietzsche's 'deconstruction' of the scientific language of cause and effect where, conventionally, 'the cause is the source and the effect the secondary given'.[6] Yet, if not for our perception of something as an 'effect', we would not be looking for its cause in the first place (as Nietzsche put it, 'the effect is what causes the cause to become a cause'); so in fact at the level of discourse it is the effect that is primary, the source or origin of our perception of what is in reality a 'secondary' cause.

The point may seem obscure, but what Nietzsche was criticizing was the way in which scientific language was/is supposed to be a mirror reflection of nature. As Ankersmit explains, he was 'playing off our way of speaking about reality against processes in reality itself'.[7] The self-contradiction ('self-reflexive paradox') involved in the effect-cause-effect example shows how language refers more to other language than to the real processes we are seeking to describe; just as in the example from Marx, when he sought to describe real productive forces and relations his language seemed to be referring to other language. This brings us back to the point I began with – that language, according to structuralists (and then poststructuralists) is 'self-referential'. It has been a point taken up by many a critic of history, as we shall see when we come to Roland Barthes. In arguing that the discourse of history (like science) is not a direct reflection of past realities, they have therefore emphasized that it is essentially a dialogue with other historians: history texts talking with other history texts ('intertextually') about competing representations of the past.

Munslow comments on how, in poststructuralism, 'the route to knowledge invariably centres upon the role of discourse and forms of representation in and through language'.[8] To apply the point to self-knowledge, we might recall Spiegel's observation that our experience of reality is a social/linguistic construct or effect of the language systems we are raised within. We learn to recognize things, and to think or express 'our' (*sic*) selves in language or through existing knowledges or discourses. It is not that we think in a manner that is entirely independently our own and then express the thought in language: we even think in/through language. So, knowledge is intertextual, by definition, in the poststructuralist view, meaning that it draws upon (or works from) many knowledges, or existing 'texts' or discourses. As we shall see in a later chapter, this perception of the linguistic determination not of the world but of knowledge of it is carried over into areas such as personal experience that have long been spoken of as if they are prior to language/discourse. Typically, personal experience is said to precede the formation of our identities, as if experience (say, the experience of 'discrimination') itself had not come to be defined as such through discourse.

With the linguistic turn came an emphasis also on how language is not transparent or straightforward, but 'opaque'. As Munslow observes, 'The linguistic turn centres on the opacity and figurative character of language, the manner in which subject positions as well as reality-effects are created within language.'[9] A simple but topical example is the word 'Muslim', the meaning of which will vary depending upon the speaker and context. A related point is one I made in the 'Preliminaries' concerning the postmodernist suspicion of 'intentionality': the confidence with which conventional scholars assume that authorial intention (with regard to the meaning of texts) can, confidently and definitively, be known.

Munslow also comments on how 'post-structuralism insists that language, as *the* cultural and intellectual form, is the medium of exchange for *power* relationships' (my emphasis). This is a reference to Michel Foucault, for whom knowledge was power and language the 'ultimate constitutor of [knowledge and] "truth"'.[10] If language is the medium of exchange for power relationships, it explains why poststructuralists focus upon *discourse* and representation – often upon representations of (say, gendered or racialized) 'difference' in terms of binarisms (that is, opposed pairs of words/concepts that are 'hierarchical' or unequal in the sense that one denotes superiority and the 'other' inferiority). Again this refers to the point above about how words refer to other words through a process of differentiation. Readers should also note that the term 'discourse' can have a broad or, in poststructuralist usage, a quite specific meaning. According to Callum Brown, author of a handy primer for students on postmodernism and history (handy for those writing on the subject, too!), 'discourse conveys the construction of knowledge in a given period (or episteme)'; it is a changing 'non-material entity, expressed in a language system (words, images or another medium) . . . that conveys a meaning, in the form of a duality (the thing and its Other)'.[11]

II

From the moment that language is involved (and when is it not involved?), the fact can only be defined in a tautological fashion. . . .

The fact can only have a linguistic existence, as a term in a discourse, and yet it is exactly as if this existence were merely the 'copy', purely and simply, of another existence situated in the extra-structural [i.e. extra-linguistic] domain of the 'real'. . . .

(Roland Barthes, 'The Discourse of History')[12]

Some leading theorists connected with the linguistic turn have already been mentioned: Nietzsche, Heidegger, Foucault, Lyotard and Derrida. Others are Benedetto Croce (like Foucault, another philosopher of history, 1866–1953), Hans-Georg Gadamer (1900–2002), and Julia Kristeva (1941–). The highly influential French cultural critic, Roland Barthes, was still another; and he is a good thinker to start with in order to get a clearer sense of the style of critiques associated with the linguistic turn and their application to history. He is sometimes referred to as a late or 'high' structuralist, indicating that he was an immediate forerunner of poststructuralism or on the somewhat blurred dividing line between the two.

Thus, in one of his famous essays, 'The Discourse of History', Barthes was another critic who emphasized how it is through language that we create reality *effects*. One could equally say that 'truth effects' are created in or through language. When Barthes spoke of how 'our civilization has a taste for the realistic effect',[13] of course it was not the popularity of 'reality TV' he had in mind, though we could take that as a further illustration of the point. He wrote this in 1967 and so, by way of illustration, he listed as examples 'the realist novel, the private diary, documentary literature, news items, historical museums, exhibitions of old objects and . . . photography'. His particular focus in that essay, however, was history – an intellectual discourse, the authority and popularity of which has been based, not unlike with 'Real Crime', 'Survivor' or 'Big Brother', upon its claim to (re-)present the 'Real'. The basic structuralist point Barthes was expressing again concerned referentiality – where the *effect* of realism is created in traditional histories through suggestions that there is a 'largely unproblematic or adequate match between reality (event, person, thing, process) and its description (linguistic expression)'.[14] Yet, history is not material reality; it is not *the past* but representations of it, however many 'facts' (*references* to real events etc.) it may contain. The scepticism Barthes expressed about conventions of history writing was largely directed, therefore, at the belief of mainstream ('empiricist') historians that they could access and reproduce the real past, or aspects of it, in scholarly texts: i.e. history as the so-called 'written past'.

As part of his critique of history's claim to realism, naturally, the status of 'facts' in history came under fire from Barthes, too, when he challenged the status of history as a distinct knowledge. The only thing that Barthes found distinctive about history concerned how discourses generally claim that their truth already lies within, while history gains the status of truth only by treating its 'facts' as substitutes for the real or true past (the referent).[15] As Barthes himself put it in the quote heading this section, history's claim to distinctiveness as a discourse rested upon the *paradox* that 'the fact can only have a linguistic existence, as a term in a discourse, and yet it is exactly as if this existence were merely the "copy" . . . of another existence situated in the . . . domain of the "real".' It is as if external reality itself were being dissolved and absorbed into the discourse, thereby becoming fact, which in turn is treated as the proof of reality.[16] This is why Barthes said in the quote heading the section that 'the fact can only be defined in a tautological fashion'. Once again, Ankersmit would say that language and reality are being confused.

Barthes contested history's facticity on more than one ground, however. He saw it as 'fictive' in the sense of its being primarily the product of the writer's imagination: the historian's creation.[17] This is what must be dispensed with, denied, or mystified in order to present one's work as reconstructed reality(s) – that is, the essentially imaginative, thus arbitrary nature of the meaning attributed to the thing, phenomenon or process under description (or the arbitrary relation between signifier and signified/referent). Barthes also insisted that 'The historian is not so much a collector of facts as a collector and relater of signifiers; that is to say, he organizes them with the purpose of establishing positive meaning and filling the vacuum of pure, meaningless series.' (We'll forgive him for his assumption that the historian is necessarily a 'he', since this was in 1967 when professional women historians were comparatively rare.) This point about facts makes sense of another of Barthes' statements: 'For History not to signify [impute meaning], discourse must be confined to a pure, unstructured series of notations', like with bare chronologies or annals, he said (that do little more than list occurrences and dates); yet, 'even if the facts happen to be presented in an anarchic fashion, they still signify anarchy and to that extent conjure up a certain negative idea of human history.'[18] In other words, the meaning of anarchy is still being ascribed to apparent 'bare facts'.

At base, what Barthes was arguing is that the modern historian's 'stock and trade' is *meaning*, not facts – ascribing meaning to events in the past (or things styled as 'events'), to processes of change, or perhaps to the life of some person in the past. He then went further than that, however, when he drew upon Nietzsche, who once said: 'There are no facts in themselves. It is always necessary to begin by introducing a meaning in order that there can be a fact.'[19] Neither accepted the empiricist/objectivist historian's self-image as mere 'collector' of facts, since this implies that there are facts ready-made out there in the real world (the real past or the bits of it contained in remaining documents), which are just awaiting collection. 'Selector' would be a better term to use because one first needs an interpretative (meaningful) question and framework in order to select the (soon-to-become) facts that will constitute evidence for the interpretation/meaning. As Munslow puts it, '"facts" are never innocent because only when used by the historian is factual evidence invested with meaning as it is correlated and placed within a context . . . which then leads the historian to generate the "facts".'[20] The point of such an argument is not that works of history contain no factual or true statements, for example that a social event (or occurrence) broadly interpreted as a 'revolution' occurred in Russia in October 1917. The problem is rather that 'the fact that something happened does not mean that we know or can adequately describe what it *means* – there is *no* entailment from fact(s) to value(s)', to its meaning, significance or importance.[21] That is, the meaning we accord an event is arbitrary, not intrinsic to it (moreover, signifying it as something, or attributing some positive or negative value to it, is a moral/political act).

Debates have long gone on about whether history texts contain more fact or more interpretation, for example in the well-known work of the early 1960s, E. H. Carr's *What is History?* Barthes, however, was doing much more than merely putting the latter proposition. For him, empiricist claims with regard to history's essential facticity were an affectation also because history repre-sented just another literary genre, no more realistic or inherently 'truthful' than, say, a realist novel. This was another way in which he contested history's claim to being a distinct discourse or knowledge. His argument calls to mind the 'ground'-breaking work of the American theorist of history, Hayden White, whose approach was in fact partly inspired by Barthes. What has been observed of White, that 'there is no distinction between history and philosophy or between history and literature', history being in his view essentially 'aesthetic and philosophic',[22] was equally true of Barthes.

Jane Austen's heroine, then, was expressing a similar scepticism when she observed that 'a great deal of [history] must be invention'. Strange that it should be so 'dull' when inventiveness delighted Catherine in other books, which is to say novels. Perhaps what for her was really dull was its dry scholarly pretensions to realism, facticity and objectivity when, clearly, so much of it was the product of the imagination of historians. 'Catherine', or rather Austen, was in fact equating history with fiction on a similar basis to Barthes or White. What is also interesting about the passage is her reference, not so much to historians' putting speeches into the mouths of heroes – for that would surely be going too far – but more to their imagining that they can be privy to their heroes' 'thoughts and designs' (intentionality). Finally, even her reference to 'heroes' is thought-provoking. Although perhaps one should not read too much into her usage of the word, it brings to mind the analysis of all works of history as 'narrative' that is invariably associated with White but is a position held by many a history theorist today. This is a reference to histories being centred on one of a number of possible literary storylines with dominant emplotments – as heroic epics or romances, tragedies, farces, and so on. (Would she have used the term 'hero' if this were not the case?)

Narrativity or narration had been another element in Barthes' critique, which just about completes the picture of why he saw history as essentially a literary enterprise. For, when history was seeking to transform itself into a genre in the nineteenth century, he points out, strangely, narration began to be seen as 'the privileged signifier of the real'. That is, apart from the fact that meaning is created in histories through narration and the ascription of 'plots', history long drew its truth- or reality-effect partly from its narrative style. Once again Barthes points to a paradox here, that 'narrative structure, which was originally developed within the cauldron of fiction (in myths and the first epics) became at once the sign and the proof of reality'. He obviously meant 'linear narrative', that is, chronological descriptive works of history. Why else would he conclude that the narrative style of history was losing its prominence already by the latter part of the 1960s, when it was already beginning to be replaced by histories (influenced by structuralist anthropologists headed by Claude Lévi-Strauss) that spoke of 'structures' (synchronic histories focussed on one point in time) rather than (diachronic) chronologies?[23] Hence, Hayden White took the point further, as I have noted, in a series of ground-breaking

works on history as *always* 'narrative'.[24] He included in this even
works of history that do not take a linear narrative approach by
developing an obvious storyline with a beginning and end. For
White, it was not that history's narrative character can actually
be avoided. His critique was not aimed at its plot structures in
themselves (though it would be nice if historians were more reflective
about their recourse to them); but rather at how they are among
ɪthe rhetorical/linguistic devices that reveal history to be essentially
a literary rather than 'scientific' enterprise.

Rather than my delving into different approaches to narrative
in history or as history, suffice it to say that, first, Barthes was a little
overconfident in pronouncing diachronic/chronological history to
be on its deathbed (he did say it was 'dying') as long ago as 1967.
It is still alive if not quite as well today as hitherto. Second, his
analysis indicates that we should be wary of taking critiques of
narrative as focussed only upon the *form* or style of a history text,
as if this is distinct from its descriptive or analytical (or moral/
political) content. This is indicated by one of White's book titles:
The Content of the Form. Even if Barthes' brief references to narration/
narrativity in this seminal essay pointed particularly to a critique of
chronology in linear narrative history (specifically to its utility for
truth or reality effects), they still bring us back full circle to meaning
in historical narrative per se. As White has so ably demonstrated,
a narrative not only ascribes beginnings and ends, but also 'centres'
– that is, when a central (essential) meaning is ascribed to historical
events or processes or human lives and their 'story' in arbitrarily
selected emplotments/meanings. (Auto/biographies or life-stories
are a classic case in point: someone's life emplotted as a heroic
triumph over adversity, or perhaps ultimately as a tragedy or farce.)

Meaning is arbitrary, as I have noted, because it resides in
language, not in the real world it seeks to describe. Derrida would
say that meaning is 'undecidable': not closed, definitive or final, but
subject to contestation.[25] This has nothing to do with 'nihilistically'
denying the real existence of the thing under description, which has
been a common misconception: to wit, 'there is no world, only text',
or 'all the world is a text'. If even the meaning of a simple statement
such as 'the chair is black' is undecidable, it is because such a
statement can have different meanings depending upon the context
(a denial of someone else's belief that it is red, or of a belief that it
is rather the table that is black). As Lawson observes, Derrida is:

> not saying that we cannot be certain that there is a chair that is black, in the sense of doubting the existence of the external world. Rather he is saying that there is no single meaning of the sentence 'the chair is black' . . . . The meaning of a sentence takes place in the play that is the web of language.[26]

Nor was Barthes denying external (past) realities when he made a similar point about history's claim to be able to apprehend 'the real' in language (in history texts): 'the real is never more than a meaning, which can be revoked when history requires it'. This, meanings being revoked (or meanings vying with each other in the play or web of language), happens all the time in history texts as historians argue with each other about interpretations of some event or phenomenon; as history theory, methodology and approaches undergo revision over time; and as world conditions and hegemonic discourses change. To illustrate the point, we might again take the example of the 'Bolshevik'/October Revolution in Russia (even what we call it is suggestive of individual interpretation!). Today the realities and meaning of this event might be much more subject to contestation than in the heady days following it when it was easier to represent it as an heroic epic. Now many more interpreters would be inclined to emplot it as a tragedy. There are other possible emplotments, too, parody, perhaps, if the point of view being reflected were that of initial sympathizers who, sooner or later, became disillusioned with or fell victim to Bolshevik abuses of power.

Meaning, therefore, lies in the realm of the historian's imagination, and in other things such as his/her morality and politics. As White or Munslow would say, it is not as if developments out there in the real past constituted stories already with only one possible meaning, plot or storyline, stories just waiting to be unearthed (or found in documents in the archives) and retold by the historian. According to White:

> Since no given set or sequence of real events is inherently tragic, comical, farcical, and so on, but can be constructed as such only by the imposition of the structure of a given story type on the events, it is the choice of the story type and its imposition upon the events that endow them with meaning.[27]

Material reality itself does not take the form of a story. Yet, this is the picture still painted so often in conventional history teaching and research, admittedly, by academics who are under pressure to be 'authoritative' by insisting upon one definitive account of some event, phenomenon, process or person in the past. Finally, to reiterate the important points so far, it was in structural linguistic terms that Barthes challenged history's realism. This was merely a reality *effect* produced (through explicit rhetoric or meta-phorical language) by its supposed grounding in 'fact' and the related 'objectivity' of the historian, as well as narration. For him, therefore, history is fictive – no more realist than the realist *novel*.

Furthermore, as his reference to Nietzsche would indicate, Barthes was no less intertextual than anyone else. That is to say, he drew upon a range of texts, sources, knowledges or thinkers, not least the above-mentioned linguist whose ideas had paved the way for the creation of structuralism as a popular intellectual trend by the 1960s, Ferdinand de Saussure. Munslow describes the move-ment as derived from his idea that:

> the relationship between all discourses, cultural forms, belief and behaviour systems can be understood employing the structure of language as the model. In practice, this means social meaning is generated according to the contrast between inherent binary opposites operationalised at the deep level of human conscious-ness and revealed in the real world in the structure of grammar, myths, [rituals] sexual relationships etc.[28]

In turn, after Saussure came a string of theorists in different fields who drew upon structuralist linguistics for inspiration, applying its precepts to their own disciplines. Thus, as another commentator has put it, the structuralist movement was characterized by a:

> peculiar distribution of roles and specializations . . . in which Lévi-Strauss secures anthropology, and Lacan and Althusser are charged with the reinterpretations of Freud and Marx respec-tively, in which Derrida and Foucault assure the rewriting, the one of the history of philosophy, the other of the history of ideas . . .[29]

Perhaps it was just an oversight that led Fredric Jameson to omit Barthes from this list of leading European structuralists. His 'high' structuralist contributions to literary/cultural theory were certainly not overlooked elsewhere in Jameson's text. For, he was among the leading theorists who inspired what ultimately came to be designated as 'postist' (postmodernist and/or poststructuralist) critiques of the empiricist/realist form of history.

The 'new cultural' or ethnographic history I mentioned in the 'Preliminaries', as popular in and from the 1980s, contributed to the development from around that time of postmodernist history. Inspired partly by founding structural anthropologist, Claude Lévi-Strauss – who also took history to task in 'History and Dialectic' in *The Savage Mind*, 1966 – and then even more by the work of American anthropologist Clifford Geertz, ethnographic/semiotic historians were (or are) not always dismissive of history's realism or entirely sceptical about its claims to facticity and objectivity. They did, however, feature in a renewed attack among historians upon linear narrative, whereupon structural-synchronic approaches to history became popular (with respect to the limited time frames studied: one point in time rather than, say, a span of centuries), as did a concern with analysing language, signs (in 'semiotic' history), myth and ritual. Hence even human action was styled as a 'text' to be read.[30] Ethnographic historians also tended to be more 'reflective' about their methods, on the printed page, not just in seminars or lunch-time discussions with colleagues, as I noted in the 'Preliminaries' chapter and as we shall see in my consideration of experimental history in Chapter 2.

III

> [I]n my understanding of it, a dialogic approach is based on a distinction that may be problematic in certain cases but is nonetheless important to formulate and explore. This is the distinction between accurate reconstruction of an object of study and exchange with that object as well as with other inquirers into it . . . .
>
> History . . . gives priority if not exclusive status to accurate reconstruction, restricts exchange with other inquirers to a subordinate, instrumental status (signalled textually by a relegation to footnotes or a bibliography), and is forced to disguise dialogic exchange as reconstruction, often in a manner that infiltrates values into a seemingly objective or value-neutral account.
>
> (Dominick LaCapra, *History and Reading*)[31]

Broadly speaking, it would seem that there are four possible positions for historians to take up in response to postmodernist critiques of the discipline. They can challenge them; or they can ignore them and continue with a practice of history that others may see as epistemologically naive and perhaps also disingenuous. It is not good enough, surely, for historians to keep protesting that 'historians . . . have always known what postmodernism professes to have just discovered',[32] whilst continuing with business as usual in their histories. A third alternative is that they can embrace them, wholly or partly, and try to work with them constructively, thereby practising a more critical form of history than hitherto – one that is sceptical of the empiricist foundations of the discipline. Finally, some who are fully committed to postmodernist principles might decide to give up on history altogether.

Giving up on 'history' can have more than one meaning, however. One logical and, I believe, defensible consequence of an acceptance of postmodernist-style critiques can be that such historians choose to write only history theory, not histories of anything, that is, unless they be critical histories of the discipline itself. This would be seen to be a problem particularly by the sort of conventional historian who sees attention to theory – especially the sort of theory that reflects critically upon one's own practice – as somehow separable from doing 'history'. American historian, Gertrude Himmelfarb, implies that such historians do not do 'real history' when she complains that in postmodernist history:

> theory has become a calling in itself. Just as there are professors of literature who never engage in the actual interpretation of literary works – and even disdain interpretation as an inferior vocation – so there are professors of history who have never (at least to judge by their published work) done research in, or written about, an actual historical event or period. Their professional careers are devoted to theoretical speculation about the nature of history in general and to the active promotion of some particular methodology or ideology of history.[33]

One can only wonder at Himmelfarb's view that, even in the academy, the so-called halls of (higher?) learning, it is not proper that some history professors or lecturers concentrate on theory. Also noteworthy is the construction, 'theoretical speculation about the nature of history in general', given that 'speculation' is a pejorative word among empiricists who do not, of course, engage in it themselves but speak only of what they 'know', purportedly sticking to 'the facts'. What is also revealing is the implication that

Himmelfarb herself is not engaged in 'the active promotion of some particular methodology or ideology of history'. Even the most unreflective, apparently untheorized works of history are positioned in various ways, theoretically, conceptually and politically (however consciously). But, as for those who do not write 'real' (*sic*) history, surely, the more theorists there are in the discipline, the better history will be for it.

My own standpoint is that one cannot do other than acknowledge the justice of central postmodernist critiques of history as a (distinct) 'Knowledge' or even impartial 'science' with its own unique set of methods with which to access Truth or past reality/s. Though I have mentioned practical constraints that can serve to prevent it, ideally, if historians who do take such critiques seriously want continually to refine their (our) practice of history, they need to try to work creatively with such critiques. This really should be done both in their writing and teaching, moreover, so that the two will not be out of step with each other. If one takes seriously the postmodernist injunction to turn one's critical eye also inward towards one's own practice ('self-reflexively'), one should be prepared to engage in self-criticism and self-doubt both in the classroom and on the written page, rather than replicating the all-knowing stance and, para-doxically, also authorial invisibility demanded by empiricism and objectivism. The latter is still often extended to the point of absurdity where the ('subjective') 'I' of the text must remain invisible whilst the text apparently writes itself, often in passive voice, in order to achieve a realistic effect.

As I noted in the 'Preliminaries' chapter, there is available an ample number of theoretical works that critique empiricist-objectivist history from postmodernist perspectives. Works that concentrate on the question of how to practise postmodernist history, however, are comparatively rare.[34] However, some authors, such as Joan Wallach Scott, Dominick LaCapra, Rita Felski, Keith Jenkins and Alun Munslow do suggest general principles that would be consistent with a non-modernist, sceptical and thereby reinvigorated praxis (theorized practice) of history. This is par-ticularly the case in the work edited by Munslow and Robert Rosenstone, *Experiments in Rethinking History*, which features examples of experimental history writing.[35] Though we would expect critics of the authoritative style of conventional history to be wary of recommending definitive methods – for, as Jenkins actually says in *Refiguring History*, only in modernist histories would we find such 'blueprints' or 'templates'[36] – here I shall nevertheless set out six commonly mentioned principles. Although I do comment on all six in this chapter, a few (points three, four and five) warrant closer consideration and are therefore discussed more thoroughly in Chapters 3 to 5, as I noted earlier. The six guidelines are:

1   a 'self-reflexive' practice by the historian (a practice that includes both self-criticism and frank admissions of one's own position);
2   an emphasis on leaving arguments open, or on the provisional nature of any argument or interpretation (an emphasis that accompanies a suspicion of closures of knowledge seen in traditional discourses);
3   a focus more upon ruptures, breaks or discontinuities than on continuities in developments or processes in the past (a focus that seeks to avoid teleological and essentialist representations of the past);
4   a recognition of 'difference' – differences of culture, race/ethnicity, class, gender, sexuality, etc. – in order to avoid earlier tendencies to universalize cultures and homogenize people (a recognition that must nevertheless accompany an awareness that often differences are not natural but rather naturalized in social processes of differentiation);
5   a rejection of humanistic views of identity, whether it be national, group or individual identity (modern humanist and individualist conceptions of identity being essentialized and static rather than discursively constituted in an ongoing process); and
6   the view that historiography, the discourse of history itself, is at least a necessary focus of the historian, if not necessarily the only proper one.

First, re (self-) reflexivity, this is a term most often used in the general sense of practising a critical form of history where one's own assumptions, interpretations, methods, contradictions, failings and/or conclusions are not excluded from the critique. However, a more precise philosophical meaning of 'reflexivity' relates to self-referring paradoxes (such as the effect-cause-effect example above, or the tautological status of the fact in the discourse of history). In *Reflexivity: The Post-Modern Predicament*, Lawson focuses upon re-flexivity – at base, 'a turning back upon oneself' with respect to self-awareness and self-criticism on the part of authors and inherent self-contradiction in any texts – as central to the stream of European philosophy represented by Friedrich Nietzsche, Martin Heidegger and Jacques Derrida. Lawson emphasizes that this stream reflects a more general ('postmodern') crisis in 'our truths, our values, our most cherished beliefs'.[37] He shows how, for all three, the pursuit of Knowledge (absolutes, Truth, definitive theories, certainties about the nature of the world), which has been the 'great enterprise' of Western philosophy/metaphysics or 'dream of the Age of Enlightenment', is doomed to failure. This is because such a pursuit is built upon self-referring paradoxes of a type they did not see even their own works as able to avoid.

A simple example of such a paradox is the problem of how one can know that 'There is no knowledge'. Another example is the way I myself express scepticism toward definitive statements, yet inevitably slip at times (or perhaps more often than not) into old habits of argument suggestive of closure. If there is no avoidance of such self-reflexive problems, one way to distance oneself from the 'great enterprise', apart from demonstrating logical failings or inconsistencies in the works of those who pursue it, is to accept and work with them. The definition I gave earlier derived from Hilary Lawson's discussion of the deconstructive method employed by Derrida throws more light also on reflexivity:

> Deconstruction, at its simplest, consists of reading a text so closely that the conceptual distinctions, on which the text relies, are shown to fail on account of the inconsistent and paradoxical employment of these very concepts within the text as a whole. Thus the text is seen to fall by its own criteria – the standards or definitions which the text sets up are used reflexively to unsettle and shatter the original distinctions.[38]

Lawson then points out that, for Derrida, this method could be applied to any text, excluding Nietzsche, perhaps, since he had already used the technique against his own texts. (This, we might note, is a strange suggestion, that if Nietzsche had already deconstructed his own texts, no one else can take it a step further or in a different direction: the matter is 'closed'.)

Still, the works of all three philosophers, Nietzsche, Derrida and Heidegger, are 'reflexive throughout', according to Lawson. 'The position of the theory or the text in relation to what it proclaims is always in question' – or always open, 'closure' in an argument or theory being what the three wanted to avoid. Put simply, these philosophers and the many scholars who follow their lead, are wary of the pretence inspired by Western rationalism that one can have the final word on anything. (This, I might add, is precisely what successive interpretations in history of some event or phenomenon argue or imply: the 'name of the game'.) In the works of the three philosophers, therefore:

> Descriptions are drawn, views held, and conclusions asserted, only later to be denied and cast aside. Nor is the denial to be seen as more valid than the assertion, for it is merely part of the continuing tension which pervades the text. No section of the text can therefore be taken at face value. No assertion is simply an assertion, for it carries within it the unsaid awareness that it cannot be asserted. In this sense reflexivity is no longer a form of self-reference, a paradoxical puzzle, or a philosophical argument, but an inescapable movement which is still present in the moments of apparent stillness.[39]

This quote would not seem quite so shocking to someone with a familiarity with other cultural traditions, say, with the logic of paradox or negation in Zen. But, it is easy to see why these philosophers would raise the ire of those who insist upon the possibility of Knowledge, or accessing Reality or The Truth, and who fear the consequences of a descent into the irrationalism, nihilism and meaninglessness they see as the alternative to 'the security of an all-embracing story'. Derrida and others of like mind, however, would see our rationalism as 'beset with contradiction', as Lawson notes, and no protection against moral wrongs and injustices, as Europe's twentieth century well illustrates. On the other hand, Nietzsche's rejection of the moral absolutes of his time does not differ significantly from the moral or cultural relativism often adhered to today, whereby many accept that truth is in the eye of the beholder and senses of morality differ in accordance with different cultures, religions, epochs and so on.

A complete avoidance of reflexive paradox is a rationalist 'pipe-dream', according to such thinkers. However, acceptance of this standpoint does not prevent like-minded scholars from continuing to try to iron out everyday contradictions in their thinking, or between the theoretical principles they adhere to and their practice of writing or teaching. To offer an example that could be taken as either ordinary self-contradiction or reflexive paradox, the fact that the 'postmodern condition' is supposed to hinge upon an 'incredulity toward metanarratives',[40] including 'metahistories', may not prevent one from slipping at times into a familiar mode of speaking in terms suggestive of universality – as if there were underlying patterns (thus logic, 'laws' or even a 'guiding hand') in the passage of time; as if there were some 'natural'/inevitable form of global development and change (toward, say, capitalism). Or perhaps I forget that even in speaking of this 'sceptical postmodern' age, or of sceptical history, I could be taken to be indulging in just such a metanarrative of 'progress'. Lawson puts it well when he observes that the new concepts employed by Jacques Derrida, enable him: 'to account for what he is doing in terms of a new epoch, an epoch in which there is no present, and thus no history; an epoch which is no longer "an epoch".'[41] Stages, ages or epochs exist in our own minds as we seek to make sense of the world, not in the world itself.

Derrida's self-reflexivity, the application of reflexivity also to his own work, is what leads him to speak in terms that the uncautious might take to be ordinary, unconscious self-contradiction. Yet Lawson says of Derrida that, in line with a suspicion of closures of knowledge, he rejects the possibility of a theory of knowledge or language; denies us the comfort of coming to a conclusion about his own work in the final paragraph of one of his texts; allows his own theory of deconstruction to deconstruct itself, and so on.[42] This is the same sort of sceptical awareness of reflexive paradox that impels postmodernists to want to avoid closures of knowledge, and to speak only in broad terms about historical/scholarly practice. Ideally, such an awareness should lead one to resist the temptation to set principles 'in stone' – a definitive or perfect method being beyond our reach.

An awareness of reflexive paradox should also lead to the recognition that even 'postist' styles of thought never completely transcend that which they 'come after' (the modernist paradigm of history sets the terms of postmodernist critique). Hence, even postmodernist histories will inevitably be pastiches of familiar and innovative ways of seeing and speaking of the past. In this connection I am reminded of Keith Jenkins' desire: 'to breathe what fresh air can be breathed into an "old discipline" by refiguring it into a discourse that gratefully accepts and celebrates . . . the inevitable failures of historical representation/presentation rather than striving to overcome them.'[43] As an advocate of self-reflexivity in a postmodern praxis of history, Jenkins would be the first to include his own failures or inconsistencies among those to be accepted; celebrating them in principle (the principle being a general resistance to 'closure', absolutes, definitive methods, the final word); whilst simultaneously, I should think, trying to iron out everyday logical inconsistencies and remain wary of sweeping metahistorical pronouncements.

Feminist literary theorist Rita Felski offers a good example of such pronouncements in her discussion of the historicity of postist discourses.[44] Here she recognizes that contemporary theorists too often ascribe a problematic homogeneity to a past from which 'a single linear trajectory from modern totality to postmodernist plurality' is drawn – conveniently, since this sort of linear narrative is frequently coupled with assumptions that the *necessary* naivety and superficiality of all past thinking has 'given way to the more enlightened, sophisticated, and theoretically self-conscious perspectives of the present'[45] (from modernity to postmodernity, history to posthistory, feminism to postfeminism, etcetera). Her implication is that, if such theorists were so theoretically self-aware, they might take more care to avoid replicating in their own works the very sorts of failings they criticize in conventional historians: not only being reductionist about past discourses through their oversimplification or wide generalizations about past movements, but even utilizing linear narratives of progress, ever onward and upward, that are suggestive of teleologies (beliefs based on hindsight in predetermined 'natural' processes and ends). A classic example of the latter is the metanarrative of Marxist historical materialism that posited an inevitable global transition from the historical stage of primitive communism to slavery, feudalism, capitalism and then, finally, socialism, whereupon 'history' (human development) will end at a stage of perfection or at least its 'highest' stage. Others, of course, would have it that capitalist liberal democracy represents the end of 'history', an equally theological (coming of the messiah) sort of view.

In short, Felski shows how some postmodernist believers in the end or 'death of History' (meaning here the study/writing/ production of history) would do well to remember that reflexive or deconstructive principles can and should be applied equally to their own assumptions. To whom does this apparently universalized 'we' refer, she asks, in their 'bland assumption that "we" no longer live historically' or no longer possess a historical consciousness? With a nice sense of irony, Felski suggests that one theorist of the end of modernity and history, Gianni Vattimo, exemplifies a broader tendency on the part of others such as Jean-François Lyotard to make sweeping 'metatheoretical pronouncements . . . [that] speak more eloquently of the European philosopher's crisis of faith in a particular metaphysical tradition than of the status of history as such'.[46] And the same could be said of postmodernist historians such as Jenkins (who takes an 'end of history' position about postmodernism's signalling 'even the end of thinking historically at all'[47]) – of myself, too, with respect to my language concerning an 'age' of scepticism, as if scholarly scepticism has carried over into the broader society to the extent of becoming hegemonic or a dominant mode of thinking. We can all slip easily into old habits of speaking metahistorically, in ways that we may not be comfortable with in our more self-reflexive moments. One may never be able to dispense with reflexive paradoxes entirely in one's practice even of a nominally deconstructive sort of history, but that does not mean that we gloss over or fail to acknowledge those we are aware of.

Felski's approach to the end or death of history issue is not unlike that of poststructuralist feminist historian, Joan Wallach Scott. Scott's recognition of inevitable 'paradox[es] at the heart of the historian's practice' still does not lead her to 'deny the seriousness or usefulness of the enterprise' we call history.[48] Neither accepts that history is coming to an end, nor that it should. Partly this is because, as feminists, they remain committed to a political practice of history that would see women and other marginalized groups appropriating the form and telling their own diverse stories. This is in contradistinction to the 'one true story', e.g., of the nation, or to the days when mainstream history was more obviously than today, essentially an 'oedipalized' (Katherine Kearns would say) discourse between men – unashamedly about and for men. Felski observes that for many women, and for sound political reasons, history is hardly defunct but has continued importance, and the same can be said for other marginalized groups. The difficulties involved in squaring postmodernist epistemological principles with political commitments is an issue that will be considered further in the later chapters on difference and identity.

I should explain that Kearns criticizes the historiographical sub-genre of psychobiography for being fixated upon the figures of Father and Son (as well as friendship between men etc.). For her this replicates the institutionalized 'Oedipal' repression, indifference to, and amnesia about mother figures and women in conventional historiography.[49] One telling example of this, she points out, was Marc Bloch's well-known work, *The Historian's Craft* (1953 Vintage edition), which featured a dedication with the opening words: 'Tell me, Daddy. What is the use of history?'. When read together with introductions by others, this represents for Kearns a classic example of history as an interchange between men in which the nameless mother/wife (Madame Marc Bloch) has 'a deferred presence'.

My explanation of point one has also illustrated how the post-modern sceptic's 'suspicion of closures' (point two) is inseparable from the expectation that critical history will involve self-criticism, at base, as well as an awareness of reflexive paradox. The discussion earlier of critiques of history's realistic effect (re narrative) should also help readers see why its postmodernist critics advise that rather than seeking to get 'the' story straight, we historians would do better to get it 'crooked'. (In other words, leave it 'open'.) According to Han Kellner: 'There is no story *there* to be gotten straight; any story must arise from the act of contemplation'[50] on the part of the historian. Apart from his denial that reality itself takes the form of a story with an inherent meaning, Kellner advises that we resist the temptation of the final word, arguing for the provisional nature of any argument, explanation or interpretation.

Katherine Kearns shares Kellner's scepticism regarding the traditional injunction of empiricist historians to get the story straight – 'straight', she says, 'as in correct, factual, straightforward, honest, and matched up to truth, and, I would add, straight as in not at all queer'.[51] (She has a fair bit to say about traditionalist critiques of postmodernist 'effeminacies', as I indicated above.) However, Kearns expresses some doubts about the gendered, implicitly masculinist assumptions of critiques of narrative: 'storytelling' as feminized as opposed to theory, science, etc. that traditionally have been treated as masculine preserves. She observes that one might be able to imagine historians capable of combining both a commitment to theory with a commitment to 'the necessity and value of narrative', but:

> This will not happen as long as even the most self-aware, analytically astute writers remain with a conceptual scheme that subordinates story-telling to some fantasy of attainable truth and that locates narrative only as relative to, at most in an asymptotic relationship with, more powerful, more 'masculine' modes of assessment.[52]

She nevertheless accepts Kellner's recommendation that we get the story crooked partly through looking at sources other than those found in archives and databases – namely, secondary texts that concentrate on 'discourse and rhetoric' in works of history (my sixth point above). Kearns acknowledges that this is a radical injunction because it would mean that distinctions that are 'fundamental and sacrosanct' in conventional history would have to be revised substantially. The first distinction she mentions is that between primary and secondary sources,[53] because privileging primary (e.g., archival) sources over secondary (scholarly interpretative) ones makes no sense in postmodernist or other histories focussed upon discourse and rhetoric in the discipline itself (where 'secondary' sources are, in effect, transformed into 'primary' ones).

Kellner challenges the traditional status of documents or (primary) 'sources' mainly because of their central place in empiricist history's penchant for the realistic effect. Here sources constitute 'evidence' for particular arguments about the past and for history's facticity and the historian's objectivity. We have been taught, he explains in a Barthes-like manner, that the historian's sources are 'particles of reality from which an image of the past is made'. A corollary of this critique of the empiricist fixation on the primary source and archive, moreover, is Kellner's insistence that significant changes in interpretations of the past do not come primarily from the unearthing of new documents, as tradition has it, but rather from changes in rhetorical (mental and linguistic) conventions.[54] The latter is often what impels historians to go looking for the former. For example, without a political conviction that the part women played in past events and processes matters, one would not bother to go scratching about in the archives for new sources on or by them (or looking elsewhere since, typically, sources by/about women were not archived in the first place). For Kellner, too, like Barthes, this suggests that 'history is not "about" the past as such, but rather about *our ways of creating meanings* from the scattered, and profoundly meaning*less* debris we find around us.' In other words, history is more about the (or *our*) present. (This issue, 'presentism', will be discussed at length in Chapter 2.)

The reference to 'meaning*less* debris' brings us to the third point on p. 33 on discontinuity. It is suggestive of another seminal thinker often associated with postmodernism, Michel Foucault. Drawing upon Nietzsche once again, Foucault was more inclined to associate randomness and contingency with processes and change in the past than determination by 'causes' (often prime or singular ones). 'The forces operating in history,' he said:

> are not controlled by destiny or regulative mechanisms, but respond to haphazard conflicts. They do not manifest the successive forms of a primordial intention and their attraction is not that of a conclusion, for they appear through the singular randomness of events.[55]

Here Foucault was reacting against teleological metanarratives (otherwise termed 'master' or 'grand' narratives) such as the above-mentioned Marxian historical materialism. This pictured human development as unfolding through successive stages that would 'conclude' with the final stage of socialism/communism, with changes (at least in orthodox Marxism) between the successive 'modes of production' being brought about essentially by material or economic causes. Hence, we often find an emphasis in post-modern histories or other critical works on the essential chaos, randomness, flux or just discontinuities at work in the passage of time, as opposed to a conventional emphasis on events that, in themselves, have an intrinsic meaning and cause other events. 'Events' actually come to be styled as such by human interpreters only 'after the event' (they have to be accorded some meaning in order to be designated an event) and, further, treated in 'grand narratives' as causes in teleological linear sequences toward the present that are based on hindsight. Even an occurrence that might seem obviously and naturally to be a 'revolution' to some could be subject to other interpretations (rebellion, anarchy, riot) implying a different essential character (e.g. 'political' event or merely 'criminal' act), different causes, and different meanings, in different overall paradigms of social change. If seen as a mere 'riot' it may not even be deemed worthy of designating as an event and cause of other events.

Following Foucault, Joan Scott posits discontinuity as one of three ways in which the object of historical enquiry could fruitfully be reconceptualized after the linguistic turn.[56] Since the three correspond with the third to fifth principles of practice outlined on p. 33, those I have selected for in-depth consideration in later chapters, here I shall draw mainly upon Scott's treatment of them but discuss them more broadly in the next three chapters. First, we saw above that Scott refutes the charge that postmodernism spells the end of (the discourse of) history, and she suggests that through an emphasis on discontinuity we can maintain 'the connection between history and time', keeping history 'forever open'.[57] More specifically, she advises that we focus upon the breaks between past and present, accounting for their emergence as 'deviations . . . from established norms' – 'not in terms of general principles of development [as with metanarratives of progress], but in terms of the specificity of their occurrence'. Further, the absence of inherent meanings in past processes (due to their randomness) does not, she says, 'plunge us into an abyss; rather, it makes the production of meaning a human, albeit historically variable and contested, activity'.[58]

The recommendation from Scott (and Foucault and Kellner) that we see the past in terms of meaningless flux is also suggestive of point four on p. 33. This concerned the recognition of 'difference' in order to avoid universalizing cultures and homogenizing people. Scott alludes to how traditional master narratives have posited global models of historical development where the real model is the so-called 'West'. In such visions cultural differences are subsumed in grand narratives of progress where those who do not follow suit, or who do not wish to, are seen to be backward or benighted, and either way inferior. Scott focuses upon 'difference' in a number of inter-related ways, first in seeing 'fundamental ruptures and, therefore, profound differences between past and present' and, second, in challenging normative Western ideas about the West's ownership of 'progress'. In the postist (or 'difference') style of feminism she represents, we also see this recognition of difference extended to gender, race/ethnicity, and sexuality, too, in contradistinction to humanist discourses marked by revealing rhetorical constructions such as the 'history of Man'. One has only to look at the usual subjects of conventional history, especially before the rise of Social, Women's/Gender and other combative styles of History, to see that, rather than really meaning all people, such rhetorical conventions revealed a relegation to invisibility of all but white, Western, economically privileged men. In other words, such constructions homogenized people, subsuming differences under 'norms' derived from Western, white, upper class men.

As I have already implied, these six points on how we might conduct a non-modernist, sceptical and reinvigorated praxis of history have a tendency to overlap. Thus, Scott's focus on discontinuity and difference as two of three ways to reconceptualize history are interrelated. Her discussion of 'processes of differentiation', moreover, is focussed upon questions of identity. This was referred to in my point five on p. 33: 'a rejection of humanistic views of identity, whether it be national, group or individual identity (modern humanist and individualist conceptions of identity being essentialized and static rather than discursively constituted in an ongoing process).' To the extent that humanism has fixed group or national identities by investing them in the past (with an enduring *core continuity* that extends to the present, in other words), once again Scott's recommendation is that we look rather for discontinuities, this time in order to avoid *essentializing* such identities.

But, why *should* we avoid attributing essences (a central or essential feature) to cultural or group identities, one might ask. Scott's answer is partly ideological: that this is more conducive to a radical, resistant praxis both of politics in general and to an unashamedly political practice of history. (I might note in passing that my first principle of practice on p. 33 – on how self-reflexivity should also involve a frank admission of one's own position – is also indicated here.) To cite an example Scott offers of how essentialized identities have had conservative political uses:

> To assume that Americanness or Frenchness consists only in an enduring set of traits or beliefs established (say) in 1776 or 1789 is to accept the ideological terms of national identity rather than to write the history of the repeated and changing ways in which the imagined community was consolidated. With the first approach, historians collude in a nationalist project by abstracting the Nation from the processes that continually produce and reproduce it; with the second approach, they demystify national identity and expose the various differences it has been used to balance and contain.[59]

In short, essentializing a nation's identity inevitably means relegating to the margins or to invisibility (and thus containment) groups whose differences render problematic the imputed essence. An obvious Australian example is the androcentric (male-centred) notion that Australian culture is centred upon 'mateship', a term ostensibly associated with equality but derived from masculinist, white (even just Anglo: beer drinking, round shouting) traditions and identities. This, we might note, was the first of the core Australian values put forward in 2006 by the Prime Minister, John Howard, when the question was raised of how we might steer Muslim children away from 'terrorism' (only the boys, presumably). Clearly, if they have to be taught this Australian value and core identity that other kids learn 'naturally', their 'Australianness' is in doubt. (A cynic might say: no wonder if they don't frequent pubs!)

Scott also questions essentialized (core, fixed) identities even for marginalized groups. As we shall see in Chapter 4, this is a point that has often been treated with suspicion by those who justifiably point to the gains made under the banner of identity politics in social movements. However, Scott makes the interesting observation that if identities (say, as Jewish, women or gay) are centred upon 'exclusion and suffering', it is a bit difficult to see how there can be a future where this is transcended. For, 'When identity becomes synonymous with exclusion and suffering, inclusion and the end of suffering portend the end of identity.'[60] She notes that such constructions of identity rest upon an ahistorical, universalized conflation of past and present, rather than on discontinuities. However, if we seek instead to historicize identity, we provide the basis for a treatment, for example of 'women', that 'is not a rediscovery of ourselves in the past'. This attempt to avoid presentism constitutes another reason for Scott's recommendation that historians focus upon *processes* of differentiation: on 'the production of identity as processes both of homogenisation and differentiation' even where its production is by marginalized groups who have used essentialized identities as political weapons in their various struggles.

This leads to Scott's third and final point in 'After History?', which concerns 'historicizing interpretation'. We should, she says, be asking questions such as how and in what historical conditions have differences of sex, or colour, or sexuality come to matter. For example:

> [I]f we document not the long history of homophobia, but the ways and times and terms in which certain sexual practices were pathologized and others normalized, we historicize rather than naturalize both homosexuality and heterosexuality. Or, to take up the question of national identity again, if we ask not what it means to be an American, but how Americanness has been defined – and by whom – [and to what ends] over time, we can write the history of the United States not as the realization of an essence, but as the story of ongoing political contestation around terms and practices that are at once durable and changeable.[61]

Not unusually, Scott's postmodernist focus is upon discourse and its intimate connection with power relations. For her, political resistance to hegemonic repressive norms and practices is best served if in our own discourse (histories) we avoid the suggestion that the differences that condition our social relationships are fixed or have remained the same over time because if they are 'natural' it would imply that they are not subject to human intervention. That way, as noted above, our political future lies open.

This concern with identity is also relevant to competing constructs of individual identity. Although it might be associated with 'postmodernism', the critique of the Western (Christian-derived) humanist-individualistic Self – based on the notion that one has a centre or 'core self' that is autonomous and remains unchanged – is not very new. One Western theorist particularly associated with the critique of the centred Self is again Roland Barthes, whose conception of the Self I shall discuss in detail in Chapter 4. Barthes had Western precursors such as Nietzsche, whilst also being influenced by Zen.[62] (Even Nietzsche, however, was one of the Western philosophers sometimes regarded as an 'honorary oriental' because of his own interest in Eastern thought.) Barthes' approach to the 'fragmented' or 'scattered' (acentric, complex and ever changing) Self partly echoed Buddhist perceptions of the individual Self as not unique at the level of consciousness, nor separable from the world around it, an approach which in postmodernism finds expression in critiques of 'interiority'. Scott, above, was also suggesting the alternative, 'exteriority', with her emphasis on identity as discursively constituted. We find the same sort of idea in Lacanian psychoanalysis, as Jameson indicates when speaking of Jacques Lacan's post/structuralist notion of the symbolic order:

> For Lacan, the Symbolic Order is that realm into which the child emerges, out of a biological namelessness, when he [sic] gradually acquires language. It is impersonal, or superpersonal, but it is also that which permits the very sense of identity itself to come into being. Consciousness, personality, the subject are, therefore . . . secondary phenomena which are determined by the vaster structure of language itself, or the Symbolic.[63]

And just as language is not learned in one fell swoop, Scott adds that identity is discursively constituted in an ongoing *process*. One's identity is, in other words, formed, and continually re-formed, through language/discourse; it does not precede language, as if somehow the individual were a self-contained blank slate upon which, at birth or even before it, identity (a centred, fixed identity) is written once and for all. Hence, the commonly heard 'defence' of homosexuality as not a choice, but 'natural' (one being born gay, and thus it 'cannot be helped') makes no sense within such a schema. Nor would it make sense in a defence of heterosexuality.

This 'postmodernist' conception of identity was developed by Scott in a well-known essay on identity or, rather, 'subjectivity' (subject formation: the formation of subject *positions*) as often resting upon the problematic empiricist category of 'experience'.[64] Here she explains how, in history, knowledge and truth have often been seen to derive from personal experience: normative history:

> has rested its claim to legitimacy on the authority of experience, the direct experience of others [historical actors under investigation by the historian], as well as of the historian who learns to see and illuminate the lives of those others in his or her texts.[65]

As to the 'evidence' of experience, she asks 'what could be truer, after all, than a subject's own account of what he or she has lived through?' Her basic point is that we should not be taking experience as given, unquestioningly, as evidence for a true story, but rather interpreting the political and other *uses* of representations of 'experience', whether by historians or historical actors.

Scott urges us to remember that the experience(s) upon which identity is often said to rest is itself discursively constituted. Let's take as an example the woman who refuses to report a sexual attack to the police because she adheres to the popular belief that in such cases a woman's own dress or behaviour must be responsible. Had she had access to alternative, say, feminist readings of such incidents of sexual violence she may have understood the experience in a different way. Yet, some time later she does come to see the incident differently (under the influence of feminist ideas), and takes it to be important in the formation of her feminist identity. So which came first: the reinterpretation or the feminism? This illustrates Scott's point that we historians should not be taking accounts of either experience or identity formation for granted, but should rather *read* them in terms of 'the complex and changing discursive processes by which identities are ascribed, resisted or embraced'.[66]

Historicizing experience, moreover, will help us to avoid essential-izing identities. If we do take 'the emergence of concepts and iden-tities as historical events in need of explanation', we automatically assume:

> that the appearance of a new identity is not inevitable or determined, not something that was always there simply waiting to be [uncovered and] expressed [as the one true self], not something that will always exist in the form it was given in a particular political movement or at a particular historical moment.[67]

Scott's approach in these two essays, 'After History?' and 'Experience', speaks particularly to three of the six general principles I set out on p. 33, on discontinuity, difference and subjectivity. However, one would not have to look very hard to find in her works[68] suggestions of the other three guidelines for a postmodernist or 'sceptical' praxis of history. She exemplifies, for example, how a reflexive self-awareness combines reflection upon one's own episte-mological, historiographical assumptions, methods and conclusions, with a frank admission of one's own political standpoints and commitments. However, one should acknowledge that the latter long predated the advent of 'postmodernism'. The principle that scholarship always is and, indeed, should be political, that is, has long been accepted by leftist scholars (Marxists, anarchists, femin-ists), in contrast to those whose empiricism and (conservative) liberal ideology encouraged them to see only their political oppo-nents as positioned or 'political' and thus lacking in objectivity. In this sense postmodernist history stands in the tradition of 'Marxist history' or 'feminist history', the very nomenclature of which indi-cates the frankly positioned nature of the works.

It is therefore for good reason that conservative historians are in the habit of tacking 'and feminists too' onto the list of those whose 'murderous' impulses they bemoan, that is, the postmodernists, literary theorists and feminists who supposedly are trying to kill off history. Perhaps Gertrude Himmelfarb does not *quite* indulge in the invective of a Windshuttle or Elton[69] (re 'fanatical' feminists, for example), though some might dispute the point. But, what she does complain of at one point is how 'the political potential of post-modernism has been seized most enthusiastically by feminist historians'.[70] Scott's propositions that history is always political and can be an instrument for feminist power (or the empowerment of Native Americans, underclass people, gays and others) she finds 'absurd'. For Himmelfarb, such propositions represent 'little more than is already being affirmed in the name of "multiculturalism"', which has had the (unfortunate) 'effect of politicizing history'. Even non-postmodernist feminists would find laughable the notion that it took multiculturalism, feminism, Marxism or postmodernism to politicize history. The only difference from mainstream history is that feminist (and other 'positioned') history is, as Himmelfarb acknowledges, 'consciously and profoundly subversive' – that is, unapologetically political.

I have already commented on the sixth and final principle for a postmodernist or sceptical practice of history that I noted on p. 33, which concerned history theory as a necessary focus of the historian, if not necessarily the only proper one. This is suggested in deconstructionist historian Dominick LaCapra's vision of history as a dialogic exchange, as expressed in the passage from *History and Reading* with which I began this section. There he noted a conventional 'distinction between accurate reconstruction of an object of study', the empiricist ideal, and 'exchange with that object as well as with other inquirers into it'. In contrast, a dialogic reading is focussed as much on an exchange with other interpreters of the past as on the past itself. Such an approach presupposes the central part that historiography (one's dialogue with other historians, or broadly with the discourse of history) plays in history production, whether it is explicit or submerged. In reconstructionist history, LaCapra then noted, the first sort of exchange, with other historians, is relegated to footnotes (or, worse, endnotes where it is even less visible) and bibliographies in a manner that 'disguises' it, representing the work as a straightforward objective re-presentation of past realities.

To clarify the point with a practical example, I could cite the manner in which history (or other scholarship) is often written. The author's intertextuality, or the extent to which s/he draws upon other texts for inspiration, is blurred by the authoritative scholarly voice combined with standard conventions of referencing. One makes an apparently confident statement of 'fact' in the text, implying that it is a fact according to some other historian only by a teensy number at the end of the sentence, and then in a foot- or endnote (which might not be read in any case) one might go so far as to acknowledge that a third historian actually disagrees that it is a fact.

In contrast, the more one discusses the work of other scholars in the main text – agreeing with it, disagreeing with it, contrasting it with one's own approach – the more one should be able to avoid the omniscient narrative voice and totalizing perspectives of empiricism. This returns us to the first principle on p. 33, because it is a bit difficult to leave the 'story' open when the inevitable dialogue/agreements/quarrels with other interpreters of the 'object of study' at hand is kept to a minimum and buried in foot- or endnotes.

We have seen how historiography or theory has been a hotly contested issue in the discipline; how historians who pay too much attention to it, or 'only do theory', have been targets of criticism. Katherine Kearns again takes a rather ambivalent position when she observes that:

> Historians who have turned to various modes of theoretical assessment seem fated to move from the enterprise of writing history to the enterprise of writing about writing history, as if, once having fallen from historiographic innocence, there is no going back. There is as a consequence an immensely rich body of post-structuralist work on historiography and an unresolved split between those who write history, those who write about historiography from various poststructuralist positions, and those who write about it out of recuperative responsibility.[71]

Kearns' sense of irony is at its best when applied to the traditionalists rather than to those who may justifiably feel that with a loss of 'historiographic innocence' there is no going back. In my view the latter is more understandable than the view exemplified by Himmelfarb's proposition that history theory is not 'real' or 'proper' history, or by Geoffrey Elton's hostility to theory. 'Talking about doing history invites a world of trouble,' Kearns observes, for 'to recognize the contradictions critically is not only to stop *doing* history, it is to threaten to stop history.'[72] I don't know about the latter but do agree that doing critical or sceptical history is no easy task; this is partly because 'there is no easy back and forth between writing about history and writing it', as she says.[73]

Yet I am not convinced that there is an 'unresolved split' between those who write history and those who write history theory. Of course, some, such as Scott, do both. We often find her reflecting upon, as I put it above, general principles that would be consistent with a non-modernist, sceptical and thereby reinvigorated praxis of history. The six general guidelines I have laid out here were of course inspired by the works of postmodernist authors such as Alun Munslow, Keith Jenkins and others not yet referred to, including numerous feminist scholars. As I have illustrated by reference to Scott, Kearns and Felski, feminist scholars have much to offer to a discussion of how we might practise a renewed critical form of history. This applies not only to postmodernists, or postmodernist historians, but also others who are not as convinced of the political utility of postmodernist epistemological principles, whether for women or for an effective (feminist or other) subversive practice of scholarship. There is little point in trying to produce 'sceptical' histories if the objects of our scepticism exclude postmodernism itself.

Suggestions for further reading

Apart from scholarly journals such as *Rethinking History: The Journal of Theory and Practice* and *History and Theory*, looking through readers is an excellent way to begin to familiarize oneself with important issues and debates in the field. They contain selected essays (sometimes abridged). One can quickly get a sense of where scholars stand, who should be read, and whether an author's style is readable or opaque. They also tend to be less androcentric than they once were. Useful examples are:

- Keith Jenkins (ed.), *The Postmodern History Reader*, London and New York: Routledge, 1997
- Keith Jenkins and Alun Munslow (eds), *The Nature of History Reader*, London and New York: Routledge, 2004
- Sue Morgan (ed.), *The Feminist History Reader*, London and New York: Routledge, 2006 (especially Part II: 'Deconstructing the female subject: feminist history and the "linguistic turn"')
- Alun Munslow, *The Routledge Companion to Historical Studies*, London and New York: Routledge, 2000, 2006

A work that offers a good overview of historiography in a lucid, accessible style (and does not exclude contributions by women or from feminist theory) is:

- Ann Curthoys and John Docker, *Is History Fiction?*, Sydney: University of New South Wales Press, 2006

For those who wish to read up on the gendering of the discipline of History (and/or the history of women's history):

- Bonnie G. Smith, *The Gender of History: Men, Women, and Historical Practice*, Cambridge, Mas. and London: Harvard University Press, 1998
- Mary Spongberg, *Writing Women's History since the Renaissance*, Basingstoke, UK and New York: Palgrave Macmillan, 2002

Also, since narrativity (history and narrative) has been a central and ongoing debate in the discipline, but I chose not to duplicate the many extended discussions of it that are available, the following reader and/or individual works really should be consulted:

- Frank R. Ankersmit, *Historical Interpretation*, Stanford: Stanford University Press, 2001; *History and Tropology: The Rise and Fall of Metaphor*, Berkeley: University of California Press, 1994; or *Sublime Historical Experience*, Groningen, 2005)
- Alun Munslow, *Narrative and History*, Palgrave, forthcoming 2007
- Geoffrey Roberts (ed.), *The History and Narrative Reader*, London and New York: Routledge, 2001
- Hayden White, *The Content of the Form: Narrative Discourse and Historical Representation*, Baltimore: The John Hopkins University Press, 1987

Finally, the new primer for students I mentioned above takes the form, in part, of an extended dictionary of postmodernism with particular reference to history, with a glossary and eight chapters, most of which are simply entitled 'Empiricism', 'Sign', 'Discourse', 'Poststructuralism', etc. However, it features discussions of many issues of interest to historians, so its usefulness extends far beyond mere definitions. The same can be said for the *Routledge Companion* by Alun Munslow. Both research students and teachers of history would find these to be handy reference works:

- Callum G. Brown, *Postmodernism for Historians*, Harlow, UK: Pearson Longman, 2005
- Alun Munslow, *The Routledge Companion to Historical Studies*, London and New York: Routledge, 2000, 2006

The latter features an introductory essay, 'History Today: Critical Perspectives' as well as an alphabetical list of entries usually a few pages long. The list includes historians and theorists (Carr, Derrida, Elton, Foucault, White, etc.) as well as styles of history and schools of thought (cultural history, structuralism) and terms and concepts (discourse, empiricism, emplotment, relativism, teleology and so on).

Chapter 2

Reinventing the wheel
The present-past nexus

I

> If it is unhistorical to permit the present to determine the past, it is surely as unhistorical to prevent the past from informing the present.
>
> (Gertrude Himmelfarb, *The New History and the Old*, Chap. 1: 'History with the Politics Left Out')[1]

> [W]e propose that historians should be more conscious of the socially constructed rules which they follow. But one of these, the rule against presentism, embodies the essential denial of the propagandistic and relativistic nature of history.
>
> (Ellen Somekawa and Elizabeth Smith, 'Theorizing the Writing of History')[2]

My reference to 'the wheel' in the title partly signals a return to an old debate in the discipline, concerning presentism. It could also be taken to signify the circularity of causation in representations of the past (or 'history', 'origins', 'tradition') that seek to show how the past has determined the present, apparently in unilinear fashion. This overlooks the fact that the past doing the determining is already the product of our interpretation, which is to say that we cannot learn the 'lessons of history' without first imputing a moral/political character to the aspect of the past which is under consideration. So, contrary to Gertrude Himmelfarb's belief that presentism should not be 'permitted' in good history, in history it is inevitable that the present will teleologically determine (our representations of) the past. Although sceptics such as postmodernist scholars may share a concern with history's teleologies and seek through various means to circumvent them as far as is possible, what differentiates them from conservatives is their acceptance that histories will nevertheless still be present-minded, and in a variety of ways, culturally, politically, epistemologically, historiographically and so on. For them 'presentist' is not merely a code-word for 'political' or, more specifically, the sorry habit that only others have of allowing their ideologies to interfere with the constructions they place upon the past. A further difference is that postmodernists often seek to engage creatively and self-reflexively with presentism in their works of history.

Toward the end of this chapter, I shall return to a consideration of the approach recommended by the postmodernist historian I contrasted with Himmelfarb earlier, Joan Scott. However, I would note in advance of that that there is a tension exhibited even in Scott's essay, 'After History?', with respect to presentism, where she implies that this can be transcended through a more careful historicist approach. In brief, it is in a conscious effort to avoid (unconscious) presentism that Scott, using the example of identity, encourages a '*dis*identification with the objects of our enquiry, a deliberate effort to separate ourselves from others who seem to be like us'.[3] She is justifiably wary of the danger of projecting our own identities, standpoints or ways of seeing back onto others (in this case, other women) in different times and places. This may be one way in which we might possibly mitigate presentism, but it will not ensure that we dispense with it entirely. Scott's approach will be discussed more fully in closing, but we should note her implication that such a method will be more true to the realities of the past. She may not be recommending the commonly endorsed method of 'empathy': the assumption that we can empathize with people in the past (get 'into their heads' or at least into their times) through use of the correct method(s). No doubt she is distancing herself from that view, which is criticized by Keith Jenkins in a section on empathy in his first book, *Re-thinking History:*

> Given then that there is no presuppositionless interpretation of the past, and given that interpretations of the past are constructed in the present, the possibility of the historian being able to slough off his present to reach somebody else's past on their terms looks remote.[4]

Yet Scott's object in proposing that we 'dis-identify' with people in the past does not appear to differ greatly from the more conventional endorsement of empathy to the extent that she sees unconscious presentism to be the barrier, not to empathy but to our recognition of the difference of the past. In principle, this is a reasonable supposition, though the question remains of whether there is any method that will enable us to avoid presentism with any degree of certainty. How can we know when we have accessed the real past through such a method? Our scepticism, nevertheless, need not prevent us from remaining cognizant of the past's distance from us, and seeking to illustrate this though a self-reflexive approach to writing history that accepts the discipline's inevitable 'omnipresent' or 'ever-present' nature. Incorporating reflections upon how our present concerns and world views are likely to colour the pictures we paint of the past is surely a preferable method to the naive confidence exhibited by some that presentism can be overcome merely by 'leaving the politics out of history'.

Ellen Somekawa and Elizabeth Smith offer a clearer contrast with Himmelfarb's proscription of presentism by going so far as to recommend that the discipline's rule against it be eliminated. They recommend this because empiricist history:

> claims that we can read documents as they were written and as they were read, and write about them in such a way that their meaning is not changed by our concerns about the present .... Historians are generally modest about their ability to achieve a perfect unity of outlook with their historical subjects. So the source of our disagreement with the profession is not that it is oblivious to the unattainability of its goals, but that by perpetuating this proscription against presentism, it actively engages in mystifying the very nature of the act of historical writing. That historians in the academy have no goals, assumptions, or purposes for writing apart from a desire to mimic accurately the experiences of past lives is clearly not a credible claim, yet such an ideal underlies the widely accepted rule against presentism.[5]

They therefore propose that we accept that history is, by nature, presentist and political, 'propaganda' being a term they are happy to apply to how its production should be seen by its practitioners. Not unlike Scott, for them history is 'the ongoing contention between competing political and philosophical perspectives'. This is what Somekawa and Smith believe historiographical debates should be concerned with, rather than with competitions over 'bias and accuracy'; or over the latest, more accurate revision that is supposedly based just on 'improved information' (newly unearthed sources) rather than changing intellectual contexts and historiographical paradigms.[6]

Further, Somekawa and Smith argue that if historiographical debates were to be centred upon the ethics or politics of an interpretation rather than on its accuracy, the grounds for imputing integrity to the historian would involve a shift of focus from his/her ability to access the truth, objectively or disinterestedly. Historians would therefore be required to believe instead in the ethical and/or political worth of the positions they take up; and to evaluate interpretations, first and foremost, in accordance with their political utility and sincerity, second in terms of their persuasiveness. Although Somekawa and Smith are wary of truth claims, their alternative of mere persuasiveness (or plausibility) rather than 'truth' would not rule out debates over facticity. Though statements of 'fact' are often not only that but are also coloured by interpretation, persuasiveness will still rest in part upon whether one accepts as 'fact' things that undeniably happened in the past (such as 'the Holocaust' or the 'Rape of Nanking'[7]), the actual occurrence of which would not be in dispute unless for dubious political purposes. Yet, as Somekawa and Smith imply, this general approach to presentism follows logically from an acceptance of the principle that there is 'no one neutral social/political position from which to view events and hence no one correct interpretation'.[8] Their point simply concerns meanings attributed to events by historians, no one interpreter of an event being able to claim intrinsic or absolute truth as if the meaning resided in the event itself. What is quite another matter is deliberate falsification through a denial of occurrences in the past, for example in the interests of anti-Semitism or a Japanese ultra-nationalism that at the beginning of the twenty-first century still wants to whitewash Japan's record of wartime aggression. Deconstructionist historians such as Alun Munslow share an adherence to this principle. In *Deconstructing History* Munslow discusses Hayden White's position on history as narrative, noting that for him it is at the moral or ideological level that our choice of plot structure and argument is determined. It is also at this level that the historian positions herself on questions such as what implications can be drawn from studying past events *in order to understand present ones*. (An anti-communist critic of post-Soviet Russia, for example, would likely explain social problems there today in terms of the legacy of the Soviet system, its entire history being emplotted as a tragedy or perhaps farce.) But, often it is not just an understanding of present conditions that is at stake, but rather a political intercession in them through self-interested constructs of the past. Either way, one cannot do otherwise than agree with White who, as Munslow puts it, 'acknowledges the presentism of history. . . . He acknowledges that no historian can stand aside from history and suspend his/her capacity for or exercise of moral judgement . . . . [This] means that there are no disinterested historians.'[9] Munslow cites White's *Metahistory* here, and it should be acknowledged that subsequently he discusses White's uncertainty as to whether it is tropes (figures of speech or, generally, linguistic conventions) that determine ideology or vice versa. I tend to assume the latter – that one's morality/ideology impels one to choose from a number of available tropic narrative emplotments, tragedy, heroic epic/romance, farce/satire and so on – though to some extent the determination doubtless goes both ways, i.e. is 'dialectical'.

This debate over whether we should be proscribing, merely accepting, or even embracing presentism is suggestive of a paradox connected with what I seek to do in this chapter. On the one hand, like Somekawa and Smith (and White, Ankersmit, Jenkins, Munslow, Scott and many others), I want to endorse the principle that history always is an ethico-political project and should be accepted as such. I see no need to try to deny or eliminate this sort of presentism that involves (*pace* Himmelfarb) leaving the politics *in* history. Where the apparent contradiction arises is with my wanting to mount a critique of conventional history for its frequent recourse *to presentism*. Ironically, however, those who proscribe consciously political history are not immune from being presentist themselves in the constructions they place upon the past. This is often in a glaringly political manner, though what particularly concerns me in this chapter is *unconscious* presentism, whether or not the teleologies in question are the direct products of the politics of historians.

There are other, conceptual or epistemological reasons for the ubiquity of teleology in history. For example, what often goes unrecognized is how conventional causation, most obviously but not only in linear narrative histories, commits one to beginning with the ostensible origin of some phenomenon that could not actually be represented as such unless from an 'endpoint', i.e. teleologically. (I mentioned this problem when discussing Nietzsche and Ankersmit on 'effect-cause-effect' on pp. 20–1.) That is, it is what we find characteristic of the phenomenon now, its essential features, that we go looking for in the past; finding one or more of these features back then, we assume that they formed part of the same phenomenon back then. But perhaps the phenomenon we know did not actually exist then. Perhaps that part of this contemporary phenomenon that we take to be central to it formed a central part of some very different phenomenon back then. Apart from this sort of teleology, there is, no doubt, an untold number of ways in which the constructions we place upon the past will always be present-minded, for (politics aside) we cannot do other than think in the languages or mindsets of our own cultures and times to an extent that we can never be fully aware of. This will be the case regardless of how hard we try to immerse ourselves in the temporal and cultural contexts of the past peoples and phenomena we investigate (the often-touted corrective methods of empathy, contextualization, historicization and so on).

My ultimate concern in this chapter is therefore not with how to avoid presentism entirely or per se. I take it to be an inevitable by-product of studying the past in the present: one of the paradoxes intrinsic to the discipline. The chapter is more focused upon a secondary paradox that troubles the discipline, one that can be circumvented. This concerns how conventional historians combine a belief in our abilities to re-present past realities with an avowed opposition to presentism, albeit whilst simultaneously engaging in it unconsciously, or without due recognition or acknowledgement of it. Glaring contradictions of this sort might be avoided if we dispensed with the habit of equating being authoritative about the objects of our enquiries with a claim to be able to find their one true story or interpretation; and frankly acknowledged more often the limits to our ability to access past realities, as well as the myriad possible effects of our present on our representations of the past. I do not mean to suggest that we do this, moreover, only in separate theoretical works reflecting on the discipline (in which authors habitually claim in response to postmodern or other radical critiques of the discipline's foundations: 'But we've always known that!' and then continue with business as usual in their other works). We need to do it in our standard works of history, too; and more consistently than just in the obligatory sections in introductions on theory/methodology.

Somekawa and Smith note the common relegation to a book's preface or acknowledgements of concerns that should be central to the work – concerns such as 'our own personal and limited perspectives, the institutional and social contexts in which we labor to produce history, and our political agendas for writing what we write.'[10] It is, of course, in the interests of maintaining the work's 'illusion of objectivity' that the author (the 'I' of the text) must remain absent from the main text, and near-absent even from the footnotes. As one of the 'founding fathers' of modern 'scientific' or objectivist history, Lord Acton, put it, good history is that in which the historian is absent and history itself appears to be doing the speaking.[11] The use of 'I', on the other hand, according to deconstructionist historian, Dominick LaCapra, 'disrupts a value-neutral façade and raises questions about the possibilities and limits of objectivity. It foregrounds the problem of subjectivity.'[12] Nevertheless, LaCapra proceeds to explain that the use of the 'I' is not without its problems, because it can serve to reinforce 'an individualist ideology', obscuring the 'intimate relation of subject and subjectivity to social positionality and the manner in which "voice" is not a pure individual or subjective issue' – not the product entirely of 'individual psyche or biography' but rather socially or discursively produced. (The postmodernist approach to subjectivity and positionality will be discussed in Chapter 3.)

The pressure in the discipline to maintain such rhetorical conventions is strong, and I would not pretend that I have managed to withstand it in my own works to date. These have not been as self-reflexive as I feel they should be, in principle, though I do not feel any discomfort at using the 'subjective' 'I', nor with positioning myself, politically. For perhaps most historians, however, such conventions seem preferable to the alternative of frankly positioned history that seems to them to threaten to lower the standard of our work by turning it into mere 'propaganda'. This is despite the fact that the distinction between good history and propaganda has long served to question the legitimacy only of histories that contest dominant ideology, as Somekawa and Smith observe. 'Good history' is that concerned with 'the truth', so the story goes; bad history is politically positioned or basically guided by one's own politics. Yet such opinions and the narrative conventions that reflect them are part and parcel of conservative liberal ideology: 'The interpretative nature of liberal and conservative histories is often invisible to people; interpretations which fit neatly into the dominant categories for understanding the world are persuasive precisely because their arguments seem to be simple empirical statements.'[13] This is because authors create such an impression, even through their style of expression. In this connection, empiricism goes hand in hand with liberalism. As Munslow concludes:

> The ultimately ideological nature of empiricist history lies in the way in which it attempts to make us all read its works as if they were realistic – this is the truth of the matter, or we really must face the facts – and thus we can respond only in certain ways.[14]

Keith Jenkins has also commented on the way in which conservatives have commonly distinguished 'ideological history' from 'proper history'. In *Re-thinking History*, he posed the question of why we would be unlikely to find in any undergraduate history syllabus a course designed in line with a self-proclaimed black Marxist-feminist perspective.[15] That is, although it may not be uncommon these days to find advanced (e.g. prehonours or honours) courses in feminist historiography, why do we seldom see ordinary undergraduate courses actually entitled something such as 'A Black Marxist-Feminist Perspective on American History' or 'An Anarchist History of the British Imperialist State'? Who has the power to effect inclusions and exclusions, Jenkins asks, when it comes to deciding what constitutes 'suitable courses'? And on what grounds would such courses not be deemed suitable? The answer is that they would be seen to be 'ideological' because they 'would come from concerns external to history per se ... would be a vehicle for the delivery of a specific position for persuasive purposes.' This does indeed imply that 'history per se' or 'history as such' is not ideological, not *for* someone nor from some particular political perspective. Hence, we don't see courses being offered under titles such as 'A Liberal History of Modern Australia' either. Amusingly, the Australian (Liberal) Prime Minister, John Howard, did me the favour of substantiating this general point when (on 21 April 2006) he was on the morning news threatening to cut funding to high schools if they did not stop teaching 'postmodernist ... rubbish' such as asking students to interpret something from a 'black Marxist racial' perspective. Presumably, his point was that a relativist approach to acknowledging different positionalities or standpoints has no part in a 'proper education', there being only one possible knowledge or interpretation of anything (one suspects that given the ongoing 'history war' over different perspectives on Australia's history of colonization, this may be what he had in mind).[16]

Jenkins rightly sees 'history per se', the view that we do history for its own sake (or for the sake merely of finding 'the' truth about the past), as itself an ideological construct. In reality, history:

> is constantly being re-worked and re-ordered by all those who are variously affected by power relationships; because the dominated as well as the dominant also have their versions of the past to legitimate their practices, versions which have to be excluded as improper from any place on the agenda of the dominant discourse.[17]

Often, people do indeed legitimate their current practices, standpoints and identities (and their future political goals) through recourse to 'history': the (presentist) meanings they attribute to the past. It may be that 'history' tells us not to repeat the same mistakes, or that in 'history' (or 'tradition') we did something better than we do now.

As Jenkins indicates, more is at stake here than a mere 'slot in the school/academic curriculum'. What is taught as history (or told or written or performed as history) is *always* the reflection of particular interests, views and concerns. Academic history often serves the interests of those in power, whether it be at the level of the state/nation/society or in the academy itself where history will often reflect dominant ideologies or intellectual paradigms. Sometimes it will contest them, too, but not always without attendant risks (academic positions, tenure, promotions, research funding and so on.[18]) Typically, it has tended to be those most suspicious of presentism, those who also purport to be impartial in their practice of history, who have just happened to be the defenders and beneficiaries of the status quo. Their impartiality, however, has involved either remaining blind to how their own ideological perspectives affect their constructs of the past, or choosing to try to render their ideological positions invisible in their books and courses partly through the above-mentioned rhetorical conventions. Whether they are loathe to endanger their status as beneficiaries or just their intellectual authority (through an acknowledgement of so-called 'bias'), it is not in their interests to accede to the sort of presentism that would require that one both position oneself and reflect upon the effects of that position on one's practice of history.

A self-reflexive approach might require them (as Somekawa and Smith suggest) to reflect also upon the 'disciplinary' effects of the institutional structures and norms within which historians labour. In what follows I shall begin with a discussion of the ubiquity of presentism or teleology in 'history'. 'History' I take to include representations of the past/'history', 'tradition' or 'origins', whether they be in academic or popular works or just everyday discourse about it. Teleology/presentism may be most apparent in 'long-sweep' chronological/linear narrative works (which of course include traditional life-writing or histories of a whole life: biography and autobiography/memoirs); and there have long been debates in the discipline about the value of this sort of history.[19] But, in some ways teleology still features in texts the authors of which seek to distance themselves from conventional narrative modes of writing – for example, through simply taking a more analytical than merely descriptive (storyline) approach, or perhaps through utilizing a 'structuralist' or 'synchronic' method focussed upon one point in time rather than a linear ('diachronic') approach. Texts and talk of history, it will be seen below, are teleological/presentist due to a range of factors, not least the merely temporal problem of someone in the present trying to access realities that are no longer existent or long gone. We do not have the opportunity to witness the past directly, 'empirically', through observation, so the empiricist claim that it can be apprehended on its own terms (recovered and 'reconstructed') makes little sense. Finally, to end the chapter I will return to the question of how historians might practise a sceptical, positioned *and presentist* form of history, the scholarly integrity of which need not be in doubt. In this connection, reference will be made to practical 'experiments in rethinking history', as long practised by some historians and also exemplified in a collection of essays by that name from the scholarly journal, *Rethinking History*.[20]

II

The historian who unreflectingly engages in an effort to locate a beginning or who subscribes to a traditionally given beginning follows the same ideological path with all its unexamined assumptions as those who spoke of that particular beginning in the first place. Believing that he has isolated a fact, he is unaware that he is the last in a long line of victims of a particular ideological project. Rather than repeating the 'mythologizing' talk of a

> beginning or rephrasing it as an objective 'fact', one ought to
> question the talk about beginnings, examine the significance of such
> talk when it occurred.
>
> (Herman Ooms, *Tokugawa Ideology*)[21]

We repeatedly hear arguments in the media being framed in terms
of 'tradition/historical precedent' or 'beginnings/origins', arguments
that feature a variety of moral/political uses, functions or effects.
A political leader may bemoan the unwillingness of migrants to
adhere to 'our' founding ethics or national identity; an indigenous
group may contest such a view by reference to their own (say, pre-
colonial) traditions; a radical feminist may wax nostalgic about
different origins again, say, a prehistorical age of 'matriarchies' in
Eurasia when women ruled or at least had more authority and
autonomy than under later patriarchy(s). Invariably, the question
of whether the picture painted of the earlier age reflects past
realities or mythologizes them is moot.

When Herman Ooms spoke of historians' going in search of
beginnings or subscribing to traditionally given beginnings he had
a specific issue in Japanese historiography in mind. This was the
way in which historians first in Tokugawa Japan (1600–1867) and
still today have represented neo-Confucianism as the political
order's ideological orthodoxy from its inception. Confucianism is
quite secular in its central concern with the social duties of individuals (say, of samurai toward lords) and modernity is often defined
in terms of its secularity. Hence, secularity is what historians
went looking for in Japan's ('early modern') past, and found in
neo-Confucianism in even the early 17th century, somewhat
problematically, according to Ooms. Although it did begin toward
the end of that century to enjoy an official favour it had not had
earlier, it did not yet begin to displace other dominant philosophies
such as Buddhism.

Ooms' warning about our taking beginnings as given has a very
broad application, and not only to formal history texts. That is, the
central issue Ooms was addressing in his book contains a number
of general lessons for historians. I might put as the first the need for
historians not to suspend their critical faculties by treating primary
sources from the period under investigation (for example, official
sources) as more than usually authoritative or 'true', rather than just
as potentially self-interested and partial as any other text. In relation
to this case, Ooms suggests that instead of treating as fact claims by
a particular line of neo-Confucian scholars that their own school

founded the period's central system of ethics, one ought to examine the significance and function of such claims. One could do so by reference to possible political strategies of self-legitimation. (The legitimation in question, it might be noted, involved dubious claims that the founder of the order, Tokugawa Ieyasu, had accorded a privileged position to the school's founder, Hayashi Razan, elevating him above other political advisors due to the greater political utility of his philosophy.) When interpreting primary or any other sources, we need to remember that talk of beginnings/origins (or tradition) could represent a political strategy of self-legitimation and thus self-empowerment on the part of the speaker.

This, however, is suggestive of a second lesson derived from Ooms' critique of beginnings: namely, that just as the speaker may not be engaging in a fully self-aware deception of others, the historian's acceptance of conventional beginnings need not be consciously ideological. Any historian's constructs of the past may be ideological in effect, but not by design. This recalls Ooms' point about those who subscribe to a given beginning following the same ideological path as those who spoke of that beginning in the first place (or just earlier than ourselves). At base, the Hayashi scholars were no more disinterested than the modern historian who unquestioningly accepts constructs of origins, perhaps of something like a nation's or people's cultural identity. Yet neither need be practising a conscious deception, since the mythologized beginnings Ooms refers to allude to how beginnings, especially when they are repeatedly said to be such, have a way of seeming *natural* and thus necessarily true rather than arbitrarily imposed:

> [B]eginnings, or even the phenomena they are supposed to be the beginnings of, are in no way naturally given. They are all perception; they are all of the mind.
>
> Locating beginnings, however, entails more than bringing clarity to a diffuse past. There is no innocence about such an undertaking. The project of going back to a beginning is engaged in only because a pressing present has drawn singular attention to some item of the past . . . .
>
> A discourse of beginnings always produces a force akin to that generated by mythological origins. Thus it appears that beginnings are often not 'real' beginnings but real talk about beginnings. Such talk of beginnings often serves concrete interests and is thus itself ideological . . . .[22]

This point about a common naturalization of beginnings/origins, whether deliberate or 'innocent', we might take to be a third general lesson suggested by Ooms' case study. Legitimation through naturalization is a common strategy or function of political ideologies. The example of its being said to be 'natural' for women to stick to domestic duties in the home comes to mind, this being the same sort of gender construct that serves to justify lower wages for women by reference to men's 'natural' role as breadwinners.

English historian, Eric Hobsbawm, once made a similar point in a work devoted to the subject of 'the invention of tradition'. There he commented on the 'curious, but understandable paradox' that: 'modern nations . . . generally claim to be the opposite of novel, namely rooted in the remotest antiquity, and the opposite of constructed, namely human communities so "natural" as to require no definition other than self-assertion.'[23] Hence, in one essay in that volume the author, David Cannadine, discussed contemporary ceremonies utilized by the British monarchy, which are popularly assumed to be so splendid because they are the product of 'a thousand-year-old tradition'. To put it another way, the English are seen to be so good at public ritual due to centuries of precedent in pageantry.[24] Cannadine noted another curiosity, which was that *historians* had paid little attention to how much the monarchy's public ritual and image had actually changed over the past two centuries – which is to say that historians, too, had unthinkingly been accepting and repeating this talk of 'tradition'. He suggested that if one focussed upon the discontinuities in monarchical tradition, one would find that precedents for modern royal ceremonies did not extend back very far at all. What he was also recommending, of course, was the historicization of past realities as a means of circumventing unconscious presentism: unconsciously projecting modern practices and meanings back onto earlier times.

Cannadine found that over the past two hundred years there had been 'four distinct phases in the development of the ceremonial image of the British monarchy'.[25] The first phase extended from around the 1820s to the 1870s, a period Cannadine describes as one of 'ineptly managed ritual, performed in what was still preponderantly a localized, provincial, pre-industrial society'. The second began in 1877, the year in which Victoria became Empress of India, and extended to the First World War. This phase represented the 'heyday of "invented tradition"' not just in Britain but in much of Europe (and outside of it): 'a time when old ceremonials were staged with an expertise and appeal which had been lacking before, and when new rituals were self-consciously invented to accentuate this development.' Self-consciously invented yet sometimes styled as old, he might have said, since elsewhere he remarks upon the British monarchy's 'new and unique capacity to call in the old world to redress the balance of the new'. For instance, the new pomp and ceremony for Edward's coronation in 1902 paradoxically signalled for contemporaries 'unprecendented circumstances' in which the British celebrated 'immemorial tradition'. Hence, one commentator of the time spoke in terms of how 'the archaic traditions of the Middle Ages were enlarged in their scope so as to include the modern splendour of a mighty empire'.[26] According to Cannadine, it was particularly from the third phase, however (from 1918 to 1953, Elizabeth's coronation), that the British began to convince themselves that they were good at ceremonial ritual because they *always had been*. And people have continued to speak of 'a thousand-year-old tradition' despite the further changes to public ceremony occasioned by the 1950s with the advent of televised royal events and so on – in apparent ignorance of the fact that the origins of the grand spectacle of modern coronations, weddings and the like lay in a period so recent as the 1870s to 1914. This Cannadine described as the phase of 'international, competitive, ceremonial inventiveness'.[27]

Like Hobsbawm, Cannadine emphasized how inventions of tradition and origins are often at their most determined following profound social, national and/or international change. It was against the backdrop of change, namely the postwar decline of empire, that British ceremonials had the function of offering a 'comforting picture of stability, tradition and continuity'. Ooms, as we have seen, draws on a quite different example to suggest the related point that talk of beginnings must be interpreted by reference to the contexts (temporal, cultural, personal, political) and positions and possible aims of those doing the talking.

This is another way of saying that talk of tradition, origins or history/historical precedent is presentist. It might seem to be natural or 'innocent', moreover, when to the contrary it is ideological. But, whether it is motivated by some pressing *political* problem in the present, or not, the picture painted of the beginnings may make little sense outside a modern framework or mental universe. Hayashi Razan probably did not see himself as founding a new Tokugawa ideological order, nor necessarily see his ideas as distinct, systematically, from those of his contemporaries, to the extent that he would intentionally aim to have neo-Confucianism dispense with its traditional ties to Buddhism, displacing its traditional authority in the process, thereby signifying the origins of Japan's secular modernity. Similarly, people in ages past – say, our 'ancestors' from whom some claim an inherited cultural identity centred on some particular essence that has somehow managed to survive down through the ages – may not have even seen themselves as part of a unified group. It is what is seen to be essential now that is being projected back onto the past where, from its supposed origins, it somehow manages to remain fixed or unchanged.

A further lesson, then, is Oom's reminder that so-called 'origins' would not have been seen then as such; they become such only with hindsight. Hindsight, moreover, means that some endpoint is not just colouring our understanding of some past phenomenon as an origin, but perhaps determining our very selection of it or, rather, our *creation* of it as a (distinct) phenomenon at all way back when. This is an ostensibly linear (forward) continuity that, in its conception, represents back-to-front causation – and that well illustrates the suspicion held by Foucault and others toward supposed continuities in 'history' (over time).

I shall discuss another Japanese example of this shortly which is very instructive: the modern nationalist construct of 'Shinto' as Japan's core religio-cultural tradition and thus identity. The modern creation of the myth of Shinto as Japan's religio-cultural origin and thus essential religio-cultural identity has been singularly successful, as we shall see. Yet its difference from the imaginative utilization of 'tradition/origins' elsewhere amidst nation-building processes was only one of degree. It formed part of a not unusual 'invention of tradition' by a modern state in the interests of creating a national identity, national unity, respect for monarchs, obedience to political leaders, and so on and so forth.

Hobsbawm discusses three overlapping types of such inventiveness in his introduction to the above-cited work he edited with Terence Ranger, *The Invention of Tradition*:

a) those establishing or symbolizing social cohesion or the membership of groups, real or artificial communities;

b) those establishing or legitimising institutions, status or relations of authority; and

c) those whose main purpose was socialization, the inculcation of beliefs, value systems and conventions of behaviour.[28]

The work features discussion of constructs of tradition in a range of post-industrial revolution contexts: re the supposedly archaic rituals of the British monarchy (discussed above); the newly constructed cultural essence/identity of the Welsh and also Scots; European invented traditions exported to colonial Africa and Victorian India; and also working class/socialist 'traditions' in Europe. Concerning the last, an essay by Hobsbawm himself on 'Mass-Producing Traditions: Europe, 1870–1914', is of interest because it exemplifies the fact that modern nation-states are not alone in participating in the teleological invention or reinvention of 'tradition'.

We should recall that Hobsbawm's first type of invented tradition was 'those establishing or symbolizing social cohesion or the membership of groups . . .'. Re political movements, he notes that we might expect inventiveness from nationalist or Catholic movements that were well aware of the usefulness of 'ritual, ceremonial and myth, including . . . a mythological past'; but not from rationalist socialist movements that tended to be hostile to such inventions.[29] This notwithstanding, May Day is among Hobsbawm's examples of invented traditions since, from around the turn of the twentieth century, May Day festivities in various parts of the world began to reflect the ever-changing character of 'tradition', its openness to reinterpretation, albeit in a way that was spontaneous, not directed from the top. Traditions such as May Day may have been reinvented partly to suit the mood of workers/socialists in different cultural environments, he points out, and also to keep abreast of socio-political change. However, labour 'tradition' could be used quite consciously as a weapon and not only against bosses and/or the state. Labour movements internationally have also invented traditions to keep 'undesirables' out of their ranks or to deny them the privileges of 'white' men. Essays in this same volume discuss examples such as white workers in southern Africa who came from Europe, Canada and Australia in the 1880s and 1890s now using 'revived and invented rituals of craft unionism . . . to exclude Africans from participation'.[30] I say 'now' because it is within the realm of possibility that in their own countries similar tactics had been used to exclude women (or non-'white' men).

Male unionists in Europe and elsewhere often created a 'historical' picture of gendered work that would serve their own economic and/or political interests. This was an idealized picture in which women either did not 'work' (traditionally and in the present) or (when it could no longer be denied that they did increasingly work

outside the home) had no 'skills' that would justify their access to full
membership as workers with the rights and privileges duly accorded
men. When 'skill' came to be redefined as a male possession, it flew
in the face of the artisanal work that women had traditionally done
before the days of production for the market. Deborah Simonton has
shown how:

> Where the location of work and home was nearly contiguous,
> these tasks [of woman as worker, wife and mother] blended, and
> the idea of male and female workers was underplayed. Tensions
> which arose with the shifting location of work, its identity as
> waged, and more capitalistic control of work contributed to
> defining gendered locations for men and women.[31]

Now real traditions of women's work and skill were downplayed
with arguments that stressed women's 'natural' lack of aptitude for
working with machines – or, later, *on* machines, since only men had
the aptitude to be mechanics (an idea that continues to this day).
Women were expected to do the 'light', repetitive work 'suited to
women' such as operating the smaller machines or (once again,
ironically) the looms, now writ larger. Similarly, typesetting was
gendered a male trade but mere typewriting female (whilst personal
computers, amusingly, have put men in danger of becoming
'feminized'). Terms such as 'work', 'skill' and, of course, 'craft' came
to be associated with men, the conventional argument being that
this had always been the case, as if it had only (or even mainly) been
men who traditionally worked in the domestic production of goods
that included craft items. The obviously presentist agenda of the
male workers who utilized such constructs of tradition was either
to exclude women workers or to maintain their superior status in
the 'shop' or trade as an extension of their authority in the
patriarchal family.

Works of feminist history such as that by Simonton on the history
of European women's work encourage us to be more wary than
hitherto of projecting modern gender constructs back onto earlier
centuries. We need to recall, for example, that there was no middle-
class 'cult of domesticity' in Europe in the eighteenth century or
earlier, nor a male 'breadwinner' ideology, which encouraged
people to think of 'work' as the realm and preserve of men; and
that women of the lower classes always have worked. Other authors
have addressed the issue of anachronistic inventions of tradition that

have commonly been used to keep women in their ['natural/ proper/traditional'] subordinate place with reference to many different cultural and temporal contexts. An example that comes to mind is anti-colonial nationalist movements of the nineteenth to twentieth centuries. When such movements exhibited their own 'nostalgia for origins' in their fight against colonial domination, ironically, the traditions that were being idealized might be more reflective of the colonial present (the traditions or ideals of colonial powers) than their own pre-colonial past. Jeanne Maracek has discussed the example of Sinhala nationalism in Ceylon/Sri Lanka where, not unlike in India and in line with the modern European cult of domesticity once again, one of the main responses to British colonialism was a gendered separation of spheres into a feminized private and masculinized public sphere.[32] Here:

> Different roles, different spaces and different orientations to past and future were associated with men and women. In the masculine public sphere, the demands and possibilities of modernization could be given free play. It was in the feminine private sphere of domestic life that cultural traditions were to be revived and preserved. Representations of ideal womanhood sustained a specific Sinhala identity anchored in the ancient past.

Men, or men of certain classes, were free to reap the benefits of Western-style modernity and 'progress'; women less so, since they were expected to be the 'repositories of tradition'. And look the part, one might add, since some Sinhala nationalists even urged women to don a modest style of dress, the sari, which was not actually traditional Sinhala dress. More generally, the irony about women's being pressed or wanting themselves to symbolize the precolonial past was that successive waves of colonizers (Portuguese, Dutch, then British) had over the centuries inculcated in Sri Lankans gender ideals and practices in all areas of life that had little to do with indigenous traditions.

In the Sri Lankan case, British law had forced European sexual morality and marital practices upon the locals, so 'pure' Sinhala womanhood was being defined under the weight of 400 years of European morality. Thus, when men in the Sinhala nationalist movement spoke of 'righteous Sinhala womanhood and their vision of an indigenous and specifically Sinhala civilization', they were iterating 'local' conceptions of all sorts of things – Maracek's list being marriage, divorce, adoption, offspring, rights of widows, women's work and sexual morality – which were in large part reiterations of Western ideals of womanhood and family. One could readily find any number of such cases around the world, where nationalist identities formed in opposition to colonial or neo-colonial domination have been conditioned by the very ideals and norms that ostensibly are being rejected. This may involve an active appropriation of aspects of the 'superior' culture in a situation where the realities of power mean that recourse to real indigenous tradition/identity cannot signify 'progress'; or it may be unconscious. One is reminded of the critique of a 'nostalgia for lost origins' by Gayatri Chakravorty Spivak in her influential essay 'Can the Subaltern Speak?' Here, as Ania Loomba expresses it, she was challenging the common 'assumption that native cultures were left intact through colonial rule, and are now easily recoverable',[33] particularly the voices of the marginalized 'subaltern' groups or underclasses.

The expectation that it is up to women and girls to carry most of the weight of ostensibly traditional identities on their 'shoulders' (or bodies, more generally) is commonly encountered still today. Southeast Asian historian Mina Roces, a specialist on the history of gender and dress, puts it nicely when she uses the phrase: women as 'the bearers and wearers of tradition'.[34] This might suggest the example of the veil which, when donned by Muslim women in the Philippines (or Malaysia or Indonesia), might lead one to wonder whose traditions are being 'worn'. This is not a *Southeast Asian* Muslim tradition of very long standing at all.

The pressures on women to symbolize 'tradition' in their bearing, public/private roles and what they wear can vary, both in the degree of individual choice or pressure/compulsion and with respect to situation: in some areas of the world the demands of ethnic tourism may be counted as one such pressure. In an essay on 'Negotiating Female Subjects in Contemporary Mayan Theatre' in Chiapas, Mexico, Cynthia Steele cites a Mexican magazine of the 1990s that celebrated Mayan women 'as the last repository of ancient tradition':

> Unlike the men, who have gone from sandals to cowboy boots, the Zinacantec ladies still go barefoot and are the iron-willed repositories of many myths and customs which the gentlemen no longer respect. They are the shield against acculturation and the umbilical cord connecting these Mayas with their past.[35]

The magazine, we might note, was devoted to promoting ethnic tourism. Steele relates how many Mayan men in Chiapas are no longer peasant corn farmers but rather take up a variety of occupations as wage earning semi-proletarians, as truckdrivers, merchants, government employees and so on. The men in the theatre group that is the focus of her article, on the other hand, also run a family museum for tourists, featuring traditional clothing and the like. Being far from traditional themselves in their (dress or) occupations does not stop them, however, from advocating the preservation of traditional gender roles, 'with men taking their place in the fields and women remaining at the cooking fire and loom'.[36]

It would seem that at least some Mayan women must be spending far more time at the loom than they did traditionally, given the tourist industry in traditional textiles. No wonder one of the women in this theatre group (albeit not for long, given the pressure to conform to 'traditional' gender roles) bemoaned the popular belief among the Maya that 'a woman's duty is to clean the house, cook, have and take care of children, fetch water and firewood, and *constantly weave*' (my emphasis).[37] This, moreover, was just after she had observed that, although women have very little role in public religious ceremonies – since 'tradition demands that women stay in their houses' – in the past they had achieved influential religious offices. What constitutes 'tradition' in this context, once again, has much to do with the perceived needs of the present.

III

> [T]he secret of their success as historians lies in hindsight and argument backwards.
>
> (Geoffrey Elton, *Return to Essentials*)[38]

As is indicated by the last few examples drawn from works of history from the 1980s and 1990s, it is now more common to find historians exercising caution when confronted with talk of 'tradition' or 'origins/beginnings'. Contrary to Elton's somewhat inconsistent claim that it explains the secret of their success (inconsistent because he is one of the conservative critics of presentism), this is because we are more *wary* of 'hindsight and argument backwards'. There have been a number of important sources of inspiration for critiques of backwards causation or teleology in history such as that conducted by Ooms. In Foucault, we should recall, one finds a suspicion of conventional determination/causation and a related suspicion of the teleology inherent in linear chronology whereby events cause other events in sequences toward the present: forces of change, as he put it in the passage from 'Nietzsche, Genealogy, History' cited on p. 41, 'do not manifest the successive forms of a primordial intention and their attraction is not that of a conclusion'. This is why he recommended that we focus on the randomness and contingency of past events rather than upon causation and continuities, and why those who follow his lead such as Joan Scott and many others emphasize discontinuity. Ooms' sources, we might note, included Foucault and Barthes (as well as Nietzsche, whose *Beyond Good and Evil* Ooms cites at the head of the first page of his book).

Poststructuralists such as Foucault and Derrida, however, were not the first to critique teleological quests for mythical origins, as Curthoys and Docker observe when discussing a 1955 essay by Michael Oakeshott: 'The Activity of Being an Historian'.[39] In an argument they rightly see to be 'strikingly similar' to critiques of origins by Foucault or Derrida, they cite Oakeshott to the effect that:

> the historian must avoid an inquiry into origins since such an inquiry 'read(s) the past backwards', looking to it to supply information about the 'cause' or the 'beginning' of an already specified situation, and thus imposing on past events 'an arbitrary' teleological structure.

This recalls Ankersmit's argument on effect and cause, as well. Curthoys and Docker relate that Oakeshott went on to note that even the historian interested in the past for its own sake must inevitably interpret it in the terms of the present, understanding 'past conduct and happenings in a manner in which they were never understood at the time'.[40]

Derrida is a theorist that I have found inspirational in connection with a critique of teleology and 'nostalgia for origins', especially his often-cited essay, 'Structure, Sign, and Play in the Discourse of the Human Sciences'.[41] There was one passage in particular that threw my critique of teleology in history into sharper relief. This passage potentially has a very broad critical application, as is indicated by the fact that the subject of Derrida's critique was the Western human sciences in general (even if his more immediate target was structuralist anthropology represented by Claude Lévi-Strauss):

[T]he structurality of structure – although it has always been at work, has always been neutralized or reduced, and this by a process of giving it a center or of referring it to a point of presence, a fixed origin. The function of this center was not only to orient, balance, and organize the structure – one cannot in fact conceive of an unorganised structure – but above all to make sure that the organizing principle of the structure would limit what we might call the *play* of the structure . . . . even today the notion of a structure lacking any center represents the unthinkable itself.[42]

It might be observed that Ooms' (or Hobsbawm's) remark about the seeming naturalness of origins is suggested here, a point which would hardly be applicable only to the *Western* human sciences. Derrida may have been discussing the way in which, in structuralist anthropology, *linguistic* structures such as differential categories of analysis were 'reified' – turned into fixed realities (as Callum Brown points out, Lévi-Strauss investigated differential categories of superiority-inferiority such as male-female in certain societies or kinship groups at one point in time, but then treated them as universally true for all time in all cultures.[43]) What I want to highlight, however, is simply that although Derrida could be taken to imply in this passage that when we think 'structurally' the centre of the structure is synonymous with the fixed origin (though the 'or' in the first sentence creates an ambiguity), a little further on in the text he spells it out: 'the center . . . can also indifferently be called the origin or end, *arché or telos*'.[44] A related point that makes immediate sense concerns how in Western science and philosophy and, indeed, in the 'deepest recesses' of 'the soil of ordinary language, things are conceived of in terms of structures that must be centred on something (some fixed essence).

With little effort, one can think of any number of linguistic-conceptual habits that exemplify this essentialist tendency. As we shall see in Chapter 4, people are spoken of in terms suggestive of a structure centred upon some unchanging essence, not unlike with the notion of the eternal soul where personality/individuality continues even beyond death. The static essence or 'centre' may be an essential character trait, although people's lives, too, are often structured around some central meaning or destiny. In addition, a nation or culture is commonly spoken of as if the sum total of 'a' people's traditions, their history, can be treated as a structure and centred/reduced to one identity that, in turn, must have its own centre to make sense. Alun Munslow, whilst discussing the presentist agenda of the authors of a work entitled *Telling the Truth About History*, argues that they set out to 'discover the truth of . . . a pluralistic and multicultural American history' that (paradoxically I think) 'will necessarily reinforce . . . America's essential democratic heritage'.[45] The paradox as I see it is that if America is indeed pluralistic and multicultural, and has been that since its inception, it would seem to rule out the imposition of any one essential heritage or 'truth'. An indigenous or African American may not agree that democracy represents the centre/essence of American history, thus also its 'heritage' and, in turn, fixed identity.

How often, however, do we hear people opine that Americans are essentially democratic, Australians 'matey' (egalitarian, tolerant, etc.), Germans arrogant, the British class conscious, and so on and so forth? With all these examples and many more besides – a century centred upon one feature/meaning, or an event, or a process – we can see how the 'organizing principle' of the structure, which is to say its centre/essence, limits the 'play of the structure', or the play of other elements within (and outside) it. An essentially democratic character imputed to a nation casts into the shadows and fixes them there other features such as inequality, repression and violence; and those who could hardly be said to be the beneficiaries of this democratic spirit are relegated to the structure's margins or perhaps excluded from it altogether. An essentially 'classist' character imputed to another nation overlooks the strength of its egalitarian and democratic traditions at the level of labour and other social movements.

Derrida's further point about how the centre is the origin which is the end ('telos') is not, perhaps, so readily explicable. But what about the way in which, in self-referential or self-representational writing, individuals' lives are constructed from the standpoint of an endpoint, as I like to put it: that is, in terms that cannot be separated from the present contexts of their writing of memoirs or autobiographies? Such a life (-story) might well be centred from beginning to end upon some particular 'destiny', say, a triumph over adversity, that could hardly be seen as such unless from an 'endpoint', i.e. with hindsight. And doesn't this also suggest that the individual in question is being arbitrarily structured, his personality or character (and, traditionally, it was a 'he' invariably, in the 'great man' genre of auto/biography) centred upon a trait such as determination or a strong will? In such representations, origins and ends are inseparable and, moreover, indistinguishable from the unchanging centre/essence that is accorded the life or person.

I had long been wary of the frequently encountered essentialism in my own specialist field of Japanese history with regard to Japan's cultural identity: Japan as 'homogeneous', its people 'groupist/conformist' rather than individualistic etc. However, as I noted above, Derrida's point about origin=centre=end (or, rather, end=centre=origin) helped to sharpen my critique of one glaringly modernist, teleological construct of Japanese religio-cultural identity: the notion that 'Shinto' represents Japan's religio-cultural essence and has done so for 'ages eternal', since the very beginnings of 'Japan'. Historians who unthinkingly accept this conventional view far outnumber those who are critical of its teleology and modern political uses.[46] It is a complex issue, but I will try to be brief, which means leaving aside largely modern Shinto's intimate relation not just to the imperial institution but also to the modern state's imperialism, racism and warmongering. I should note, too, that Japan also participated in what Cannadine referred to as the phase of 'international, competitive, ceremonial inventiveness' that extended from around 1870 to 1914. In fact, the Japanese state drew partly upon the British example for its own invention of modern public imperial ceremonies that were unprecedented in their publicity, scale, pomp and splendour (especially the mourning rituals for the Meiji emperor in 1912[47]); whilst simultaneously incorporating imperial Shinto rituals, not all of which were as archaic as represented and now were subject, in any case, to modernized meanings.

It was in the modern context of the restoration from 1868 of Japan's emperors to secular power (at least in name) following many centuries of bushi (shogunal) rule that nationalists sought to create for Japan a dominant religion based on kami worship and now called 'Shinto' that could be seen to be Japan's own, not originally 'foreign' like Buddhism. To this end, the government quickly promulgated a law to 'separate the kami from the buddhas', as if many, many centuries of syncretism at the level of institutions, theology, and popular belief and practice could be undone so easily by state decree, in one fell swoop. (Kami are spirits, ghosts and gods, but even an extraordinary living human being can be regarded as a kami, as the notion of the 'living god emperor' would indicate.) At the level of Buddhist doctrine the orthodox view had long been that kami are the phenomenal form of buddhas (should they choose to take one), which is itself indicative of the traditional inseparability of Buddhas and kami, Buddhism and kami worship. It also explains why, historically, before modern times, a shrine devoted to kami worship was often part of a temple-shrine complex run by Buddhist priests, the shrine priest being one of them but low in the clerical hierarchy. As for the people, buddhas and kami were both part of a religious world view and practice where one simply prayed to buddhas and kami for different purposes: buddhas for things of the next life, kami for things of this life.

It is important to understand that, although there had been since medieval times a few scholarly sects of Shinto (which I will call 'imperial Shinto') that were tied closely to a few important imperial shrines, these had had no popular following. A Japanese person might well be a self-proclaimed devotee of a particular Buddhist sect (say, Zen or Pure Land) but nobody was a follower of 'Shinto' in the same sense. Only Buddhism had a distinct creed or theology and its own nationally organized institutions and clergy. Hence, if premodern Japanese religion can be said to have had any 'centre', it was obviously Buddhist, albeit a form of (Mahayana) Buddhism that from ancient times had continually been subject to change, partly through incorporating many pre-existing folk religious practices, as was the case elsewhere in East Asia, too.[48] Traditionally, in other words, there was no such thing as 'a religion' called 'Shinto' before the modern state tried to invent one, and speaking in such terms (to say nothing of speaking as if it was the unchanging core of Japan's religio-cultural identity) is decidedly anachronistic.

The issue, moreover, cannot be reduced to a question of merely quibbling about words. Some might argue (as indeed some have) that even if premodern people did not think of 'Shinto' as a distinct religion, of course they did practice kami worship in shrines all around the country; and that because this predated the introduction of Buddhism to Japan in ancient times it is still legitimate to think of 'kami worship' as Japan's original, 'indigenous' religion. Original it may have been, but it was no more purely 'Japanese' than Buddhism, Confucianism, Daoism and so on, since whatever folk religion there was in early Japan came with the successive waves of migration from the mainland and Pacific. To speak even of 'kami worship' as Japan's own indigenous religion is also to suggest some degree of unity or cohesion when doubtless what existed was a range of disparate, unsystematized, unorganized beliefs and practices –

animism, shamanism, ancestor worship, Daoism and so on. Using this phrase when speaking of premodern religion may be an advance on using the term 'Shinto', but is still somewhat misleading.

The English term with its capital letter, we should note, tends to encourage people to think of 'Shinto' as a separate religion from archaic to premodern times. In Japanese, on the other hand, the two characters that make up the word are read as 'shin-tō' now, signifying the modern meaning associated with that word, but historically there were other possibilities. If one looks up 'historical' character dictionaries (produced in modern times) one still might find 'shindō', 'kami no michi' and perhaps 'kannagara no michi', all being said to mean 'Shinto': 'The Way of the Gods'. Yet the second character did not always mean 'The Way of . . .' in the sense of a religion or an ethical code (as in 'bushidō', the way of the warrior). When used in early to medieval times together with the first character for 'kami' sometimes it, too, meant 'kami'; or it simply meant 'ways' or 'conduct' as in what the kami do, what they get up to, etc. Japan historian, Kuroda Toshio, has showed how the two characters had a range of meanings for ancient to medieval Japanese. This renders nonsensical the habit modern Shinto priests or nationalist scholars have had of applying the modern meaning of 'Japan's own religion of kami worship' to the very occasional appearance of the word(s) in Japan's oldest extant texts: the imperial myth-histories or genealogies, the Nihongi and Kojiki. [49] Amusingly, one ancient meaning was even 'Daoism', so if we were to utilize this more properly archaic meaning, it would suggest that Chinese Daoism is Japan's own, indigenous, original, purely Japanese religion!

What the modern Japanese state attempted to do was not only to effect a separation of kami and buddhas – and, before long, of Buddhism from a recreated and vastly expanded imperial or now 'state Shinto' – but also to lump virtually all of Japan's disparate, ostensibly non-Buddhist religious traditions together and rename them 'Shinto'. The government then tried to create this newly amalgamated 'Shinto' as *the* single state religion. In this it failed largely due to Western pressure for freedom of religion, but also because of popular resistance and the traditional power of the Buddhist establishment. Henceforth, State Shinto was not formally defined as a 'religion'. This was reasonable since it was decidedly political, centred upon encouraging a new popular veneration for the imperial institution (and the mythology surrounding its origins in the age of the gods etc.) in the service of the state; as well as drumming up popular support for nationalism, militarism and, before long, overseas aggression. The fact that State Shinto was now officially not a religion after all meant that people could be forced to participate in its reinvented imperial-national rituals in newly amalgamated and, partly newly created institutions. This (re-)invention of tradition was able to claim at least a modicum of 'tradition' in the sense that it included the reorganization and consolidation of existing shrines all around the country into a national hierarchy. Yet, in the process, some actual local traditions of kami worship were destroyed by the state, too, in cases where a village had more than the one 'necessary' shrine. Real traditions of very long standing had also suffered when the state decree to separate kami from buddhas (and some ambitious shrine priests) encouraged widespread attacks on Buddhist temples, icons and clerics.

In the final analysis, although State Shinto was dismantled at the end of the Pacific War by the Allied occupation authorities, what proved to be more enduring was the myth of 'Shinto' as Japan's ancient 'religion' (and, in turn, religio-cultural identity). Ask just about anyone, excluding the more historically aware Japanese, to name Japan's own indigenous religion and the answer is likely to be 'Shinto'. Yet this is a view of origins which is just as mythological as the claim that Japan's line of emperors extends back through 'ages eternal' to the age of the gods. Most Japanese history texts are also at fault, moreover, in the teleological language they use about ancient or medieval 'Shinto' (by which they mean kami worship) and Shinto (i.e. shrine but Buddhist) priests. Modern readers might well wonder what is 'wrong' with one history text that comes to mind, for it does represent an exception to the general anachronistic rule. In this rather weighty tome on late medieval village life in Japan, the index does not feature the word 'Shinto' at all. In the text there is reference to 'Shinto deities' at only one point (a linguistic slip?), though there are several references to kami, kami worship, shrines, and so on.[50] Other historians would do well to follow suit.

Returning to Derrida, then, and his ends=centre=origins schema, it was due to the demands of modern Japanese emperor worship and nationalism that 'Shinto' began to be represented, teleologically, as Japan's origin and thus timeless essence. When even scholars, historians of Japan among them, take as given these particular origins, they speak as if Japan's entire course of religio-cultural development can be conceptualized as a structure defined by a core that has remained unchanged down the centuries. In doing so, they follow the same ideological path as those who spoke of that particular beginning in the first place, as Ooms put it, joining 'a long line of victims of a particular ideological project' – this being one that served the interests of modern Japanese jingoism and militarism. There are good reasons, therefore, both at the political and epistemological levels, to cease our talk of Shinto as Japan's origin.

One could go on interminably raising examples of constructs of 'history', 'tradition' and/or 'origins' being put to present political uses in society, today and in the past; and this alone should give historians pause. Readers should begin to see why Ooms would recommend that we focus our attention not on beginnings ('origins' or 'history' or 'tradition') but on *talk of them*. Perhaps the only truly surprising aspect of the work I was drawing upon above, *The Invention of Tradition*, published in 1983, is that Eric Hobsbawm would admit in its closing pages that the aim of the book was to 'encourage the study of a relatively new subject'.[51] What was unsurprising about it was that scholars could document so many cases of invented traditions (and just from the limited sample of British/European history in the age of imperialism, moreover). Doubtless he did not mean that no historians had ever discussed the issue, but rather that history texts devoted to it were then rare. (Cannadine, we might recall, also noted that historians had rarely studied changes in British monarchical ritual, which contributed to the ease with which people have spoken of 'thousand-year-old traditions'.) Now, it does not seem quite so unusual to find works with titles such as *The Teleology of the Modern Nation-State*, comprised of essays surrounding the theme of modern teleological representations of origins/tradition, and devoted among other things to showing how a:

> conflation of the national story on the local does great harm to the historical record ... [and also] serves the interest of the contemporary nation-state which is only too happy to invent its own 'ancient' past and use it to continue to retain control over how the local stories may be told. This sort of anachronism is the handmaiden of the nation-state discourse.[52]

Now, under the influence of theorists such as Foucault, Derrida, Spivak and the like, historical works that treat discourses of origins/

tradition with suitable scepticism are somewhat more common. One can only wonder why *invented* tradition was such a new topic as late as the 1980s. Hobsbawm acknowledged that political self-legitimation, not just in modern politics and law but even in traditional societies has often been through recourse to 'custom' or 'precedent', whether that be real or imagined.[53] I am reminded of the Hayashi scholars discussed on p. 63–4; and a Japanese parallel is again suggested by Hobsbawm's reference to how peasant movements typically used 'historical' precedent as a weapon against lords when claiming some right or common land. Hobsbawm may be right in distinguishing modern inventions of tradition from the traditional recourse to precedent on the basis of the former often being a response to novel situations such as times of rapid, dramatic social change – the Japanese case of Shinto also suggests this – but both represented similar political strategies. This, in turn, can only add to our sense of wonder that modern and premodern *constructs of* 'tradition' or 'origins' or 'precedent' have not warranted more attention in historical scholarship. Surely, one of the primary tasks of the historian should be to reflect upon the inevitable problems that arise from the past-present (or, rather, present-past) nexus in history production. Historians would not be producing new works focussed entirely upon modern teleologies unless they believed there is still a need for them because historians are among those who unthinkingly accept those teleologies. Perhaps the proscription of presentism in themselves blinds historians to it where it should most be contested?

IV

> [W]e need to escape from the most insidious temptation hiding within the very concept of learning from history. That temptation lies in seeing history as essentially relevant to the present; the technique which operates that temptation is known as present-centred (sometimes presentist) history . . . . it selects from the past those details that seem to take the story along to today's concerns and so reconstructs the past by means of a sieve that discards what the present and time-limited interest determine is irrelevant. The method is totally predictive: it produces the result intended because it is designed to do so.
>
> (Geoffrey Elton, *Return to Essentials*)[54]

Elton and other historians of recovery warn against consciously present-centred history. Their alternative is history 'for its own sake' (in its own terms), history 'with the politics left out'. The question, however, is whether in their determination to be unpartisan or objective in simply retelling 'the story' of some aspect of the past, they run a greater risk of becoming victims of the 'ideological projects' of others. This is not so likely to happen with the self-reflexive, critical history advocated and practised by postmodernists.

Joan Scott, for example, is committed to a 'reconceptualized' practice of history that she sees as more effective, *politically*, in the present and for the future: a history *for* women and other marginalized sectors of society/the world. She would not deny that her work is present-minded or 'present-centred' in this sense. (Her means to this end is a method inspired by Barthes, Foucault and others that, as we saw in Chapter 1, focuses upon discontinuity, processes of differentiation and historicizing interpretation.) She also insists in 'After History?', however, that 'the analysis of processes of differentiation is not a matter of applying a predetermined grid to events of the past.'[55] To reconceptualize identity, for example, we can provide the 'basis for an analysis of women that is not a rediscovery of ourselves in the past' by historicizing it. This would require inverting the question conventionally posed about how women were treated in the past and asking instead: 'how and in what circumstances the difference of their sex came to matter in their treatment.'[56] In her '*discourse analysis*' approach, Scott does seek at least to mitigate the teleologies intrinsic to history; to counter unconscious presentism in our representations of the past. To that extent she has something in common with Elton, who refers to presentism as an 'insidious temptation' but (like Himmelfarb) takes it to be avoidable. The latter describes presentism as 'reading history backward, of seeking in the past the sources of those ideas and institutions we value in the present, thus ignoring the complexities, contingencies, and particularities that make the past peculiarly past.'[57] This also might have been Ooms speaking, except for the fact that, like Scott, he recommends a discourse analysis approach (switching our focus to *talk of* beginnings) in an effort to lessen the modernist teleologies that have inhered in linear chronological approaches to history in his field.

Scott's approach may go some way toward circumventing what I have called the 'omnipresent' (or 'ever-present') nature of History production, but it cannot help us to transcend it altogether. To continue with her example of identity, clearly, our reading of these processes of representation in the past will still be conditioned by our current concerns and modes of thinking even if we do manage to historicize identity; even if we do, that is, recognize that identity formation then was not what it is now, and thus remain wary of projecting our own identities back into the past. Furthermore, Scott's style of history, as she recognizes herself, will still involve recourse to the empiricist reality effect criticized by Barthes – where 'interpretations are treated as "facts" of history', as she puts it. She is, after all, still putting forward an interpretation concerning the *realities of past processes of representation*, albeit with the acknowledgement that the insights gleaned from her methodology are no more closed or final than anyone else's insights; that she has no special claim to 'the truth'. The critics of postmodernist history are not so cautious.

However, what Scott proposes with her discourse analysis and historicist approach is that we make interpretation itself (and 'facts', including our own 'facts') the object of our inquiries. Even if this 'precludes neither judgment nor the need for standards of evaluation [and] the discipline will continue to have to furnish ways to distinguish persuasive from unpersuasive readings,'[58] paying attention to 'facts' necessitates a focus on signification (interpreting for meaning), which in turn requires that we attend to how human 'subjects and their objects of knowledge' are constituted. Undeniably, such a method represents an advance on unreflexive history because it should serve to highlight historians' own interpretations and conceptual differences from the past, a point on which I shall quote Scott in full:

> Historical consciousness is in this approach always double; it is a process of confrontation between or among interpretations. It recognizes that recounting the 'facts' of another age without analysing the systems of knowledge that produced them either reproduces (and naturalizes) past ideologies or dehistoricizes them by imposing present categories.[59]

This returns us again to the problem of unconscious presentism or taking history's teleologies (say, 'talk of beginnings') as given. Arguably, Scott's *self-reflexive* historicist method should at least lessen this, by forcefully directing readers' attention to it instead of trying to let it remain invisible. The same can be said of Greg Dening's 'reflective ethnographic' approach, which I shall discuss in closing.

Compared with empiricist reconstructionist history, a self-reflexive method has the advantage of being more likely to confront us with history's inevitable paradoxes and our own contradictions. Within such a framework, how can one be sceptical of conventional history's reality effect – its claim to be able to recover past realities through simply finding the available evidence/facts – without also turning the sceptic's gaze upon one's own 'facts' and interpretations? How can one fail to be less presentist in practice than the conventional historian who would not 'permit' (politically motivated) presentism in herself, whilst she simultaneously bemoaned newly popular styles of history in the 1980s (social history etc.) that only wanted 'to explore the lowest depths of life' (*sic*)? As opposed to concerning themselves with the 'irrational' aspects of life, she enjoined historians to stick to conventional political histories about 'rational' institutions such as governments, the law, the polity, etc. For Himmelfarb, the problem with the new styles of history then was that they dismissed great political ideas and institutions that, apparently unproblematically represent 'our' heritage.[60] She wanted historians to *ask only questions of the past that the past asked of itself*, but it would seem that *her* 'past' is no less indistinguishable from her politics than Scott's.

Similarly, since the 1960s when he published his well-known work, *The Practice of History*,[61] Elton has continued to inveigh against the 'insidious' habit of present-centred history – as if his is not that – and to advocate empiricist methods of recovery or reconstruction. That is clearly demonstrated in that early work where he modestly admitted that 'not all the past is recoverable', adding that 'the study of history is necessarily confined to that part of it of which evidence either survives or can be reconstructed in the mind.'[62] But, what is perhaps most famous about this passage (or infamous, depending upon one's point of view) is the assessment that followed of history being not the 'whole of mankind's past life' but only the 'surviving past':

> Historical study is not the study of the past but the study of present traces of the past; if men have said, thought, done or suffered anything of which nothing any longer exists, those things are as though they had never been. The crucial element is the present evidence, not the fact of past existence; and questions for whose answer no material exists are strictly non-questions.

Although he did acknowledge that both finding new evidence and utilizing certain historiographical techniques can enable the historian to 'reconstruct that which is lost from that which is still around', he still judged histories of 'ordinary people', the poor lower classes, or all of 'mankind' to be illegitimate if the evidence for the study of such problems does not exist. Apart from his empiricist assumptions that history is the past and that evidence is simply out there waiting to be unearthed by the objective historian, what he was dismissing was what others even then were more inclined to think of as the *importance* of social history and the consequent necessity of finding ways around the problem of the paucity of extant sources by or dealing with the lower classes.

Himmelfarb, some years down the track, was still mounting a rearguard action against the 'subversive' feminists (Scott), Marxists (even Hayden White, *sic*, was a little too 'Marxist' for her liking), postmodernists and anyone else that practises or goes so far even to recommend 'political' history.[63] Of course, her own work even at that point, in 1992, was still 'impartial': not presentist nor positioned. Clearly, the sort of approach she was defending in 1992 was simply more in tune with an earlier intellectual and political present than that of those who, especially since the 1980s, have been challenging historiographical convention in various ways. By 1992, however, more postmodernists were adding their voices to those of feminist and leftist historians who had not only popularized social history, but had long been suspicious of the overconfidence with which traditionalists laid claim to the truth/facticity of their own accounts and their own lack of partisanship. In the classic liberal view, everyone but oneself is political. Hence, for Himmelfarb, it is only postmodernists (who in her view are necessarily leftist) who 'tell it' (history) just as they like.

Elton's use of sexist language in the above quotes from his earlier work may have been a reflection of the unthinking androcentrism of the day, but it is ironic, none the less: 'the historian' is a 'he', 'mankind' represents the whole of humanity, and it is 'men' who say, do, think and suffer things. As Australian feminist historian, Judith Allen, once pointed out, if we were to follow Elton's 'non-partisan, non-presentist' treatment of questions for which there are no extant sources as non-questions, we would be hard put to produce many histories of women.[64] Women who had the education and leisure to leave behind written works and the social 'importance' to ensure that they would be valued and preserved were comparatively rare. But, if feminist historians since the 1960s had heeded Elton's empiricist rules of evidence, or concentrated on Himmelfarb's 'rational' institutions alone, today there would not be the wealth of sources available that deal with women in history, women of all social classes and ethnic groups, around the world.

Allen's main point in that essay was that it was not only the foci of mainstream history that were androcentric, with regard to judging what or who is 'important' enough to study, but its methods as well. Unlike Elton, she was disinclined to say, 'Well. Tough! If [insufficient or only 'improper'] sources do not remain of them, for historians they did not exist!' She recommended that feminist historians find ways to get around the problem of silences and gaps in the extant records with respect to women. Apart from redefining what constitutes a proper primary source (as many have done), one could, for example, use deduction or inference – which is not necessarily prohibited in positivist History unless taken to be mere 'speculation' unsupported by the 'given' evidence – combining that with due caution as to the reliability of positive evidence in extant sources such as official records. For example, Allen cited suspiciously low rates of abortion in police records of Australia and New Zealand from the late nineteenth to early twentieth century, in which were also found unusually high rates of 'accidents of pregnancy', 'spontaneous miscarriages' and/or 'maternal deaths due to pregnancy or childbirth'. She therefore argued that we might reasonably infer that the incidence of abortion then was much higher than reported or discovered by the authorities. (So much for the 'existing evidence'!) Such an inference would be strengthened further if safe methods of preventing conception were not then widely available, which they were not. Similarly, a lack of positive evidence in official records of the incidence of rape can hardly be taken to mean that it did not occur, though from that particular silence – one might say from this 'negative evidence' – we can reasonably infer other things about community attitudes toward rape and women's unwillingness to report it. Allen would say that we need to think about *how and why* such silences or omissions in the historical record came about, and what they might signify about women/society in the past.

There is a further problem with accepting Elton's dictum that 'if [wo]men have said, thought, done or suffered anything of which nothing any longer exists, those things are as though they had never been.' This might lead us to assume that women in the distant past never did any number of things simply because records of such things are not extant or scarce, or because the only positive evidence remaining is that which said they *should* not. This is rather like assuming, as histories have done often enough, that if a law or dominant behavioural code said that women (or peasants or merchants) must not do something, they did not. The obvious question is why did the laws or codes come about in the first place and, in some cases, even keep being reiterated by the authorities. As I suggested above, one can readily find in history examples of primary sources (especially official records) being treated less than critically, as necessarily authoritative or 'factual'. Doubtless, this is partly why Scott would recommend that we *interpret* 'facts' or treat them, too, as the objects of our enquiries rather than simply taking them as given.

One might well ask, then, whether Allen's approach was any more positioned than Elton's. And to which do we ascribe the more scholarly integrity? The political presentism that inhered in her avowedly feminist history at least had the virtue of self-awareness and frankness. When in 1991 Elton acknowledged that 'the secret of [historians'] success . . . lies in hindsight and argument backwards',[65] surely here, too, he was contradicting his denial of presentism in his own works. Argument backwards from what, we might ask, if not from their own present? Isn't the first step missing from his formula that historians 'always reason from the situation they study to its prehistory – from what is [was] to how it came about'? Why do they select it for study, if not partly for its meaning for them in the present? The usual response may be for the importance or meaning it had in the past – that we study history 'for its own sake' or 'only ask questions of the past that it asked of itself' – but Elton speaks as if historians were not only time travellers but ones whose minds can be swept clean before they travel.

In *Is History Fiction?* Ann Curthoys and John Docker trace the empiricist-objectivist approach we find in Elton back to ancient Greece. Normally, the original inspiration for this style of historiography would be said to be the nineteenth century's Leopold von Ranke: the so-called 'father of scientific history'. Yet Curthoys and Docker associate the preconceptions and methods of von Ranke with those of Thucydides, contrasting these with the rather different style of Herodotus who lived earlier in the fifth century BCE. In *The Histories*, they conclude, Herodotus practised a 'critical' sort of history that 'anticipates contemporary literary and contemporary theory in many ways'[66] – in brief, with respect to his 'doubled' view of history as a discipline or field of enquiry with its own research methods and as storytelling, too (so an 'art' as well as a 'science'); his freethinking cosmopolitanism and hence commitment to writing about all sorts of areas of life and all sorts of people; his 'structural looseless' (use of various methods and emplotments); and his relativism (multiple stories or voices) and epistemological doubt. What all this suggests, including the reference to 'critical history', is that Herodotus also had something in common with Nietzsche, that famous nineteenth-century opponent of von Ranke.

Curthoys and Docker describe Nietzsche's views on such 'scientific objectivists' as follows:

> What nations do not need is the nineteenth-century kind of history that claims to be a 'science', where historians regard themselves as 'objective', as 'pure thinkers who only look on life' . . . . Nietzsche suggests that the ideal of objectivity, as in a history that believes itself to be a 'reproduction' or 'photograph' of the 'empirical nature of things', is a modern 'superstition'. He strongly urges the historian to 'interpret the past' out of the 'fullest exertion of the vigour of the present'.[67]

They also cite his cynical attack in *Genealogy of Morals* (1887) on 'ascetic' historians whose 'major claim is to be a mirror of events [and] reject teleology', who 'disdain to act the part of judges [and] neither affirm nor deny' but 'simply ascertain, describe'.[68] Their conclusion is that Nietzsche's insistence that the historian interpret the past in line with the concerns and desires of the present both echoed Herodotus and prepared the way for a dissident stream of twentieth-century reflections on history that extended from Benedetto Croce, R. G. Collingwood and Walter Benjamin to Foucault (and Barthes, Lévi-Strauss, White, Scott and others already mentioned). Avowedly presentist but self-reflexive, sceptical history has been around for quite some time, in short.

V

> [H]istory is both a metaphor of the past and a metonymy of the present.
> The texted Past is always beached in presents that always reinvent it.
>
> (Greg Dening, *History's Anthropology*)[69]

I said in the introduction to this chapter that, in closing, I would consider some experiments in writing sceptical history. This I shall do briefly, albeit with the acknowledgement that there have been many, many more imaginative works produced in the field, especially since the 1980s, than can be discussed here. Curthoys and Docker describe the 1980s and 1990s as 'a kind of Herodotean period of extended thinking about history as a literary form; and of historians engaging in literary experimentation in imaginative and innovative ways' that included 'micro-narratives, multiple points of view, and also fragmentation, montage, and genre-crossing'.[70]

Greg Dening, a specialist in Pacific Studies, is known both for his leading role in the 'Melbourne School' of ethnographic history and for his experimental works in history. To rephrase the often-cited first quotation above, which is from his *History's Anthropology* of 1988, history is not the past but something that seeks to stand for it; it is also part (and parcel) of the present. Though in this earlier work Dening distanced himself from deconstructionism with which he has long had much in common, but which he then believed would make 'a jungle of history's enchanting garden', he also insisted that 'there is in history no resurrection'.[71]

Although, ideally, his object in this work may have been the recovery of the actual experience of his subject – the astronomer on the supply ship Daedalus, who was one of three Europeans killed by Hawaiians on a beach on Oahu in 1792 – Dening's claims as to what he might realistically achieve were more modest than those of reconstructionist historians:

> In this history of the death of William Gooch, I simply offer an ethnographic reflection. I owe William Gooch . . . the realism of a crafted story . . . . I owe him presence in the ways of life he actually experienced. But I am a product of my times as much as he was of his. The realism I crave for him is crafted too – by my ironies, by my show of doubt as well as certainty, by display of exhaustive research, by all the tropes that persuade you that he not I is present.[72]

Clearly, his methods are also more complex.

Dening's works are unusual in the extent of their self-reflexivity, or the degree to which he, the author, is present in the text, reflecting upon the story he is telling. Typically, in them a descriptive narrative is interspersed with interpretation and also reflective sections where he discusses his research experiences, inspirations, findings and methods. Dening knows that his style of writing history can be 'slightly disturbing to others',[73] perhaps because among his 'shows of doubt' is the fact that he will not allow his readers to imagine that his present does not impinge upon the aspect of the past he is attempting to recreate or, rather, 'perform'. Unlike Elton, Dening acknowledges the inevitably 'one-sided and selective' nature of history production:

> Having a Von Rankean ambition or even an ethnographic one to describe 'what actually happened' becomes difficult when the same event is possessed in culturally different ways. Both the British and the Hawaiians made history of the death of William Gooch. It takes something of an eternal *Nunc* to claim that the past of neither is what actually happened, but that it is what we invent from our vantage point. In vain do the ghosts of Gooch and Hergest peer over our shoulder and say 'but we were there'. The Past is never likely to recognize itself in History, any more than natives are likely to recognize themselves in ethnography.[74]

An 'eternal Nunc' or now (as in 'God is the eternal Now') he describes earlier as a cosmological mind-tease for mortals, a paradox. But, clearly, his desire to do justice to his subject, William Gooch, with realism, with an attempt to describe 'the ways of life he actually experienced' is a far cry from Elton's call for an understanding of the past 'for its own sake/on its own terms', apparently without reference to the present.

Dening does not deny the present-mindedness that must inhere in his or anyone else's works of history, and indeed he often reflects upon history's present-past nexus or paradox. Hence, in his works we do not find the glaring self-contradictions witnessed in those historians who oppose presentism while simultaneously practising it, apparently unconsciously. In the passage cited earlier he followed the remark about deconstructionism with the observation that he knew 'the lethargy that too much reflection creates' (a wink to those historians who feel that theory has no place in history). That notwithstanding, he ends the paragraph with the following acknowledgement: 'how can I pretend that Roland Barthes, Michel Foucault and Victor Turner have not spoken', and Marshall Salins, too. This is a reference to how, in the wake of their ground-breaking works of theory (in different disciplines), 'Ethnography now with no reflection is no ethnography at all.' That is, without Dening's presence in the text alongside that of William Gooch this would not be an ethnographic history worth its name.

Dening's self-reflexive method enables him to leave his interpretations of the past more open than those in histories of recovery or reconstruction. Not unlike with Joan Scott, it involves more recognition of the distance ('difference') of the past, an awareness of both its necessary complexities and those of trying to interpret it. Though Dening is not committed to a political practice of history in as explicit a way as Scott or Somekawa and Smith or, indeed, Keith Jenkins,[75] his approach exemplifies a sort of history that is still frankly positioned, epistemologically, thus sceptical *and also presentist*. These, moreover, are qualities that few would see as impugning his integrity as an historian even if they do not warm to his 'complicated' style.

Unsurprisingly, Dening is among the authors included in *Experiments in Rethinking History* (2004), the above-mentioned collection of essays edited by Alun Munslow and Robert A. Rosenstone, which were drawn from the first several issues of *Rethinking History: The Journal of Theory and Practice*. In fact, Dening's essay is one of four included in part one of the book, which is simply entitled 'Self-reflexive'.[76] The editors begin their introduction to Part One with the words: 'Self-reflexivity is, of course, central to experimentalism in history. It is the self-conscious understanding of the authorial and imaginative roles played by both historical actors and the historian.'[77] At base, as I noted in Chapter 1, it is the recognition (and discussion) of the self-referring paradoxes, as well as the ordinary everyday contradictions and difficulties routinely encountered in one's practice of history – for example, with respect to engaging in 'a literary-creative act even when the aim might seem to be reconstruction'.[78] 'History is not the past', as Dening is fond of emphasizing, but rather 'theatre', something we 'perform', playfully, inventively or imaginatively; the realities of the past are gone and we cannot capture them in our history texts. Munslow and Rosenstone observe that it is to highlight the inevitable presentness of history that the starting point of any self-reflexive practice of it must be 'our engagement with the past'. Citing Dening, they believe that history is only lost when, among other things, 'authors cannot recognize or refuse to display their own presence' in their history texts.

Dening is no naive realist or reconstructionist, but he does exhibit the sense of 'responsibility toward the past' that Munslow and

Rosenstone see as characteristic of their self-reflexive authors, despite the experimentalism of their writing. This can be seen in an interesting illustration in another of Dening's works, *Mr Bligh's Bad Language*, where he discusses the enthusiastic response of students to his 'patently presentist, relativist notion of history'. Wanting to convince them that history is something we make rather than learn, he confesses that:

> I want to persuade them that any question worth asking about the past is ultimately about the present. I want to persuade them that any history they make will be fiction – not fantasy, fiction, something sculpted to its expressive purpose. I want them to be ethnographic – to describe with the carefulness and realism of a poem what they observe of the past in the signs that the past has left.[79]

His students' enthusiasm he puts down to how his approach seems 'soft' – 'no hard facts to learn' – and to how 'it warms their prejudice that history is just opinion, one as good as another'. Yet their opinions are shaken somewhat by viewing old films about the incident they are studying, the mutiny on the *Bounty*. These, Dening says, they see to be 'irresponsible, negligent of the rights of an historical past to be properly represented', but also funny in their sorry failure to grasp either the differences between the present and the past or the differences between cultures. In a good comment on the often-heard criticism of postmodern or otherwise sceptical history, that it irresponsibly encourages us to represent the past however we like, he concludes that his students 'discover that their own presentism, relativism and fictions have responsibilities' to the difference of the past and other cultures, a discovery he sees as 'cultural literacy . . . . acquired somewhere between theatre and living'.[80] His implication is that the said films (history in the reconstructionist mode) exhibit the cultural imperialist and ethnocentric biases of their times in a way that a 'relativist and presentist', self-aware practice of history could not. This is reminiscent of Scott's warnings about treating as realistic an unconscious projection of ourselves back onto the past.

In another section of that same book on experiments in writing history, Part Two entitled 'New Voices', are a few pieces whose authors' reasons for experimenting are similar to those of Judith Allen. For, they include a desire to redress silences or other slights in the historical record toward women. We might well ask whether this merely represents our own current feminist concerns, or whether it reflects a sense of duty toward women in the past.

One of these authors, Robin Bisha, opts for 'pseudo-auto-biography', a life-story written as if the historical actor in question, an eighteenth-century Russian noblewoman, were telling it herself.[81] The voluminous correspondence available, Bisha says, 'reveals little of the inner world of the correspondents', whilst conventional secondary sources such as a recent biography do little more to throw light on the role of the women in the affairs of society and governance despite the undeniable 'importance of women in the cultural and political life of Petrine Russia'.[82] Clearly, these factors plus another she mentions, the recourse to 'unsubstantiated legends' and gossip or rumour even by scholars of repute, elicits in Bisha a sense of responsibility toward her subject. The same might be said of Judith Zinsser, who criticizes standard biographies of the French scholar the marquise Du Châtelet, for beginning 'her' story with Voltaire, her one-time lover. Zinsser suggests that this is but one way in which historical treatments of her personality and achievements have been skewed.[83] Not unlike with Bisha, her sense of responsibility includes rigorous scrutiny of the available sources, and developing a familiarity with the subjects' temporal and cultural contexts in order to remain true to them as far as is possible. However presentist one's feminist or other agenda may be, one cannot, in other words, tell any story about them that one feels like.

In Zinsser's prologue to a full-length work on the marquise, she begins by contrasting a few possible ways of beginning a narrative about her subject's life. Each of them represents for her a 'true' or 'real' (that is, plausible) account of the marquise's last months. This is an approach she apparently replicates later in the work, of which she says:

> I have chosen a different approach to biography. Instead of writing one chronological narrative, I am dividing the biography into three separate but complementary sections. Just as in this introduction, each presents the marquise from a different perspective, each comes from different kinds of sources, and includes speculations based on my own experiences. Each has a different purpose and answers different questions.[84]

Zinsser explains that she chose this method in response to the challenges posed by our studying the historical record, since the

more we do that 'the more spaces we find . . . between the "facts",
that in turn pose questions defying simple answers'. Letters, for
example, are 'separate "facts", surrounded by vast spaces that biographers must fill in' from their reading of other historians, as well
as from their own experiences and understandings. In the biography's third section she addresses the question of why her subject's
history has been so 'neglected', so 'skewed and fragmented',
focussing her attention upon the views of her bequeathed to us by
past historians. She acknowledges her own 'agenda', on the other
hand, in wanting to throw some light on the question of 'how the
marquise du Châtelet could have been alternately admired,
ridiculed and forgotten'; and wanting to 'do justice to all aspects of
her unorthodox interests and achievements'. She therefore combines
a sense of duty to the life, personality and achievements of her
subject with an awareness of the limits of facticity and of what she
calls the 'truisms of historiography':

> In this section, I demonstrate how the same 'facts' have been
> joined into many narratives and used to create contradictory,
> disparate images. Here I explore the truisms of historiography:
> that each century must write the narrative in its own way, that
> historians write within a framework bounded and crisscrossed
> with preconceptions. All of us have implicit or explicit agendas
> that determine what subject we have chosen to research and
> recreate. All historians have a particular story to tell that
> reflects our own questions about our own times, even about
> ourselves.[85]

Zinsser therefore joins her voice to those of others who recognize
that their historical narratives and analyses cannot be other than
present-minded, which is not the same thing as accepting that they
will be 'irresponsible'.

Finally, I commented in Chapter 1 on one further scholar whose
approach takes for granted both the presence of the historian in the
text and the intertextual nature of history production. Dominick
LaCapra describes his 'dialogic' method of reading, writing and
interpretation as parallel to 'a certain mode of deconstruction'.[86]
Contrasting the conventional empiricist 'distinction between
accurate reconstruction of an object of study' to 'exchange with that
object as well as with other inquirers into it', his dialogic approach

underlines the dialogue between historians that forms an important part of any work of history. In empiricist history, however, this can be quite submerged, representing one more 'rhetorical convention' designed to strengthen the appearance of an objective representation of past realities. (I remarked in Chapter 1 on how the author's intertextuality is blurred by the omniscient scholarly voice combined with standard historical conventions of referencing.) After all, it is not so easy to present one's interpretation as a straightforward 'retelling of a/the story' when one spends a considerable amount of time drawing explicitly upon the work of other interpreters or, 'worse', acknowledging that they have had their differences and disagreements. LaCapra sees dialogism as precluding a 'totalizing perspective' on the past because, while it is not meant to displace accurate reconstruction:

> it accords an important place to the 'voices' and specific situations of others at the same time as it creates a place for our 'voices' in an attempt to come to terms with the past in a manner that has implications for the present and future.[87]

LaCapra thus enunciates principles of 'good' (i.e. reflexive) practice adhered to also by others – leaving interpretations open, acknowledging one's intertextuality, and demonstrating one's presence both in the text and in the present – whilst also opening up a space for a variety of experimental approaches. Interestingly, however, he follows this passage with the remark that when we are interpreting historical texts and actors it is still important to provide quotations, extensively enough so that any possible counter-reading or interpretation is enabled (not to provide evidence for the one possible reading). He does not, in any case, reject out of hand all historiographical conventions. Hence, for him, a dialogic reading must be combined with an attempt to be true to past realities; and even objectivity can be rehabilitated. His conception of 'responsibility' to the past includes 'a post-deconstructive notion of objectivity' that does not occlude dialogic exchange with past texts and peoples as well as other interpreters. It also involves attempts (in a manner reminiscent of Scott) to check the projection of ourselves back onto the past through methods such as 'contextualizing techniques, requiring meticulous research and the attempt to substantiate [our] statements' or arguments.[88]

VI

In conclusion, I hope I have demonstrated in this chapter just how common unconscious presentism is in history, whether it be in people's (including historians') unthinking acceptance of given beginnings/origins, or constructs of tradition, or teleologies of the modern nation-state. To this list we can also add the obvious present-centredness, politically and epistemologically, of those who criticize the nasty habit of presentism in others, speaking as if it can entirely be transcended (for example, merely by divesting it of politics). We have seen how even postmodernist or otherwise sceptical historians have sought ways to soften it, however – through historicizing interpretation; focussing upon discontinuities rather than conventional linear chronology and its teleological causation; and utilizing a discourse analysis approach to 'talk of beginnings' (or talk of tradition, origins, or even facts). I would add to the list: leaving our interpretations open partly through the incorporation of reflexive self-doubt. Such methods are more likely to be effective when coupled with a reflective approach that highlights the present-past nexus in history writing by requiring the presence of historians in their history texts. Among other things, this would mean, as Scott says, that they reflect upon the status of their own 'facts' as well as those of others – not dispensing with facticity but remaining aware of the blurred boundary between fact and interpretation in all history texts. Even where the status of a fact is not in dispute, it is the 'space between facts', as Zinsser put it, that history is mostly about.

As for the question of integrity, a postmodernist or sceptical approach to such things need not be 'irresponsible'. It can be both scholarly and imaginative (as any history must be), fictive in the sense of being a creative work of 'art': not 'science' but not pure fantasy either. Personally, I accept Somekawa's and Smith's proposition that the historian's integrity need not hinge upon one's ability to grasp 'the truth', disinterestedly or objectively. We could see integrity as residing in the utility and sincerity of the historian's ethical/political and, indeed, historiographical stance. On this basis as well as others, they will be seen to be persuasive in their interpretations (or not). What is implicit in this redefinition of historiographical integrity, moreover, is that frank self-awareness (or self-criticism or 'decon-struction' of one's own work) *on the printed page* is an absolute requirement. A number of other radical historians discussed in this chapter share such a view: that we must be self-reflexive in our praxis of history with respect to many things, not least its inevitable, multiply derived present-mindedness.

Suggestions for further reading

It is always good practice to go back to the sources, to read 'classics' or important works for oneself. I shall include a few here that I have not discussed, first on teleology and origins/beginnings:

* Michel Foucault, 'Nietzsche, Genealogy, History', in Paul Rabinow (ed.), *The Foucault Reader*, London, Penguin Books, 1984 (the essay will easily be found elsewhere as well)
* Edward Said, *Beginnings: Intention and Method*, Baltimore: John Hopkins University Press, 1975

On those and related issues such as 'pres-enting the past', Greg Dening's works could be consulted. They are useful also as well-known examples of experimental and reflective history. On the other hand, they well illustrate the theoretical and methodological concerns of the ethnographic or 'semiotic' history discussed here and in Chapter 1.

* Greg Dening, 'A Poetic for Histories: Transformations that Present the Past', in Aletta Biersack (ed.), *Clio in Oceania*, Washington: Smithsonian Institution, 1990; or 'Reflection: History as a Symbol Science', in *The Bounty: An Ethnographic History*, Melbourne: Melbourne University History Monograph, no. 1, 1998; or *Performances*, Melbourne: Melbourne University Press, 1996

Also, for interesting works on history and time, see:

* Julia Kristeva, 'Women's Time', in Kelly Oliver (ed.), *French Feminism Reader*, Lanham, Boulder, New York, Oxford: Rowman and Littlefield Publishers, Inc., 2000 (discussed in Chapter 3)
* Elizabeth Deeds Ermarth, 'Beyond the "Subject"', in Keith Jenkins and Alun Munslow, *The Nature of History Reader*, London and New York: Routledge, 2004 (in Part Four, 'Endisms'), pp. 281–95 (or Ermarth's book, *Sequel to History*, Princeton, Princeton University Press, 1992)

Part Four of this reader focuses on the debate over the 'end of [the discourse of] history', with which readers might like to become acquainted. It includes essays I have referred to already, by Joan Scott and Rita Felski, as well as by authors I shall discuss in subsequent chapters, Ermarth and Dipesh Chakrabarty. I would suggest that the debate is particularly pertinent to this chapter, however, as it is itself an example of teleology in histories of history.

Chapter 3

Negotiating 'difference'

I

> Postcolonial scholarship is committed, almost by definition, to engaging the universals – such as the abstract figure of the human or that of Reason – that were forged in eighteenth-century Europe and that underlie the human sciences . . . [Frantz] Fanon's struggle to hold on to the Enlightenment idea of the human – even when he knew that European imperialism had reduced that idea to the figure of the settler-colonial white man – is now itself part of the global heritage of all postcolonial thinkers.
>
> (Dipesh Chakrabarty, *Provincializing Europe*)[1]

> Since the 1970s poststructuralist theories . . . have radically challenged approaches to difference which see it as grounded in biology, human nature or in universal structures of the psyche . . . [A] strong argument can be made that the different forms of post-structuralist theory share a postmodern impulse in their approaches to language, meaning, subjectivity and power. Above all they challenge ideas of fixed meaning, unified subjectivity and centred theories of power.
>
> (Chris Weedon, *Feminism, Theory and the Politics of Difference*)[2]

In Chapter 1 I set out six general principles for a 'postmodernist' or, more broadly, a sceptical practice of history, three of which were particularly relevant to my discussion of teleology/presentism in Chapter 2. A central part of that discussion was focussed upon unconscious teleology, particularly in conventional approaches to linear causation involving quests for origins. Given the frequency with which origins and tradition are obviously invented, it can be seen why so many postmodernist and other critics of modernist empiricist history would recommend that we switch our focus to ruptures or breaks in the passage of time/events – to discontinuity(s). A second guideline for a sceptical praxis of history that was especially pertinent in Chapter 2 was the need for self-reflexivity on the part of the historian, with respect to frank admissions of one's own position(s), uncertainties and contradictions. In agreement with Somekawa and Smith and others, what I take to be more indicative of scholarly integrity than disinterested truth claims is the frankness with which the historian acknowledges his/her commitments – for example, to an epistemological and political, *radical* praxis of history. The third principle of practice underlined in Chapter 2 was intimately related to the above-mentioned demand for the historian's presence in the text, reflecting upon his/her uncertainties and contradictions as well as history's intrinsic paradoxes. This was the desirability of leaving arguments and conclusions more open to avoid 'closures of knowledge'.

This chapter is focussed upon one further principle listed in Chapter 1 that is often put forward as a means of practising sceptical or radical history: a focus upon 'difference'. What is meant by this can vary from a call merely for more recognition of cultural, racial/ethnic, gender, sexual or other differences – which may be explicitly informed by a critique of humanist universalism or may not – to a central concern among postmodernists with 'processes of differentiation' (to use Joan Scott's phrase). This refers to the ways in which difference is discursively constructed rather than being naturally given. Hence, we often find authors speaking of those who are 'racialized', since the definitions of black and white, for example, have varied depending upon context (Greeks or the Welsh as 'black' etc.); just as feminist scholars for some time have been using 'gender' as a verb to indicate that it is a social construct, speaking of how people (and all sorts of things: the Occident/Orient, nations, colonizers and subject peoples) are 'gendered'. However, these days many feminist and queer theorists go further to question the conventional feminist 'sex-gender' distinction, arguing that even so-called 'biological sex' (male and female) is not natural but, rather, culturally determined. British feminist scholar, Chris Weedon, indicates this in the quote above where she mentions poststructuralist challenges to conventional notions of difference that are popularly assumed to be 'grounded in biology, human nature or in universal structures of the psyche'.

Whether writing works focussed on modern or historical discourses, what authors seek to do with their critiques of differentiation is to lay bare the political implications, uses and effects of binaristic constructs of difference. Their object is to deconstruct conventional binaries that have implied hierarchies of value and therefore also to expose their operation in relations of power. There are many possible examples: positive and negative opposites such as 'the West' and its inferior 'Other', the East; white/black, man/woman, masculine/feminine, active/passive, mind/body, rationality/emotionality, etc. Such binarisms are also interrelated.

At a basic sort of level, this contestation of binaristic logic is partly what is meant by a third usage of 'difference': Derrida's deconstructive concept of 'differánce'. However, more specifically, this refers to the endless 'play' or 'deferral' (non-closure) of meaning in language. Derrida's prime concern was with textuality or writing, moreover, rather than speech. Weedon notes how Derrida distanced himself from Saussure's structuralist linguistics also because of its 'logocentrism' according to which 'signs':

> have an already fixed meaning recognized by the self-consciousness of the rational speaking subject. Derrida ... replaces the fixed signifieds of Saussure's chains of signs with a concept of '*différance*' in which meaning is produced via the dual strategies of difference and deferral. For Derrida there can be no fixed signifieds (concepts), and signifiers (sound or written images), which have identity only in their difference from one another, are subject to an endless process of deferral.[3]

Meaning may appear to be fixed in representation, that is, but this is 'a temporary retrospective fixing', for what is signified by a term or phrase depends upon the discursive context. Weedon gives the example of 'woman', the meaning of which is subject to continual rereading or reinterpretation. To add a couple more examples to the list she gave: it continues to vary from woman as figure of sin/evil (say, in monotheism's primary religious texts) or woman as dangerous or subversive (to established morality or patriarchal institutions), to the modern notion of woman as moral 'ideal' (say, moral exemplar), to woman as victim (or 'object of male sexual desire', the 'male gaze'), and so on and so forth. The virtue of studying history is that we are more likely to be able to recognize the historicity of such terms, the ways in which their meanings shift according to time and cultural/political contexts.

What all this points to is the dismissal by poststructuralists of the fixedness and transparency of meaning in texts/discourses and, by extension, also of authorial intention. The reference is to how authors are not fully in control of their language or the meaning(s) they want to put across – there is 'slippage' as meaning is *deferred* – and even where they might be in control, the meaning(s) of the text will still be subject to different interpretations on the part of readers. This, too, is what the 'deconstructionist' must be alert to – this and other things such as figuration (common rhetorical/metaphorical modes of expression), the use of which by writers will once again not always be fully conscious. This is partly why some have spoken of the 'death of the author', which will be discussed in Chapter 4.

Though there has been some debate about whether Derrida and Foucault properly qualify as postmodernists or poststructuralists, they usually head the list of theorists regarded as such. We have seen how postmodernist historians have followed Foucault's lead in emphasizing discontinuities in 'history' (or the passage of time) rather than the conventional approach to linked sequences of cause and effect in linear (e.g. 'progress') chronological and teleological models. What has perhaps been more central to his popularity, however, was his rethinking of *power* in terms that challenged orthodox Marxism. Though one often encounters the implication that this was the product of original genius on the part of Foucault, his approach to power was partly inspired by Nietzsche and, in some respects, it also reflected the thinking of sectors of the 1960s 'New Left'. Even traditional anarchism critiqued power in all its guises or workings (including in sexual relationships, among comrades, etc.), not just at the state level, or in relations between bosses and workers.

Weedon offers a useful summary of the 'guiding principles' proposed by Foucault that can be used 'to identify the nature and workings of power in any area of social and cultural analysis'.[4] In the interests of even more brevity, however, I shall treat it selectively, repeating only the aspects of his theory of power that I see to be pertinent to this discussion:

> 'Power is not something that is acquired [or owned/possessed], seized, or shared', it is a relationship. . . .
> Relations of power inhere in all . . . types of relationship (economic relations, sexual, knowledge relations).
> Power is not only restrictive and repressive, it is also productive.

Power comes from below [too, not just from above, from the state, etc.] and from a number of different sources . . . .

Weedon's point seven – 'Where there is power, there is resistance, and . . . this resistance is never in a position of exteriority in relation to power' – relates both to the third on power's productivity (power relations produce resistance, which is intrinsic to them) and to the first, since if power is a relation rather than a possession, resistance, too, is a manifestation of power. Thus, the one resisting is not outside power.

Clearly, if we were to write a history of, say, peasants, taking heed of these propositions, it would look rather different from traditional accounts in which lords always seemed to be 'calling the shots' and great men were, single-handedly, the makers of 'history'. Even within undeniably repressive structures of power or unequal relations of power, those on the bottom rungs of the social ladder could doubtless find many ways to resist and have some control over their own lives. In an essay entitled 'The Life of Infamous Men', Foucault once wrote of how in France petitions to the king for a judgement on a complaint against a third party represented a sharing in so-called 'absolutist' power: 'Everyone could make use of the enormity of absolute power for themselves . . . and against others'; everyone had the potential to become 'a terrible and lawless monarch for another' by using petitions, the 'mechanisms of sovereignty'.[5] In order to undermine dichotomous conceptions of power, Foucault discussed how an individual, who might seem powerless in the face of apparently overwhelming power, can 'appropriate this power, at least for a moment, channel it, tap it and inflect it in the direction one wants . . . make use of it . . . "seduce" it'.[6] Thus, seemingly powerless people can be more than the victims or objects of power: they can be the subjects both of 'power' and of 'history' (that is, its makers); they, too, that is, contribute to bringing about change. (I am aware that Foucault's manner of speaking here, and my repeating it, suggests a reification of power, a treatment of it as some external, tangible, almost physical thing. This could perhaps be taken as an illustration of slippage or deferral in the language even of the 'best' of us.)

I should comment on an aspect of Weedon's point two above: the reference to power inhering in knowledge relations. Foucault's emphasis on *knowledge as power* has also proved popular, particularly among those suspicious of empiricism's claim to absolute, transcendental Truth and objectivity or impartiality. At base, what he emphasized was that to engage in the production of knowledge(s) – say, history or science – is to intervene in relations of power in a variety of ways. Even the most 'innocent' or seemingly disinterested knowledges serve or contest entrenched interests. I am reminded of Edward Said's famous critique of 'Orientalism' first in a book by that name – the term meaning in his usage modern eurocentric 'knowledge' of the Orient or East – for which Foucault was an important inspiration. Both writers, we might also note, have been very influential in postcolonial theory and history, which I will be discussing in this chapter.

Finally, another aspect of Foucault's work that has been inspirational, particularly among postmodernist feminists, historians of gender/sexualities and queer theorists, has been his analysis of 'the' (i.e. Europe's) history of sexuality(s). What was related to that was his emphasis on what Weedon calls 'embodied subjectivity', so Foucault helped inspire a common focus in scholarship on 'the body'; and perhaps the central underlying theoretical reason for this is a need to 'unpack' the traditional mind/body binarism of Western thought. Though Chapter 4 is concerned with identity/subjectivity, I should note at this point that influential feminist/queer theorists such as Judith Butler have drawn upon Foucault in theorizing the body and the imprints upon it of power. It should come as no surprise that poststructuralist feminist and queer theorists would want to appropriate his model of power; for, as Weedon says, Foucault developed this 'in the context of a consideration of how sexuality has functioned to shape and regulate bodies and subjectivities over the last three centuries'.[7]

One thing Foucault emphasized was discontinuities in the European history of sexualities, whereby same-sex practices came to be seen as an *identity* (people being defined/centred, and also medicalized or pathologized, in terms of sexual desire and practice, as 'homosexual' or 'lesbian') only in modern times. Again, the point is that markers of differentiation such as sexual desire and practice as well as 'feminine' or 'masculine' behaviour are not universal and unchanging. The modern 'homo/hetero' binarism that so many like to see as 'natural' has not existed in discourse throughout time and across cultures. In both ancient Greece and early modern Japan (among samurai), for example, constructs of ideal or pure masculinity could hinge upon male same-sex practices – or so-called 'bi-sexuality' in the sense that men who practised 'pederasty' (or 'comrade love' between older mentors and youths) normally also had wives, most importantly, perhaps, to produce male heirs to further patrilineal family lines.[8]

Apart from Derrida and Foucault and others mentioned above, among the postmodernist scholars who have had a considerable impact upon the human sciences are a number of postcolonial theorists. Gayatri Chakravorty Spivak's work exemplifies how deconstruction has been seen by some to be a 'new, more progressive' theory that is useful for feminism: 'in so far as it offers a method of decentring the hierarchical oppositions which underpin gender, race and class oppression.'[9] Spivak is known particularly for her critical response to a group of postcolonial scholars connected in the 1980s and later with the journal, *Subaltern Studies*, which comprised ex- and neo-Marxists and, increasingly, poststructuralist scholars in the field of Indian/South Asian history. In wanting to give voice to those traditionally excluded from history, 'subaltern' or marginalized social groups, the initial project of these scholars ran parallel to that of the 'history from below' of British Marxist historians such as Eric Hobsbawm and E. P. Thompson[10] and social historians elsewhere. Spivak, however, focussed upon the 'difficulties and contradictions involved in constructing a "speaking position" for the subaltern', doubting that subaltern voices can be recovered that are 'original', authentic or pure rather than teleological, essentialist fictions[11] (as I noted in Chapter 2 in connection with a nationalist 'nostalgia for lost origins').

In what follows, I shall discuss 'difference' critiques and the critical theories that have informed them, with a view to considering how these critiques already are impacting upon, or might potentially influence further, a radical praxis of history. I will also turn the deconstructive gaze on difference itself, which is to say that I will reflect upon possible pitfalls and dangers associated with this conceptual category. A central problem, for example, is how scholars who are 'Western' can take heed of cultural difference without exoticizing the 'Other'; without essentializing other cultures or ethnic groups (or, indeed, our own). This is partly what the poststructuralist focus on processes of differentiation, discourses or 'talk of difference' is seeking to avoid. As I have noted, the ascription of an essence to any nation or particular group involves a reduction of heterogeneous elements to one single feature that in turn serves to marginalize anyone that does not conform to the essence or ideal. Some scholars have also been addressing the issue of 'reverse, inverse or self'-orientalism whereby, ironically, so-called 'Eastern' critics of eurocentrism take as given traditional Western orientalist notions of what characterizes the entire 'East' – the East as 'intuitive' in contrast to the West as 'rationalist', the East as groupist and authoritarian as opposed to a free individualistic West, and so on – albeit whilst inverting the eurocentic hierarchy of value to assign superiority to these supposed Eastern essences. Hence, in such constructs *the* East can become 'properly' hierarchical (respect for elders, social superiors, etc.) rather than authoritarian in its collectivism; and *the* West selfishly materialistic, and libertine or licentious rather than 'free' or 'free-thinking'.

On the other hand, should our focus happen to be sexual difference, say, in women's histories, the problem we encounter is how to differentiate 'woman' from 'man' without essentializing her (and him) on the basis of 'sex', 'nature' or 'biology'. These categories are themselves just social categories or constructs, according to many theorists. Though some feminist poststructuralist theorists have grounded woman's difference in her sexual body (or, more precisely, in the language that differentiates it), others have insisted that such works still imply a natural or essential womanhood. Any attempt to define true womanhood may reproduce the often-criticized humanist tendency to universalize women on the basis of norms that are, in reality, Western, white and middle class. As feminist historian Linda Gordon once put it whilst expressing concerns about the sexual difference approach in women's studies that was growing stronger in (from) the 1980s, 'the emphasis on a *unique* female voice almost always becomes an assumption of a *homogeneous* female voice'.[12] This points to a second standard usage of 'difference' in feminist scholarship where it means not female-male difference but an emphasis upon differences among women.

II

> with us there is nothing more consistent than a racist humanism since the European has only been able to become a man through creating slaves and monsters.
>
> (Jean-Paul Sartre, 1961)[13]

Whether in connection with class, culture, empire, nation and race/ ethnicity, or sex/gender and sexuality, increasing numbers of scholars since the 1980s have been directing their critiques at Western humanism. Poststructuralists and/or postcolonial scholars, those who are broadly termed postmodernists, have been in the forefront of this critique. Although it mounts a challenge to other aspects of humanism , too, such as its commitment to Enlightenment Reason and what Weedon calls 'unified subjectivity' (or essentialized ident- ity), what is most relevant to this chapter is humanism's supposed universalism. What we do not want to be doing in our histories is reproducing the eurocentrism or racism, or phallocratic exclusions of traditional humanism.

Humanism was/is a discourse stemming from the Enlightenment that in its many expressions purported to be about 'humanity' (human nature/psychology/Reason) and ideals for all humanity such as 'progress' (defined in European terms) as well as equality. In practice, its critics insist, it has not been all-inclusive but premised rather upon multiple binarisms and exclusions – of the colonial 'native', women, the lower classes, peoples of 'the East', or non- heterosexuals, to name just some. Among other things, it has treated the so-called 'West' or 'First World' as normative: Western experience, development, ideals, and also the Western individual (-istic) subject. Invariably, this subject was, implicitly at least, white, male, heterosexual and of the privileged middle to upper classes. This reveals the self-contradictory nature of humanist ideals, since this abstract, universalized vision of the human had not prevented its advocates from differentiating between colonizer and colonized, white and non-white, men and women, and so on, in terms of con- ventional hierarchical opposites of superior and inferior, advanced and backward, or adult-style maturity versus childlike innocence (hence the need for paternalistic colonial protections).

Illustrating that it has not only been so-called postmodernists who have been trenchant critics of humanism, Jean-Paul Sartre once delivered the following savage indictment of its racism. Here I shall quote it more fully than above:

> Chatter, chatter: liberty, fraternity, equality, love, honor, patri- otism and what have you. All this did not prevent us from making anti-racial speeches about dirty niggers, dirty Jews, and dirty Arabs. High-minded people, liberal or just soft-hearted, protest that they were shocked by such inconsistency; but they were either mistaken or dishonest, for with us there is nothing more consistent than a racist humanism since the European has only been able to become a man through creating slaves and

monsters. While there was a native population somewhere this imposture has not shown up; in the notion of the human race we found an abstract assumption of universality which served as cover for the most realistic practices. On the other side of the ocean there was a race of less-than-humans who, thanks to us, might reach our status a thousand years hence, perhaps . . . .[14]

This indictment of Western hypocrisy appeared in the Preface to Frantz Fanon's famous work, *The Wretched of the Earth*.

Though liberal-humanism is probably most often critiqued on these grounds, it is not the only Western metanarrative of 'progress' and European superiority that comes under fire, but Marxism, too. To illustrate the point, we might consider the following passage from *Provincializing Europe* by postcolonial theorist and deconstructionist historian of modern South Asia, Dipesh Chakrabarty:

> One simply cannot think of political modernity without . . . concepts that found a climactic form in the course of the European Enlightenment and the nineteenth century.
>
> These concepts entail an unavoidable – and in a sense indispensable – universal and secular vision of the human. The European colonizer of the nineteenth century both preached this Enlightenment humanism at the colonized and at the same time denied it in practice. But the vision has been powerful in its effects. It has historically provided a strong foundation on which to erect – both in Europe and outside – critiques of socially unjust practices. Marxist and liberal thought are legatees of this intellectual heritage.[15]

Chakrabarty goes on to say that in South Asia, for example, among the many legacies of Enlightenment Europe or, rather, their appropriation by the colonized was 'the very critique of colonialism itself'. Marxism, though it was itself among the 'legatees' of Enlightenment humanism, has of course often inspired struggles against colonialism or neo-colonialism in the so-called 'Third World'. Ironically, this can be said even of the 'metahistory' of historical materialism – the theory of universal stages from 'barbarism' (or primitive communism) through slavery and feudalism, then capitalism, and ultimately to communism/socialism – since some peoples outside Europe were keen to appropriate for themselves some of its markers of 'progress' or 'advancement'.

[handwritten margin note: criticid of Marxist theory]

The paradoxical nature of 'Third World' appropriation of Marxism is implied in that very nomenclature: Third as opposed to First or Second World. Marxian historical materialism, too, was founded upon notions of Europe leading the world. Only it could lay claim to 'civilization' and even a true history, since that required the ability to 'advance' (progress invariably being defined, then as now, in terms of Western norms). However trenchant a critic of Anglo-European colonial practices he was, Marx's theory of the 'Asiatic Mode of Production', and the theory of 'oriental despotism' associated with it, hinged upon an assumption that without the help of Europe 'backward' areas of the world would continue to 'stagnate'. Colonialism was therefore 'objectively progressive' because ultimately it would help to bring about social revolution, for example in India, and thus enable its transition to the next 'higher' stage of history: capitalist liberal democracy.

In his work, *Orientalism*, Edward Said noted this contradiction in Marx's thinking, citing him on the 'double mission' that England had in India: 'one destructive, the other regenerating – the annihilation of the Asiatic society, and the laying of the material foundations *of Western society* in Asia' (my emphasis).[16] Perhaps Marx was not far wrong, however, when he predicted that colonialism, both its destructive material practices and the European notions of superiority that even he was subject to, would help lay the groundwork for its own demise. Amidst those colonized by European nations there were those who aspired to Enlightenment humanist ideals, yet, since their exclusion from authority, self-determination and equality rested upon this sort of eurocentric paternalism, many soon recognized the ambivalent character of those ideals.

The case of Marx calls to mind another sympathetic, well-meaning critic of colonialism and neo-colonialism, Frederic Jameson. In an essay entitled 'Jameson's Rhetoric of Otherness and the "National Allegory"', Aijaz Ahmad once took Jameson to task for unthinkingly homogenizing the 'non-West' in line with worldist categories, 'universalist' (but really Western) norms and conventional East-West binarisms. This could easily have been a critique of some Western historian of the 'third world', but it was a response to an essay on 'third world literature' by Jameson. In this he apparently called for this to be taught in English or literature courses in the US as an 'antidote' to, as Ahmad expresses it, 'the general ethnocentricity and cultural myopia of the Humanities as they are presently constituted in these United States'.[17] Ahmad's long-term sense of comradeship with Jameson was shaken, he said, by a sense of discomfort with the text once he came across a sentence beginning with: 'All third world texts are necessarily . . .' Although one has to call such literature something, he acknowledged, he also insisted that the 'Third World' is a 'polemical' construct 'with no theoretical status whatsoever'. That is, 'there is no such thing as *a* "Third World Literature" which can be constructed as an internally coherent object of theoretical knowledge.' The rest of the offending sentence, we might note, was: 'to be read as . . . national allegories.'[18]

Ahmad then proceeded to argue against the language of worldism said to permeate the text, which had led Jameson to define the so-called Third World exclusively in terms of its Western-induced experience of colonialism and reactive political category of 'the Nation'. Hence, *the* 'Third World' intellectual/writer also had to be defined in terms of his/her nationalism. Why was it, Ahmad asked, that Jameson defined the First and Second Worlds in terms of systems of production, capitalism and socialism, respectively, yet switched the terms in the case of the Third World to the experience of externally imposed phenomena: colonization? (I shall resist the temptation to argue with the notion that socialism or capitalism was never imposed . . .) This explains why, for Jameson, the Third World had no other choices, ideologically, but its nationalisms versus 'global American postmodernist culture': his westcentrism and nationalism/postmodernity binary opposition ruled out another real possibility, of going the way of Second World socialism.[19]

Yet 'Third World' intellectuals/writers themselves might well centre their own experience/identity on any number of other collective identifications. Class, gender, caste, religion, trade union, political party, village and prison were the ones Ahmad mentioned. They might combine any one or more of these with an account of *individual* experience.[20] 'The nation' or the experience of colonialism-nationalism may not be invoked at all, or not be central in 'Third World' authors' narratives. In sum, Ahmad, a Third World author himself, was disconcerted by his First World 'comrade's' failure to recognize the heterogeneity of 'Third World literature', or of the 'Third World' and its peoples in general. He felt that Jameson's humanist 'rhetoric of Otherness' – that is, defining 'you' in terms of 'us' (what we are not) – had turned Ahmad from inspirational comrade into 'civilizational Other'.

Ahmad is not unlike Chakrabarty, who recognizes that humanism, both in its liberal and Marxist expressions, also provided 'a strong foundation on which to erect . . . critiques of socially un-just practices' in the 'Third World'. Yet this does not stop them from mounting a critique of its eurocentric legacies in liberalism and Marxism and, indeed, (in Chakrabarty's case) in the discipline of history, too. [For him, a 'post-modern' praxis of history must necessarily engage with history's eurocentrism.] This the editors of *The Nature of History* noted in their introduction to the extract they included from Chakrabarty's *Provincializing Europe*. According to Munslow and Jenkins, the central question he addressed in the work was 'what would a history look like if it was properly "past the modern"', political modernity having been dominated by Western European concepts, discourse, theories and praxis.

III

In another paper by Chakrabarty entitled 'Minority histories, subaltern pasts', [he addressed a related issue commonly referred to by critics of humanist universalism: the problem of trying to rectify the exclusions humanism was based upon with liberal-pluralist (or multicultural/assimilationist) strategies of *'inclusion'*.] Here Chakrabarty was specifically addressing the difficulties involved with attempts to rectify history's traditional exclusions: namely, pluralist attempts on the part of historians of South Asia to 'include' subaltern or subordinated groups in the history of a nation. Discussing the trend toward social history or 'history from below' in the Western democracies, he commented upon how by the 1980s histories from below were adding indigenous peoples, 'ethnic' groups, gays and lesbians and other marginalized groups to the list of 'minority' subjects already being included since the 1960s: the industrial proletariat, peasants, women, slaves and convicts.[21] Hence, by the latter part of the 1990s a virtual 'cult of pluralism' had ensued in history. Somewhat paradoxically, however, in defence of this even the postmodern critique of Western 'metanarratives' had come to be used as a weapon against the typically standardized, single 'grand narrative' of a nation. (The alternative was seen to be multiple possible narratives and voices, in 'minority histories' and the like.) Here Chakrabarty was implying an irony, for if 'Minority histories . . . in part express the struggle for inclusion and representation that are characteristic of liberal and representative democracies', if they 'make the subject matter of history more representative of society as a whole', they are part and parcel of the mindset of liberal-humanist modernity which is, ostensibly, the prime target of postmodernist critiques. We have here a reflexive paradox once again. [The *mere inclusion* of minorities in the pages of history, in other words, falls short of targeting the humanist, liberal-pluralist foundations of the discipline (and, of course, the exclusions intrinsic to liberal-humanist capitalist democracy) in convincingly postmodernist terms.]

Chakrabarty illustrates this when he observes that minority histories mainly constituted resistance only in the early days when they were still excluded from mainstream history. Once they were 'in', their oppositional stance tended, apparently, to become redundant. This does not mean that he fails to acknowledge the changes wrought in the discipline since the advent of social and women's history, or 'histories from below', however, for:

> History has not been the same ever since a Thompson or a Hobsbawm took up his pen to make the working classes look like major actors in society, or since the time feminist historians made us realise the critical importance of gender relations and of the contributions of women to social processes. So the question of whether or not such incorporation changes the nature of historical discourse itself can be answered simply: 'of course, it does'.[22]

That notwithstanding, he then insisted that 'the answer to the question: did such incorporation call the discipline into any kind of crisis? would have to be, No.' I should acknowledge that Chakrabarty proceeds in this paper to discuss the epistemological difficulties and paradoxes that arise when one seeks to incorporate colonial minority histories (whose actors may see their own actions as supernaturally caused or motivated) into a discipline founded upon European historicism and Reason (linear sequences of rational cause and effect in what he calls a developmental 'unity'). However, his critical stance on mere inclusion is more pertinent to my discussion of analytic methods of contesting traditional exclusions based upon a binaristic, hierarchical logic of difference that were often practised while simultaneously mouthing humanist ideals.

This calls to mind similar critiques mounted by other theorists of difference, albeit with other 'subaltern' or subordinated groups in mind. Feminist theorists and/or historians have also been arguing for quite some time that, in the interests of real social justice, feminist scholars need to go further than women's mere inclusion in traditional androcentric theories, discourses or academic disciplines – to critique their very foundations. 'Difference-' or 'postfeminism' has been in the forefront of the trend in cultural or critical theory to counterpose to humanist/pluralist discourses of inclusion a focus upon difference in all of the senses outlined above: both a respect for difference and a focus upon the repressive effects of conventional discourses of differentiation; and an emphasis both on sexual difference and the many differences between women.

'Post-feminism', I should explain, is a term that is often used rather loosely to mean anything that has postdated and supposedly differs markedly from and transcends the Second Wave of feminism that began in the 1960s. Here it has a more specific usage referring to two main streams of postfeminism: poststructuralist feminism and postcolonial feminism. The latter is a feminist branch of postcolonial theory, the deconstructionist side of which is counted among a few major variants of poststructuralist feminism; so the boundary between these two main streams can sometimes be blurred (as is the case, for example, with Spivak).

An influential, psychoanalytic form of poststructuralist feminism has focussed upon sexual/gender difference between women and men under the influence of the so-called 'French Feminists': Julia Kristeva, Luce Irigaray and Hélène Cixous. Their works have involved a borrowing upon but rethinking of the theories of Freud and Jacques Lacan, particularly the latter, on 'the acquisition of gendered subjectivity, unconscious processes and the phallocentric structure of the symbolic order' of language (and social processes and institutions, law, etc.). As Weedon explains, most psycho-analytic feminists have looked to Lacan for inspiration, though not uncritically. In general, their approach:

> involves the assumption that women have no position from which to speak in the symbolic order and that feminine potential is repressed in favour of a patriarchal version of femininity in which male desire and male interests define and control female sexuality and feminine subjecthood.[23]

To return to the issue of inclusion, poststructuralist feminists have led the way in reappraising the sexual equality approach central to some earlier styles of feminism in the First and early Second Wave. They found this wanting because its demands for 'equality' did not go nearly far enough. First we should recall that the ideal of human equality was one of the legacies of Enlightenment humanism said by Chakrabarty to have provided a strong basis in and out of Europe from which to challenge socially unjust practices. As he expressed it:

> Where the Enlightenment seems special is in its universalization of different versions of the idea of equality, which allowed the colonized to charge the colonizer with self-contradiction . . . [for] he, the European had made a travesty of his own principles of human equality.[24]

Needless to say, it was not just the 'colonized' who demanded equality of those who preached it, but feminists, too, in and outside of Europe/the 'West', on behalf of women. Poststructuralist sexual difference feminists, however, have seen equality feminism as replicating humanist universals in the sense of its being predicated upon assumptions of women's 'sameness' with men.

According to its feminist critics, since the First Wave equality feminism had played down women's differences from men in order to demonstrate that they are just as ('equally') capable, rational, worthy, and so on; or would be if they had the same opportunities. This can be seen particularly in the demands of liberal feminists since the eighteenth century, but in some respects in those of socialist feminists of later centuries, too (both reformists and revolutionaries). In various parts of the world, socialist feminists would often insist that male socialists treat them equally, as comrades rather than as (mere) women; and that they were equal threats to the state and socio-political status quo.[25]

As historian Linda Gordon has emphasized, however, neither equality/sameness feminism nor 'difference' feminism is very new:

> If one uses the notion of 'difference' as an organizing principle, one can periodize the entire history of feminism in terms of the domination, in alternation, of an androgynous and a female-uniqueness view of women's subordination and liberation. The eighteenth- and early nineteenth-century Enlightenment feminists, religious *and* secular, tended toward an androgynous vision of the fundamental humanity of men and women; that is, they emphasized the artificial imposition of femininity upon women as part of a system subordinating, constricting, and

controlling them, with the result that 'women', as an historically created category, had their capacities as well as their aspirations reduced. By contrast, the later nineteenth-century feminists tended toward a female moral superiority view. They applauded what was different in women, and while they were not always biologistic in their assumptions about how we became different, the process of differentiation was less interesting to them than the result: a world divided between a male principle of aggression and a female one of nurturance.[26]

Her reading of past feminisms contains some lessons for feminist theorists who treat past feminisms as heterogeneous, implying that 'difference feminism' is a new development.

I should explain that maternalists of the First Wave exemplify the latter view. For them motherhood was indeed 'the fundamental defining experience of womanhood', as Gordon notes, an experience that purportedly led women to be necessarily superior, morally, in their nurturing, peace-loving natures. Yet similar attitudes to women's difference, uniqueness and superiority were also held in the Second Wave, particularly in 'radical feminism' (one of the three main streams of Second Wave feminism, together with liberal and socialist feminism). In its later guises it was/is also termed 'cultural feminism' at times because of its emphasis on a (existentially and morally 'separate') women's culture that could include a vision of separatism from men as an ideal lifestyle, not just political strategy in activist groups or movements. This renders nonsensical the teleological distinction that is commonly made between feminisms of the First and Second wave, on the one hand, and postfeminisms that seemingly invented 'difference', on the other. Moreover, there are further reasons for questioning this 'progress' sort of narrative, connected with the socialist wing of feminism and its traditional class (difference) analyses of women.

The other main stream of postfeminism, postcolonial feminism, owes more to traditional socialist feminism than is usually acknowledged. First, it has rethought male-centred postcolonial discourses (including histories) surrounding the nation, culture, race, power and empire in terms that pay more attention to issues of women, gender and sexualities. In doing so, postcolonial feminists have also distanced themselves from humanist Westcentric metanarratives of 'progress', as put forward not only by liberals or Marxists, but also some earlier feminists. The First and Second Waves (in toto) are often said to have taken the superiority of the West for granted and universalized women – that is, treated them all as the same in line with underlying Western norms, standards and values. A commonly cited example is the Second Wave slogan of 'sisterhood is powerful' usually taken by its critics necessarily to imply the notion of a global 'sisterhood'. Where it did imply that, it rested upon the premise that all women share similar experiences and oppression and thus have or should have the same concerns. Although postcolonial feminist scholarship now does not always focus directly upon women, since gender analysis includes attention to constructs of masculinity, too, postcolonial feminism came into being defined by a central emphasis upon differences between women. This featured a stronger, if not a new emphasis on women's differences. Obviously, for socialist feminists around the world, class differences between women always had been a central focus, since Marxism/socialism had always been centred on class inequalities, and 'class struggle'. Traditionally, socialists have been more inclined than liberals to oppose inequities stemming from imperialism and racism as well. As we shall see below, the traditional socialist emphasis on class has tended to be largely displaced in postfeminism(s) by a focus on other differences, especially 'race'/ethnicity and sexual preference. Hence, in today's feminist histories, too, issues of class tend to be sidelined or ignored. This is a good comment on the way in which the foci, methods and analytical categories of history (and other scholarship) change with the times: each age or period features its own trends or dominant forms of historical knowledge.

Concerning inclusion, then, the sort of feminism that has typically featured demands for the 'mere' inclusion of women has been feminism of equality or 'sameness' or 'androgyny', especially liberal feminism. According to this, women were to be fully included both materially in the existing social system and in the theories or discourses, including academic disciplines such as history, from which they had traditionally been excluded. Conventional theory, 'malestream' and feminist, was the specific target of one well-known critic of equality feminism, the Australian theorist, Elizabeth Grosz, of the psychoanalytic sexual difference school of poststructuralism. In 1986, Grosz discussed in a seminal paper the limits of feminist theory to date:

> [I]t became increasingly clear that it was not possible simply to include women in those theories where they had previously been

excluded, for this exclusion forms a fundamental structuring principle and key presumption of patriarchal discourses . . . . Moreover, even if women were incorporated into patriarchal discourses, at best they could only be regarded as variations of a basic humanity. The project of women's equal inclusion meant that only women's *sameness to men*, only women's *humanity* and not their *womanliness* could be discussed. [author's emphases] Further, while women could not be included as the objects of theoretical speculation, their positions as the subjects or producers of knowledge was not raised. In other words, in adopting the role of the (male) subjects of knowledge, women began to assume the role of surrogate men.[27]

Hence, following the lead of French feminist, Luce Irigaray, Grosz argued that what was required was women's *exclusion* from conventional theories (and discourses, disciplines, institutions of learning) that were intrinsically androcentric.

Not unlike Chakrabarty, by 'exclusion', Grosz did not mean that we accept the traditional means by which women had been excluded from public life, positions of authority, a presence or voice in the pages of history, and so on. Nor did this renewed feminist emphasis on sexual difference mean leaving behind us the feminist critique of hierarchical gender constructs that had served to keep women 'in their place' by emphasizing their 'natural' differences. Though Linda Gordon characterizes earlier difference feminists as less interested in the process of sexual differentiation than its socio-political effects, this could hardly be said of poststructuralists such as Grosz (or, indeed, Joan Scott). Rather, with the advent of the sort of sexual difference feminism headed by the French feminists, the critique of conventional sexual differentiation (or of gender constructs) became more central and, undeniably, more refined. When she advocated women's 'exclusion', Grosz was mainly making the point that inclusion should be on our own terms, for only that way would open up the possibility of women's autonomy, agency and self-determination.

By the mid-1980s when Grosz published that paper and post-feminisms were on the rise, feminist historians had already been challenging for some ten years what is popularly known as the 'add women and stir' approach to women's history. This was also a critique of mere inclusion, which held that it was not enough to add women into the existing androcentric mix, thereby failing to question the patriarchal foundations of the discipline. In effect, this would just reproduce humanism's treatment of women as mere variations on a universal theme ('variations of a basic humanity', as Grosz put it), the basis of which was actually male and thus already gendered. Hence, the virtual silence about women that characterized academic history before the days of Second Wave feminism and the entry of many more women historians into the profession. For, why would it be necessary to incorporate more of a focus upon women into the pages of history if, essentially, they did not differ from the human 'norm'?

Amidst the growing trend in women's history from the 1970s in various countries, at first feminist historians' professional training in humanist assumptions and empiricist methods led them to believe that their works would just 'fit into the field of history as a whole'.[28] As Bonnie Smith explained in *The Gender of History: Men, Women, and Historical Practice*, their (then empiricist) belief was that adding women to the existing field would have the effect merely of rendering the full picture of the past more complete and thus more truthful.[29] Some, however, soon suspected that even 'ingredients such as periodization would change as matters important to women displaced men's events, and that the cast of historical characters and many traditional interpretations would alter too.' If, as Smith argues, the development of modern history's 'scientific' methodology and, indeed, its whole professional practice have been 'closely tied to evolving definitions of masculinity and femininity' – in a number of ways not least the gendering of academic history as masculine and amateur history as feminine[30] – then the advent of a whole field of academic women's history would likely spell more profound changes in the discipline than just a switch of focus to women, their mere inclusion in the pages of history. Mary Spongberg (in her *Writing Women's History since the Renaissance*) has also commented upon how women's history began to move beyond being merely 'compensatory and restorative', seeing as androcentric: 'the evidence used by historians, the nature of historical investigation, periodisation and even the nature of time itself.'[31] Hence, a wider, more fundamental challenge to the discipline was soon being mounted by feminists.

We saw in Chapter 2 how Judith Allen had contested the implicit androcentrism in Elton's positivist method. On another front, Spongberg's reference to time is suggestive of a well-known essay by Julia Kristeva, 'Women's Time'.[32] In this she basically argued that linear time is masculine and cyclical (recurring, repeating, 'cosmic') time feminine, the latter partly for obvious biological reasons: in female subjectivity, 'there are cycles, gestation, the eternal recurrence of a biological rhythm which conforms to that of nature . . .'.[33] Readers should note that this naturalist vision of female subjectivity is not what we would expect of a 'poststructuralist'. Female subjectivity, she later says, intuitively renders problematic: 'a certain conception of time: time as project, teleology, linear and prospective unfolding; time as departure, progression, and arrival – in other words, the time of history.'[34] For Kristeva, in short, conventional historical time was men's time. Another 'poststructuralist' might question this apparent centring of women's subjectivity on biology, wondering if it is really this sort of ('women's') bodily/biologically based 'intuition' that explains why, as Smith observes, feminist historians were soon challenging even conventional periodization or eras or time frames. Perhaps it was more because of history's obvious all-round phallocentrism; and periodization is of course central to history. These feminist historians, in any case, were rethinking the ways in which the past has conventionally been carved up into sections or stages interspersed by events of great significance for change, advancement or 'progress' in the affairs of 'humanity'.

Thus, already in the mid-1970s, the well-known and respected American feminist historian, Joan Kelly-Gadol, had the following to say about conventional male-centred periodization. She noted how a focus upon the issue of women's status in different societies at different times was leading feminist historians to challenge this. What such a focus meant for feminist historians was that they should:

> look at ages past or movements of great social change in terms of their liberation or repression of woman's potential, their import for the advancement of her humanity as well as 'his'. The moment this is done – the moment one assumes that women are part of humanity in the fullest sense – the period or set of events with which we deal takes on a wholly different character or meaning from the normally accepted one. Indeed, what emerges is a fairly regular pattern of relative loss of status for women precisely in those periods of so-called progressive change . . . . if we apply Fourier's famous dictum – that the emancipation of women is an index of the general emancipation of an age – our notions of so-called progressive developments,

such as classical Athenian civilization, the Renaissance, and the French Revolution, undergo a startling re-evaluation.[35]

Conventional eras in Western history can and often have been contested on various grounds, as Reina Lewis pointed out in her *Gendering Orientalism* in 1996. Periodization can vary depending upon the field of enquiry (the example she gives being how the origins of modernism differ depending upon whether the field is art history or literature); or upon whether it is English or French (or other) history that is being written; postcolonial histories, on the other hand, may reject imperialist periodization; whilst 'women's history challenges the masculinist exclusions of his-story'.[36] Carving up the world's past into 'ages' and 'stages' (the classical age, the age of Reason, the feudal or modern age, and so on) makes sense only in terms of master narratives (metahistorical approaches) that are intrinsically eurocentric, androcentric and imperialistic. Of course, Kelly-Gadol's approach had its dangers, too, if it meant merely replacing the androcentrism with a 'Woman'-centred vision, leaving the imperialist side of conventional periodization intact.

But, as for rethinking the past in terms of 'her-story[s]', too, other feminist historians of her time were already going a little further than Kelly-Gadol. She had argued only that the existing periods or ages be rethought in terms of their effect upon and thus meaning for women. Though doing this serves to make the point that traditional notions of progress in history have been founded upon phallocentrism, clearly, a more radical step is to dispense with conventional ages and stages altogether, replacing them with landmarks of change/progress for women (for women, moreover, not just of one class, 'race', etc.). The well-known American cultural historian, Natalie Zemon Davis (the first to introduce a women's history course in Canada in 1971),[37] had already recommended this, in fact, when she suggested in the 1970s that Europe's history might well be carved up in line with significant changes in reproduction and sexual morality and practice.[38] Indeed, if changes in women's lives were prioritized or even treated as equally important as change in men's lives, one of the primary markers of Western 'modernity' might well be the advent of safe, effective contraception! For, without this, postwar women in Western capitalist societies would not have been entering or remaining in the workforce (and public life in general) in the numbers they have been; there would have been no 'sexual revolution', and so on.

Chakrabarty may have been right when he concluded that the mere incorporation of women and minorities into the pages of history did not occasion a 'crisis' in the discipline as a whole. Yet, arguably, the feminist emphasis on women's differences from men (and on that together with class or ethnic or other differences from the 'norm') did begin to shake the foundations of the discipline well before postmodernism gained fame/infamy as the most radical challenge yet to history. Feminist historians quickly went further than women's mere incorporation into a fundamentally male-defined and centred discipline that not only reflected men's interests but also served them. Of course, even without their direct challenges to the intrinsic masculinism of history's foci, themes and purportedly 'scientific' methods, some male traditionalists would still have been voicing their fears that too much historical research about women would endanger history's claim to 'balance' or a lack of 'bias' and end in 'politicizing' (*sic*) the discipline.[39] We might recall that conservatives, Elton, Windshuttle and the like, and Gertrude Himmelfarb, too, have been in the habit of adding feminists to the list of the 'Marxists', literary critics and postmodernists responsible for lowering the tone of, or endangering, or even 'killing' the profession. This is for good reason, since feminist historians (not unlike other politically radical historians) have long been questioning many of the discipline's basic precepts, including its so-called disinterestedness and proscription of presentism, as we saw in Chapter 2. With due respect to Chakrabarty, the question is whether we could have gone on for long merely incorporating women and other marginalized groups into history without confronting the Anglo-European, phallocratic and class biases implicit not only in the topics and subjects normally studied, but also in history's epistemological and methodological foundations.

Radical historians since the 1970s have mounted such challenges in various ways, helping to pave the way for deconstructionist or other postmodernist histories of difference/differentiation. Feminist historian, Joan (Wallach) Scott, was already advocating both a gender rather than women's history and a poststructuralist-difference approach in 1988 when she published *Gender and the Politics of History*. For her a more critical sort of history than hitherto would focus upon the 'processes of exclusion achieved through differentiation', as we have seen (but with reference to later essays).[40] This has long represented for her a central part of a method, inspired theoretically partly by Derrida and Foucault etc. and partly by feminist theory, that would subject to scrutiny the very categories of analysis we take for granted, categories such as 'women, men, equality, difference' *and 'history'*, *too*; and do so, moreover, in terms of their implication in hierarchical power relations. We cannot write women into history, she said in the concluding pages of that work:

> unless we are willing to entertain the notion that history as a unified story was a fiction about a universal subject whose universality was achieved through implicit processes of differentiation, marginalisation, and exclusion. Man was never, in other words, a truly universal figure . . . . One aspect of these processes involved the definition of 'women', the attribution of characteristics, traits, and roles in contrast to 'men'.

Scott then distanced herself from much of women's history to date in typically 'postist' terms. Its authors needed to be reminded, she felt, that the differences they had documented in 'women's experience or women's culture' had not come about due to essential, 'natural' qualities that inhered in the female sex. They had rather arisen as 'the expression of female particularity in contrast to male universality': in other words, as a reaction against the humanist treatment of males as normative. And the risk involved in that, of course, is that 'female particularity' might still be defined in terms of maleness, albeit as its binary opposite. Here she was expressing a poststructuralist suspicion of essentialism with regard to an equally universalized category of 'wo-Man', insisting that women's experience and their subjectivity(s) do not precede language/discourse but are discursively produced and differ in accordance with location, position and time. Doubtless, in part she was reacting against the radical or 'cultural' (sexual difference) feminism of the Second Wave, including its French psychoanalytic variants. Finally, for Scott, too, a postmodernist critique of traditional processes of differentiation and marginalization/exclusion would necessarily call into question the politics of equality, *inclusion and pluralism*, even in feminism. As she pointed out, inequality persists even when physical (e.g. legal) barriers have been removed, thereby contradicting the paradigmatic liberal-humanist (progress) 'story of democratisation as a story of access' – that is, the belief in an automatic, increasingly improved access to power and/or the material benefits of society for ever greater numbers of people.

IV

To reiterate, it is particularly in the writings of postist (postcolonial and poststructuralist) scholars, female and male, that we find a renewed focus upon difference/differentiation amidst a critique of humanist universals. We witness in their works a related scepticism toward liberal-pluralist (or 'multicultural'/assimilationist) strategies of inclusion where they inhere in academic disciplines such as history, too. As the poststructuralist ('linguistic turn') focus is on language: discourse, rhetoric or 'categories of analysis', Grosz, Scott, Chakrabarty and others contest the founding principles of traditional academic disciplines: including concepts such as 'fixed meaning, unified subjectivity and centred theories of power', as Weedon put it in the quote heading this chapter.

However, Scott and Grosz exemplify the fact that different variants of poststructuralist feminism are not always in agreement. Grosz, writing in the mid-1980s and echoing the approach of 'French feminist', Irigaray, wanted to embrace a new radical form of sexual difference, a new 'autonomous femininity' where women could 'write, read and think *as women*', not surrogate men.[41] Although one cannot help but have sympathy for such a position as a critical response to humanism, and though Grosz did insist that this opening up of a 'new discursive space' for *women's* writing, reading and thinking would encourage a 'proliferation of voices', one can also see why some feminists would be wary of its potential for essentialism – involving 'fixed meaning' and a unified and centred identity for a universal category of 'Woman'. With such an approach, there is the danger both of reproducing traditional gender binarisms – arguably, as seen in the French feminist emphasis on things such as women's 'natural' (?) distance from conventional/male rationalism – and, as Linda Gordon warned, of 'homogenizing women' through attempt to define 'Woman', thereby marginalizing any who do not fit the definition of the category.

In her early work, *The Poetics of Women's Autobiography*, Sidonie Smith raised a question that is thought-provoking, perhaps especially for literary historians or historians of women's self-representational writing. It concerned how we are to interpret the common narrative differences in self-writing by women and men. Her question concerned the usefulness of a 'psychobiographic' approach (influenced by the French feminists) to 'a women's/feminine writing'. She called into question in 'nature/nurture' or nature/culture terms the fact that in women's autobiographical writing it had so often been the case that the Self was constructed in relational rather than masculinist individualistic ways. Traditional literary/autobiography criticism had failed to take account, she said, of the ways in which women have tended to re/present their selves narratively through relationships – for example, with a significant 'Other' such as 'husband, child, God' – rather than through separateness, distinctiveness or individuality.[42] For Smith the question was whether this has been the product of 'psychobiography', on the one hand, or social/gendered expectations, on the other: 'Is female preoccupation with the Other an *essential* dynamic of female psychobiography or a *culturally conditioned* manifestation of the ideology of gender that associates female difference with attentiveness to the other?' she asked (my emphases). Certainly, individualism was a central part of the humanist (male, middle- to upper-class) European norm or ideal, and there is little doubt that ideologies of gender have constructed and reinforced individuality as a male possession in many ways.

However, strictly speaking, the question Smith was putting *need* not be about the 'nature versus nurture' issue. That is, notwithstanding Kristeva's reading of women's intuitively different understanding of time, arguably, the psychoanalytical approach to women's sexual difference does not usually present a naturalized, biologist picture of 'Woman'. Generally speaking, in Lacanian and feminist psychoanalytic (and poststructuralist) thinking, psychosexual development comes with a child's entry into language. Through it s/he learns to differentiate purportedly masculine and feminine behavioural attributes that, in a phallocratic world, are discursively derived from the presence or 'lack' of one particular bodily marker: the 'phallus'. Hence, we could say that both of the alternatives Smith sets up are about 'gender' as a social (or sociolinguistic) category and method of differentiation and hierarchization. It is not the case, then, that a 'psychobiographical' approach in our historical analyses of women's writing or gender differences in writing need be biologist: it need not involve a direct-line sort of determination from physical body to 'womanly' behaviour, thinking or writing. Nevertheless, Judith Butler has become an influential poststructuralist critic of this style of feminism on the grounds of its apparent biological essentialism, and her queer feminist stance will be discussed in Chapter 4, which concerns identity/subjectivity.[43]

As I have noted, Chris Weedon is another who is ambivalent about psychoanalytic feminism because she believes that it universalizes women by reducing them to 'a version of their sexuality'.[44] Weedon spells out the difficulty that many poststructuralists may have with a 'fixed Freudian [-Lacanian] model of psychosexual development'. We are supposed to read all sorts of problems concerning women in terms of this fixed (universalist, ahistorical) model, she says – re women's subjectivity/identity, their access to language, the constitution of their desire/pleasure, the marginality or centrality of discourses concerning them, or the power or interests these serve or oppose.[45] The unconscious, she suggests, encompasses a lot more than 'psycho-sexual organization' or the 'organization of sexual difference'. To quote her more fully:

> In Lacanian-based psychoanalytic criticism historically produced language constructs rather than reflects meaning but it constructs meaning according to particular pre-given structures of meaning, defined in relation to the primary signifier of sexual difference, the phallus, and the unconscious structures which found the patriarchal order. In feminist poststructuralism, however, there can be no ultimate fixing of femininity, masculinity or unconscious structures. They are always historically produced through a range of discursive practices much wider than those of the immediate nuclear family and both the symbolic order [of language] and the unconscious are marked by difference, contradiction and pressures for conservation or for change.

In short, the problem with this sort of psychoanalytic approach is not that it sees language/the symbolic as merely reflecting a pre-given, natural difference between two sexes; it does create it. This binaristic construct of sexual difference is a part of language, as Weedon says, and to that extent its approach is poststructuralist. What does not seem very consistent with poststructuralism, however, is reducing gender constructs and the patriarchal order to one particular underlying 'pre-given structure' of meaning production in a way reminiscent of other universalistic metanarratives, even if the Freudian/Lacanian model is sometimes said to be specific to Western capitalist patriarchy.

A practical example might be useful at this point, to demonstrate the usefulness (or lack of it) of psychoanalytic theory to readings of gender difference in our histories. Although I am loathe to single out for criticism a work that is notable also for its erudition, this 'metanarrative' style of analysis is exemplified in an essay I often set for student reading. I do so first to demonstrate to students of world women's and gender history the diversity of styles of gender and sexualities analysis in history today. Second, however, I use it also to raise the question of how plausible its psychoanalytic analysis of one individual 'witch' is as an explanation of either her own motives for confessing (or state of mind) or the European witch-craze phenomenon. The author, Lyndal Roper, denies that she set out 'to apply psychoanalysis to . . . derive conclusions about an entire society' or, implicitly, about a trans-cultural phenomenon; her intention was merely 'to draw on psychoanalytic ideas in order to reconstruct the mental life of an individual'.[46] Yet, immediately before this she argues that 'a *phenomenon* [my emphasis] such as witchcraft . . . in which the individual agency of both the witch and her victims is of the essence . . . demands explanation not only in sociological but in psychological terms.' Presumably, what she means is that to understand the cases particularly of those individuals who confessed to some rather fantastic crimes such as copulating with 'the Devil', we need to utilize a 'sociological' or contextual social-historical analysis historicizing the phenomenon, together with a case-by-case, individual psychoanalytic method. However, the thrust of Roper's analysis of Regina Bartholome's case in Germany in 1670 implies that similar cases could also be rendered explicable by the same sort of psycho-sexual, 'Oedipal' explanation of conscious and unconscious motives and action.

At one point Roper argues that there is 'no mileage in teasing out the "real" from the fantastic' in Regina's confession in standard historiographical fashion, for it is impossible to know where the dividing line between reality and fantasy was.[47] Roper's concern is rather with 'the psychic logic of her tale', a tale that wove together diabolic and sexual themes – concerning her sexual desires, affairs and related actions, and not only with Satan. She herself had first introduced him into the story, by the way, effectively turning it into one of 'witchcraft'. (She had first been imprisoned for lesser crimes such as reacting to unrequited love by threatening to kill the new bride of the object of her affections.) Personally, what I find rather fantastic is the author's suggestion that in all Regina's love-affairs (or was it, rather, just in her account of them whilst in prison?) she was acting out a psycho-sexual ('Oedipal') 'father'-fixation. Roper herself suggests the centrality of a different sort of fixation upon father figures that is explicable in terms of both systemic socio-political structures of patriarchal-paternalistic authority and the immediate context of Regina's imprisonment and interrogation. Regina apparently expressed insubordination and even 'rage' toward a whole range of father figures, including God and the Devil, her judges and own biological father; which one could read as a simple lashing out at all those seen to be in control of her life and immediate situation, rather than as 'multiple symbolic incest'.

Often, Roper overlooks possible pragmatic explanations for Regina's behaviour in her determination to explain, psychoanalytically, even the 'collaborative' fantasy of witchcraft between the accused and her interrogators. For instance, even if the torture was mild in this case, perhaps it was the fear of further torture and more pain that led her to admit to what her accusers expected or wanted to hear. Or perhaps, once she was on 'stage', her performance became more theatrical in tandem with the avidness of her audience's attention to any mention of devilish influences or interventions – especially when in connection with sex. The latter is unsurprising given the common discursive connection of the day between femininity, sex and Satan exemplified, for example, in belief in the occurrence of demonic witches' orgies or 'sabbaths'. (In that religio-cultural, temporal context, 'Wives of Satan' of course represented the logical 'flip-side' of 'Brides of Christ'.) And perhaps in her youthful naivety, Regina's admitting to having been 'seduced by' the Devil was a defence of her sexual and other misconduct, an abdication of personal responsibility for her crimes. If so, it was a dangerous strategy, one that led to her execution as a 'witch'.

We seem to be caught between two modern means of making 'sense' of early modern, European Christian mindsets and behaviour: the common-sense rationalist and Freudian-Lacanian psychoanalytic. Our recourse to modern means of comprehension of one sort or another may not be avoidable, but I am more inclined to heed Weedon's warning concerning how neither femininity, masculinity nor unconscious structures can be universalized, fixed and reduced to central, underlying psycho-sexual factors (or any one factor) in such a way. I would rather leave the 'story' and its meaning(s) a little more open. Although, not unlike Scott, Roper does acknowledge that meaning is historically and culturally produced and subject to change, so that our separation of the 'real' from the fantastic would make little sense to Regina or her accusers, what we do not receive from her analysis is the impression that Regina's state of mind, motives and actions or, indeed, her 'unconscious' could have been subject to multiple pressures, and discursive and other more immediate contextual influences.

As to the utility of Roper's approach for *feminist* history, that is, a feminist political project, clearly, she wanted to depart from a tendency in early Second Wave feminism to depict woman as victim. She wanted to negotiate (sexual) difference differently; to offer an explanation that would take more account of women's, thus Regina's own agency. Hence, her central question was why did Regina implicate herself in such a serious crime. We should not, indeed, always and only be painting women as the victims of capitalism, imperialism, misogynistic religions, patriarchy, father figures, men, or whatever. But nor, however, should we be losing sight of the ways in which women are often in situations that render them simultaneously *both* victims *and* agents, rather than *either* one *or* the other. Even if Regina made her own choices, choices that landed her in even more trouble, even if she found ways to resist authority, was she (and others like her) not victimized? Obviously, an overemphasis on women's agency can be self-defeating for a feminist project, especially when in connection with such an appallingly misogynistic and violent historical phenomenon, in which women's status as the primary victims in the vast majority of areas affected cannot be denied. (The figures usually cited vary between 70 and 85 per cent, but I do not recall having seen anyone make the point that often female and male family members of accused female witches also fell foul of the witch-hunts.)

Perhaps Roper could have done more to illustrate the likely complexity both of Regina's motives and actions and the power dynamics of her situation. Ideally, this should be done in terms that take more account of the wider socio-political effects of a phallocratic discourse that gendered woman, the feminine and the feminine body as essentially sexualized and, partly for that reason, particularly prone to evil. (This was part and parcel of the gendered binarisms central to monotheisms, the positive side of which rendered godliness/heaven/spirituality/mind/purity, etc. as intrinsically or essentially male.) These terms surely should have included the way in which women can often themselves internalize misogynistic constructs. In my view, negotiating (gender) difference in general and in connection with specific past phenomena such as the witch-craze requires more than 'reducing women to a version of their sexuality', as Weedon put it. Arguably, to do so is to replicate the very style of thinking that contributed to the witch-hunts in the first place and, further, to introduce yet another 'universal' under-pinned by yet another reductionist conceptual 'norm'.

V

> Taking difference seriously necessitates the adoption of a politics of *partiality* [author's emphases] rather than a *politics* of inclusion. A politics of partiality implies that feminism must emphasise and consciously construct the limits of its own field of political intervention. While a politics of inclusion is driven by an ambition for universal representation (of all women's interests), a politics of partiality does away with that ambition and accepts the principle that feminism can never be an encompassing political home for all women . . .
>
> (Ien Ang, 'I'm a feminist but . . . .')[48]

Turning to feminist (or women's, not necessarily 'feminist') post-colonial scholarship, it should first be remembered that feminism, too, not only liberalism and Marxism, has been critiqued for fall-ing prey to humanist universalism and the politics of inclusion. First and Second Wave feminists have been among those targeted by postcolonial scholars, not so much for glaring, explicit or conscious racism but for their unthinking treatment of whiteness as a universal norm. For example, Australian Indigenous scholar, Aileen Moreton-Robinson, has pointed out that taking heed of differences among women should involve treating whiteness, not just blackness, as a category for analysis with respect to how, typically, only non-'white' women are racialized. In her *Talkin' Up to the White Woman: Aboriginal Women and Feminism*, of 2000, Moreton-Robinson discusses the pervasiveness of whiteness as an 'invisible norm' in white feminist writing, indicating that whiteness, too, should be interrogated:

> Recent feminist literature about Indigenous women and feminism disrupts and historicizes the universal category white woman, but it does so from the subject position middle-class white woman. Indigenous women's subjectivity and experiences are often missing or subsumed within the literature, which tends to speak *for* Indigenous women. The specifics of Indigenous women's accounts of white race privilege and domination, which can offer insights into incommensurabilities and limits to knowing [the] 'Other', are invisible. As important as this litera-ture is to feminist theorizing and pedagogy it is limited because

it does not make problematic how the social construction of the subject position white woman is represented . . . . Whiteness is so pervasive as an invisible norm that race, as difference, still belongs only to women who are not white in Australian feminism.[49]

Thus, negotiating difference in history, too, should rightly involve a treatment of whiteness as a category of analysis or critique. This means that race, race privilege and racism should be a topic for discussion in histories of white women, just as the history of a white woman/women of the upper classes could hardly be conducted without reference to class privilege and difference. Implicitly, moreover, one of Moreton-Robinson's points is that, just as attention to the historical rather than eternal nature of constructs of sex/ gender and sexuality will serve to illustrate that such things are still subject to change, taking heed of the relatively recent nature of white domination and the attendant racialization of peoples will help to undermine racism today.

Moreton-Robinson follows the above passage by commenting upon how Australian feminism since the 1990s has replaced a politics of 'unity in diversity' with a 'politics of difference'.[50] The latter, she notes, has been influenced by 'challenges from Indigenous women, women of colour, immigrant women and lesbian women', and informed also by 'postmodern, deconstruction and poststructural theories'. Since that time other scholars have indeed spoken out on behalf of 'non-white, non-Western women in "white/Western" societies',[51] mounting a similar sort of challenge to a liberal feminist politics of 'unity in diversity' or 'politics of inclusion'. Ien Ang, for example, has argued in an essay entitled "'I'm a feminist but . . ."' – "Other" women and postnational feminism' that mainstream Australian Second Wave feminism may have left assimilationism behind, but it still acted 'like a nation' in wanting to embrace 'multiculturalism'. Since any politics of inclusion is always founded upon ideas of 'commonality and community', feminism must cease seeing itself and acting as a 'nation', she warned, in order that difference not be absorbed within a 'pre-given and predefined space'.[52] Far better to leave space for the sort of ambivalence that would see not just 'Other' women hesitant about identifying themselves as feminists, but some 'white/Western' women, too, in recognition of the way a/the feminist identity has often been totalized, homogenized or stereotyped. The ongoing media hype that surrounds 'feminists' who necessarily think this, do that, or are responsible for something else doubtless contributes to the unwillingness of many (for example, young women) to define themselves as such. The word 'Feminist' is therefore a very good example of how identity categories are subject to ongoing contestation.

In a widely known work of postcolonial feminist scholarship, *Third World Women and the Politics of Feminism*, Chandra Talpade Mohanty, mounted a similar critique of Western feminism. She was more careful than some not to speak as if 'Western feminism' were a singular, unified entity.[53] However, noting in her introduction that feminist scholars have often spoken of an entire undifferentiated category of 'third world women' in terms of 'underdevelopment, oppressive traditions, high illiteracy, rural and urban poverty, religious fanaticism, and "over-population"', she observes that corresponding terms of analysis have been used to study US-based black, Asian and Chicana women as well.[54] Not unlike Ien Ang and Moreton-Robinson, she therefore calls for more recognition of the heterogeneity of 'third world' women and third world 'feminisms'. She notes that many women engaged in such struggles prefer not to identify as 'feminist' because of the Western norms, values and demands associated with the term. Another author, Yvonne Corcoran-Nantes, in an essay on women's activism among the urban poor in Brazil, concludes that often in developing countries 'gender issues take a secondary role or may not be considered at all'; whilst her study of these women in Brazil found that 'female' consciousness had developed around 'strategic gender interests', for her 'whether they choose to describe these as feminist or not is irrelevant'.[55]

Just as 'Western women' or 'white women' (or, indeed, 'white Western feminists') do not automatically constitute a unitary group with any one coherent set of interests, so, too, do 'third world women' define their own interests in terms of their widely varying experience or discursive/political positions. As Mohanty notes, the latter form alliances and are also divided on the basis of 'class, religion, sexuality, and history'. Echoing the common postcolonial (-postmodernist) critique of humanist universals and norms, she recommends that Western feminists cease 'defining third world women in terms of their "problems" or their "achievements" in relation to an imagined free white liberal democracy' – that is, unless they want to continue removing third world women 'from history, freezing them in time and space'.[56] Other than respecting difference, Mohanty asks how we are to redress the silences in the historical record with regard to how third world women have engaged with feminism, whilst still framing our questions in line with feminist historiography.

What she proposes is a model of an 'imagined community' of oppositional struggles by third world women – not a 'real' community but an 'imagined' one because it points to *potential* political 'alliances and collaborations across diverse boundaries'. Speaking of the utility of such an approach for feminist histories of third world women and feminism, she says:

> The idea of an imagined community is useful because it leads us away from essentialist notions of third world feminist struggles, suggesting political rather than biological or cultural bases for alliance. Thus, it is not color or sex which constructs the ground for these struggles. Rather, it is the *way* we think about race, class, and gender – the political links we choose to make among and between struggles. Thus, potentially, women of all colors (including white women) can align themselves with and participate in these imagined communities. However, clearly our relation to and centrality in particular struggles depend upon our different, often conflictual, locations and histories. This, then, is what provisionally holds the essays in this text on 'third world women and the politics of feminism' together: imagined communities of women with divergent histories and social locations, woven together by the *political* threads of opposition to forms of domination that are not only pervasive but also systemic.[57]

If, then, we were to take a leaf out of this particular book, we would write a history of third world women and 'feminism' taking as our starting point – for example, our very selection of historical subjects for study – *similar thinking* about race, class and gender and thus similar political struggles against global imperialist capitalist patriarchy. Rather than beginning with a pre-given category of the 'Third World' defined by all that 'we', in our 'imagined free white [affluent, classless, progressive, etc.] liberal democracy[s]', are not, our history of third world feminism would naturally include the study of subjects engaged in struggles against *the 'third world' within: our own 'third world'*. This would represent a rather different feminist politics of 'inclusion', if we can term it that at all.

Ien Ang would suggest not. The same is true of Mohanty who argues that ideological differences 'mediate any assumption of a "natural" bond between women', there being 'no logical and necessary connection between being "female" and becoming "feminist"'.[58] To return to the quote that heads this section where Ien Ang urges Western feminists to dispense with their universal sisterhood assumptions, feminism can never be even a potential 'encompassing political home for all women',

> not just because different groups of women have different and sometimes conflicting interests, but, more radically, because for many groups of 'other' women other interests, other identifications are sometimes more important and politically pressing than, or even incompatible with, those related to their being women.[59]

Aileen Moreton-Robinson would probably have no objection to this, since Indigenous women scholars and activists in Australia have long been emphasizing this very point in disagreement with well-meaning white feminists (for example, in Women's Liberation from the 1970s) who sought to include them in their ranks.[60]

Moreton-Robinson made a further point in the passage I quoted on pp. 129–30, concerning 'speaking for' the 'Other' woman. Even if recent literature on Australian Indigenous women and feminism 'disrupts and historicizes the universal category white woman', she observed, it does so from the subject position of middle-class white woman. This is because white feminist academics are, in effect, speaking for Indigenous women without paying sufficient attention to the latter's 'own accounts of white race privilege and domination'. The limits to knowing the 'Other' are therefore left invisible, she said. What she was perhaps implying was not only that Indigenous women's representations of their experience and subjectivity are often being overlooked, but also that white academic feminists could be more self-reflexive when/if they choose to try to 'represent', 'know' or speak of the 'Other' woman. This is an issue often raised in other cultural contexts, too, for example in South Africa. Here Shireen Hassim and Cherryl Walker, among others, have addressed this 'representation debate'.

In the synopsis with which they began an essay on the relation of Women's Studies to the women's movement in South Africa, Hassim and Walker noted that women's studies there had been criticized by black academics and activists in the following terms:

(a) the underrepresentation of black women academics, (b) allegations about white academics' misappropriation and mis-representation of black women's experience, and (c) questions about the accountability of academics to their subjects of study and/or the broader women's movement.[61]

The authors who, as they themselves put it, are 'located on different sides of the black/white divide' also suggested that the debate about representation in South African women's studies – re 'Who can speak for whom?' – is more complex than usually acknowledged. For example, although white academics must take seriously charges of racism or ethnocentrism and reflect upon the ethics of their scholarly practice, so, too, must 'black academics and activists . . . confront the divisions of class and culture among black women'.

Hassim and Walker expressed reservations about the way in which the category of 'race' was being used by some black feminists, predicated upon a reductionist black/white divide. In the case of South Africa, they pointed out that:

> Clearly black women are not a homogeneous social group, with a single set of interests and an undifferentiated experience in common. There are some very important cleavages of class, language, ethnicity and geographical location (urban/rural) that cannot be brushed aside. The assumption that there is an all-embracing sisterhood among black women, based on a common experience of oppression under apartheid, is no less fallacious than the by now totally discredited notion that sisterhood is global.[62]

They also asked what counts as 'black', since those claiming a 'sisterly' connection with other 'black' women have conflated black as defined under apartheid (non-whites, including Indians and so-called 'coloureds') with black as a 'pseudo-ethnic' category (meaning real 'Africans', excluding Indians and 'coloureds'). As for black academics specifically, Shireen and Walker challenged the common assumption that they can 'automatically and unproblematically be sensitive to and understand all the struggles of all black women'. Such an assumption may well lead other women to charge them with an 'inclusiveness' that is insensitive to class and other differences. Shireen and Walker therefore conclude that black South

African intellectuals (academics and activists) need to exhibit the same degree of 'self-reflection' they rightly demand of white academics and activists.

In answer to the question that we practitioners of history might pose of how a white academic could write a suitably reflective, say, oral history of black women, Shireen and Walker offer some pertinent suggestions. They demonstrate that the difficulties connected with the issue of who can speak for whom are considerable, but also suggest that they are not insurmountable. First, given the common charge of white scholars' appropriating the experience of the Other, this historian should look carefully at her own intentions to write such a work to see if she is guilty of pursuing her own interests (publications and promotion, for example) by ' "speaking for" those who could and should speak for themselves'.[63] Shireen and Walker also insist, however, that this does not mean that 'only the oppressed can speak about their lives', as we will see below; and it does not mean that an outsider view cannot be perceptive and worthwhile. Second, should this historian go ahead with the research project, further self-reflexivity is required concerning issues such as the need for the scholar to reflect upon her own position in the 'politics of location' – discussing, for example, the ethics of and limits to her attempts to represent the 'Other', and the relations of power inhering in her own position as the subject of knowledge and that of her informants as the objects of knowledge. The ethics of accountability to one's informants, in other words, needs to be considered.

Though the idea of accountability to one's informants is far from new in feminist studies, a further suggestion offered by Shireen and Walker is more in line with postmodernist thinking. This is that scholars be more wary of taking experience as 'the only source of understanding'. Their suspicion of the category of 'experience' is not framed in quite the same terms as Joan Scott's – for she, as we will see in Chapter 4 in connection with the critique of humanist-empiricist constructs of identity, was tempted to abandon it altogether given 'its usage to essentialize identity and reify the subject'.[64] Yet, Hassim and Walker share with Scott a concern with how the category of experience serves as a way, not just of 'establishing difference and similarity' but of 'claiming knowledge that is "unassailable"', as Scott put it. Specifically, they call upon academics to:

challenge the dangerous claim that only the oppressed can speak about their lives or, alternatively, that only researchers with a shared racial identity can do so. Fundamentally, this is a claim that there is only one 'true', authentic understanding of social reality/history and that is *the* view from below.[65]

Like Scott, their concern, too, is with 'the absolute privileging of experience as the sole arbiter of knowledge' that they see being advanced by some South African intellectuals.

In Scott's case, however, the intellectuals being targeted for taking as given the 'authority of experience' were historians (American and other), feminist historians among them. She notes that, paradoxically, even some who have developed 'sharp critiques of empiricism' still want to defend 'some reified, transcendent category of explanation' such as 'experience', which is one of history's foundational empiricist categories.[66] Asking what a history without such foundations would look like, a history in which we could write about identity without essentializing it, she follows Spivak in suggesting that we 'make visible the assignment of subject positions', not to capture 'the reality of the objects seen' but rather:

> to understand the operations of the complex and changing discursive processes by which identities are ascribed, resisted, or embraced . . . . To do this a change of object seems to be required, one which takes the emergence of concepts and identities as historical events in need of explanation.[67]

For Scott (once again), experience must not be taken as given, natural or 'true' by the historian, but rather 'historicized'.

In sum, then, whether the history that is being written happens to be about 'third world women' (or men, too), Indigenous women in Australia, black women in South Africa, or black, Asian and Chicana women in the United States, authors need:

1 to be wary of well-meaning attempts at inclusion;
2 to respect difference whilst also recognizing the internal heterogeneity of such groups;
3 to be self-reflexive about our own positioning as scholars (and other things such as race privilege, if it applies) in relation to our subjects/informants;
4 to recognize the limits to knowledge about the Other and thus leave our 'stories' about her/him open; and

5   to pay attention to how the categories of experience and identity are not natural, but discursively formed and subject to change.

A further and final point often alluded to by postcolonial scholars concerns what is usually termed 'intersections': the need for us first to remain cognizant of how people are positioned in multiple ways, in terms of race/ethnicity, gender, class, age, geographic location and so on (terms that shift in relation to each other depending upon time and context). Whether it is individuals or groups themselves doing the positioning with respect to identity, or whether they are being racialized (having a race such as black or white, or perhaps 'Middle Eastern', assigned to them) or gendered or represented in other differential hierarchical terms, the important point so often emphasized in 'postist' scholarship is that such terms cut across and condition each other. Constructs of masculinity differ depending upon (constructs of) race and/or class; constructs of racial identity differ depending upon (constructs of) sex/gender. Thus, racism is frequently gendered and sexualized, sexism racialized, and sexism and racism conditioned by class and other factors as well, the result being a complex web of intersecting identifications and oppressions for those subject to multiple positionings. Conventional gender constructs of 'woman' might, for example, be similar in some respects whether applied to 'white', Asian or African-American women, but they will differ in some respects, too, when racism enters the 'equation'.

A postcolonial feminist work I referred to briefly above, *Gendering Orientalism: Race, Femininity and Representation* by British scholar, Reina Lewis, may be taken as exemplifying this concern with intersections. The author situates herself in 'a critical movement that has undercut the potentially unified, and paradigmatically male, colonial subject outlined in Said's *Orientalism*'. Her approach differs from others in that movement, however, because she analyzes Orientalist images *by* nineteenth-century European women (the English writer George Eliot, and French painter Henriette Browne) rather than Orientalist representations of the 'Other' woman.[68] She decided upon this approach, she says, because analyzing women's production of such images and their reception better facilitates an understanding of 'the interdependence of ideologies of race and gender in the colonial discourse of the period'. Her argument was that women's differential or unequal access to the positionalities of imperialist discourse 'produced a gaze on the Orient and the Orientalized "other" that registered difference less pejoratively and less absolutely' than Said suggested was the case with 'the' sovereign imperial/Orientalist subject. Lewis set out to show how:

> the positionings within Orientalism open to women cultural producers were always contingent on the other shifting relational terms that structured the presumed superiority of the Western Orientalist . . . women's work was read through a grid of differences that, although it often foregrounded gender, was equally reliant on domestic differentiations of class, religion and nation.[69]

We might reasonably expect individuals who were positioned as superior in colonialist East/West binaries yet rendered inferior in the gendered differentials of European society to have an 'alternative take on difference' (at least some of the time), as Lewis says. And taking such an approach to the complexity of women's positionings, it might be pointed out, does still distance us from the romantic imagination of early Second Wave politics and scholarship where women most often had to be victimized, not victimizer. Women could/can, indeed, be 'Orientalists' or imperialists, even if not so resolutely (so 'pejoratively' or 'absolutely') at times due to being subject themselves to negative terms in hierarchies of difference.

VI

> [A]mong all the temptations I will have to resist today, there would be the temptation of memory: to recount what was for me, and for those of my generation who shared it during a whole lifetime, the experience of Marxism, the quasi-paternal figure of Marx . . . the Marxist inheritance was – and still remains, and so it will remain – absolutely and thoroughly determinate. One need not be a Marxist or a communist in order to accept this obvious fact. We all live in a world . . . that still bears, at an incalculable depth, the mark of this inheritance, whether in a directly visible fashion or not.
>
> (Derrida, *Specters of Marx*)[70]

There are a number of dangers or pitfalls associated with 'difference' approaches, one of which I have already commented upon. Apart from issues such as how an emphasis on sexual difference may lead one to essentialize women (and men), or homogenize all women, there are also risks associated with overemphasizing cultural difference. In our desire to avoid in our histories a humanist-style universalization of people on the basis of standards that are Anglo-European, we may fall prey to an exaggeration of difference, exoticizing other cultures and losing sight of transnational similarities in the lived experience of people. It pays us to remember a point I made earlier that, invariably, new intellectual trends are strongly reactive and lend themselves to exaggeration. We do not have to adhere to metanarratives of global historical development to recognize that capitalism, for example, affects many peoples around the world similarly in their working lives; or that some repressive gender norms have long crossed geographical or cultural boundaries. Negotiating difference in our histories (where we are 'white, western and middle class') should not mean overlooking the differentials of power and privilege between women, but nor should it mean representing the 'Other' woman as different in being necessarily more unfortunate or backward than ourselves.[71] Our focus upon difference should not be to the exclusion of a recognition of similarities, for example with respect to the repressive effects that can accompany anyone's being categorized as a 'woman'. That being said, we also cannot lose sight of the fact that often women's similarities have been emphasized by white women seeking 'to muster support for a particular (white feminist-defined) cause'; or ignored in an effort 'to prove that other women are more oppressed'.[72]

In connection with cultural difference, some authors have focussed productively on how non-Western representations of the Self can reproduce Western stereotypes of the (inferior) Other. They suggest that, rather than simply taking as given and repeating these Orientalist stereotypes, perhaps in an effort to respect difference (or the differences that others lay claim to), scholars of the so-called East or West would do better to deconstruct their 'complicit exoticism' and replication of the binaristic-essentialist logic of Orientalism. This, moreover, should involve asking what political purposes this 'self-Orientalism' serves. In an essay on 'Complicit Exoticism: Japan and its Other', Iwabuchi Koichi discusses the tendency especially in Japan's postwar discourse of 'Nihonjinron' (a discourse surrounding 'the Japanese': the 'uniqueness' of Japanese identity) to appropriate Western perceptions of 'Eastern'/Japanese difference, albeit whilst inverting the original hierarchies of value.[73] In this discourse 'Japan' has often been treated as superior in its purported homogeneity, group-orientation, and intuitive logic and methods of interpersonal communication (that no outsider can possibly understand), as opposed to the divisive heterogeneity (read: class divisions not apparent in this 'harmonious' homogeneous society), selfish individualism, materialism and rationalism of its Other, 'the [undifferentiated] West'. Iwabuchi acknowledges that this sort of self-Orientalism was not new in postwar Japan. However, by the 1980s the discourse was 'no longer the monopoly of intellectuals' but becoming part of popular culture; indeed, selling best to the Japanese themselves. With this fervid popular consumption of 'the gaze of Others appreciating Japanese otherness or exoticism', Japan was becoming 'pleasurably "exotic" to the Japanese themselves'.[74]

As for the political interests served by this 'complicit exoticism' or 'self-Orientalism', Iwabuchi discusses how it was also a strategy used earlier by the pre-war and wartime Japanese state and its apologists 'to counter "undesirable" consequences of modernisation'. The popularity then of individualism or trade unionism, to defend people's rights, was countered by recourse to inventions of 'Japan's' tradition; or to traditional values such as a paternalistic ('harmonious') familism that was extended to companies and to the nation (in the family-state ideology of the 'emperor system'). This was in order to 'repress people's demands for "democracy" or human rights, by attributing social conflict and dissent to western "disease"' (as if Japan had not had ample traditions of its own conflict and dissent).[75] As Iwabuchi indicates, the 'Japanese' traditional values now being inculcated in all classes derived from a mere six per cent of the premodern population, the ruling bushi or samurai class, whose authoritarian Confucian values included demands for loyalty to superiors and respect for hierarchical order – in short, paternalistic and repressive attitudes toward women and the lower classes (and even lower samurai). This 'samuraized' construct of Japaneseness came into being amidst the creation of a modern nation and inculcation of a national consciousness in the populace. It was an earlier example of 'the suppression of heterogeneous voices within Japan' mentioned by Iwabuchi in connection with the postwar self-Orientalist exclusion of minority groups (Ainu, Koreans and Burakumin/Untouchables), women and the working class in the interests of social 'homogeneity' and 'harmony'. Self-Orientalism, he observes, is 'a strategy of inclusion through exclusion, and of exclusion through inclusion', a strategy that comes of asserting the difference of 'we Japanese' from 'them, the westerners'. [76]

The resultant homogenization of 'the' Japanese is partly what leads Iwabuchi to dismiss self-Orientalism as a 'serious challenge to western Orientalism' and to regard the two as marked, rather, by 'a profound complicity'. For, the one responds to the other, and both resort to the same sort of logic. Utilizing a perspective focussed upon the complicit essentialism and homogenization in both enables us, he says:

> to open up 'a dimension of power/knowledge alliance *within* the nation and *between* nations'; [revealing] how the discursive construction of dehumanised Others has been subtly utilised by the power bloc to instill nationalistic sentiment into people's minds; how the heterogeneous voices of people within the nations have been repressed through the homogenising discourses of an imaginary 'us' verses 'them'. [77]

If we want to 'demystify "Japaneseness"' or, more generally, to 'transcend *eurocentric* Universalism of "the West" and *ethnocentric* Particularism of "the non-West"', Iwabuchi recommends that we eschew their 'collusive, binary opposition of self/other'. This means that we must deconstruct the ways in which Western Orientalist discourse and nationalistic self-Orientalisms 'strengthen and require each other', representing 'opposite sides of the same coin'. Further, if we seek to distance ourselves from essentialist and nationalist fictions concerning our own cultural traditions and identity:

> we have simultaneously to debunk reciprocal imaginings of other communities as monolithic entities, and recognise the fragmented, multiple and mobile nature of all identities. We have to ask 'what process rather than essences are involved in present experiences of cultural identity'.[78]

In that last sentence Iwabuchi was citing James Clifford's *The Predicament of Culture* (Harvard University Press, 1988), but his call to circumvent the essentialism inherent in holistic representations of cultural identity is reminiscent of the recommendation by Scott and others that our focus be on 'processes of differentiation' and the part they play in relations of power. The example of inverted or self-Orientalism discussed by Iwabuchi illustrates the problem-fraught, reductionist nature of a focus upon 'real', 'essential' cultural differences.

Edward Said believed that an important critical task of the intellectual is the 'effort to break down the stereotypes and reductive categories that are so limiting to human thought and communication'; to 'confront orthodoxy and dogma' rather than reproducing them.[79] This was in the BBC's 1993 Reith series of lectures, where Said also insisted that this task not be undertaken out of a misguided sense of 'disinterested objectivity or transcendental theory', but in a manner that is 'skeptical, engaged' and, moreover, devoted both to 'rational investigation and moral judgement' in the interests of some standpoint. Himself a Palestinian (which everyone knew was 'synonymous with violence, fanaticism, the killing of Jews'), Said therefore embarked upon his critique of essentialist fictions such as 'East' and 'West' and 'racialized essences like subject races, Orientals, Aryans, Negroes and the like'. [80]

A second problem with difference approaches is a rather selective critical focus only upon some sorts of difference or heterogeneity combined with a blindness to others. In Chapter 1 I suggested that we should be wary of a reflexive paradox pinpointed by Rita Felski, which concerned the tendency in postmodernism for scholars to critique aspects of modernism (or empiricist history's modernist foundations) whilst, simultaneously, adhering themselves to linear narratives of progress with respect to postmodernism's transcendence of modernity.[81] The example she gave was of a common homogenization of feminism's past whereby, despite the focus upon other sorts of 'difference', this is not extended to the recognition of heterogeneity in past thinking and movements. Difference comes into play temporally, she implied, only when these are represented as intellectually benighted compared with the 'enlightened' thinking of today.

A sceptical view of this tendency would recognize that there are various reasons for this. For example, scholarly careers are built upon claims to originality – even if the ideal of pure originary genius is actually a tenet of humanist individualism, as opposed to the greater acceptance of 'intertextuality' among postmodernists. Nevertheless, originality is still what scholars usually lay claim to when, in publications, CVs and the like, they stake out a claim for the newness and thus superiority of their analyses or approaches. All too often, in order to be convincing, moreover, such claims will involve the

(convenient) sort of homogenization, overgeneralization and reduc-
tionism pinpointed by Felski. How often in the popular postist styles
of today's feminism do we see past feminisms being reduced to the
one catchphrase such as 'white middle-class feminism' and all that
that implies? How often, in a world that supposedly has seen the
'death of Marxism', have the widely varied traditions of Marxist
theory and scholarship been reduced to one crude, highly deterministic ('base-superstructure') model, again in order to demonstrate
the superiority of that which has transcended it?

This suggests a further problem with difference approaches that
is connected both with my point above about selectivity and the
so-called death of Marxism, which traditionally has been centred
upon the concepts of class conflict and struggle. As I noted earlier,
there is a comparative lack of attention being paid today to class
in history and other fields – compared, that is, with a focus upon
race/ethnicity, colonialism/the nation, culture, religion and gender/
sexuality. The blindness to class in feminist scholarship is not
criticized as often as it might be, perhaps partly because of the
wealth of socialist feminist literature on class earlier, during the First
and Second Waves. But, it is undeniable that, unlike in the 1970s
to eighties when the influence of Marxist scholarship was at its peak,
class is seldom a central focus now in the early twenty-first century.
(This is not to say that one needs to be a Marxist to recognize the
importance of class differences. That proposition would be guilty
of selectivity of another sort by reducing all of socialism to Marxism.
On the other hand, accepting it would echo the absurd lengths that
Cold War scholarship went to, to avoid being 'tarred' with a 'red'
or even 'pinkish' brush, partly by avoiding any Marxist-sounding
concepts or terminology such as 'class' or 'feudalism'.)

Chris Weedon, however, does include a chapter on class in her
work on feminism and the politics of difference, while observing on
its first page that:

> Of all the categories used to distinguish difference – gender,
> sexual orientation, race, ethnicity, religion, culture – class has,
> in recent years, become perhaps the least fashionable. This shift
> away from considerations of class can be understood in a
> number of ways. It is due in part to the increasing postmodern
> scepticism towards general theories of history and society. In
> the case of Marxism, which has generated the most important
> theories of class over the last 150 years, doubts about its

viability as a social theory have been reinforced by the collapse of socialist systems around the world – systems which claimed to be working towards truly classless societies.[82]

On that last note, one would think that the longstanding *liberal* pretensions to classlessness in developed capitalist societies has much to do with today's class blindness in scholarship. This goes together with a comparative lack of interest in critiques of capitalism and analyses of socialist groups or movements, even those of the past, so historians are not exempt from this trend. In part, post-colonial theory's central focus upon colonialism/neo-colonialism and nation/empire renders this explicable, but one wonders how critiques of cultural imperialism, nationalism, ethnocentrism and racism can so often be divorced from class and capitalism. Yvonne Corcoran-Nantes illustrates the point well when she says in her essay on women in Brazil:

> for low-income women practical gender interests take priority in their political struggles and it is here that they have built the necessary basis for unity and solidarity. Class oppression, to which their gender subordination is directly related, has forced women to organize around issues related to their very survival and that of their families.[83]

Nevertheless, in a reader in feminist postcolonial theory, despite the common emphasis in this upon 'intersectionality', we find among the thirty-five or so papers, very few that are centrally concerned with class differences between women or even with the ways in which class intersects race and gender.[84] This is a far cry from the days when there was a wealth of material on class and gender being produced by socialist feminist authors. Although still today there are probably more self-identified socialists in the ranks of postcolonial scholars than in other branches of learning, this lacuna in feminist postcolonialism exemplifies a wider trend. Clearly, what has happened is that we have 'advanced' from a situation where class analyses were often privileged over other considerations of difference, to the other extreme whereby class is too often ignored.

One problem that stems from the comparative disinterest now in socialism and thus in its history, too, is a resulting blindness, for example in feminist theory or even histories of feminism, toward the traditional differences of socialist feminists. Perhaps this is partly because in various ways it is not so easy to fit them into generalizations about 'white middle-class feminism' and its precepts. Felski's comments are pertinent here, concerning how contemporary theory (specifically poststructuralist feminism) often ascribes a problematic homogeneity to past thinking in 'a single linear trajectory from modern totality to postmodernist plurality', the former necessarily being theoretically naive or superficial compared with the latter.[85] One example I have mentioned is the common assumption that postmodernist feminism is a feminism of 'difference' unlike earlier feminism, as if class and other differences among women had not always been central in one of its main wings around the world, socialist feminism, whether it was of the Marxist, social-democratic or anarchist variety. (Socialist feminism, I should also emphasize, remained more influential in Second Wave women's movements in Britain, some parts of Europe and Australia than in North America.)

It is not unusual for those who centre their analyses on modernity/postmodernity, and thus liberal humanist feminism versus postmodernist feminism, to overlook the socialists. This we see in one work on feminism and self-representation, *Feminisms and the Self: The Web of Identity* by Morwenna Griffiths.[86] Griffiths sets up two basic models of historical feminist representations of the Self: the modernist unitary and essentialist (centred and fixed) individualistic Self which she associates with liberal and separatist/radical feminism; and the acentric, 'dispersed' or multiple and changing Self associated with postmodernist feminism. So where do all the socialists fit in, one might well wonder.[87] (These different conceptions of the Self will be discussed in detail in Chapter 4.)

If in scholarship class, capitalism and socialism are being overlooked, we might find it unsurprising that most history students, too, evince little interest in such topics. I have found that however much reading I set for students on class capitalism and/or socialists, the disinterest remains. On the other hand, they readily recognize that people have differed in accordance with culture, race/ethnicity, religion, and sex/gender and sexuality; and that social systems have commonly been built upon racism, heteronormativity and male domination. To cite some practical examples, when teaching world women's and gender history, I continually need to remind students that women of the lower classes in Asia whose labour was needed in the fields would hardly have been subjected to footbinding, full veiling/cloaking or seclusion in the home; or that not all women in nineteenth- to twentieth-century Europe lived in accordance with the cult of domesticity of the privileged classes. This class-blindness is difficult to counter, despite the fact that I include in student reading texts that certainly do not overlook class – Merry Wiesner-Hanks' *Christianity and Sexuality in the Early Modern World* being one that springs to mind.[88] Similarly, when teaching the history of feminism, I find that students will overlook in their essays the workings of capitalist industry even in analyses of female body image or pornography. Some, moreover, apparently feel that an essay on the national or transnational history of feminism is complete with little to no mention of the role of socialist feminism in it. This is despite the fact that, in the course I am thinking of, set course readings include works by socialist feminists such as Alexandra Kollontai and Sheila Rowbotham; and on the role of socialist feminism even in struggles for suffrage around the world.

Weedon mentioned an 'increasing postmodern scepticism towards general theories of history and society' as the first reason for the unfashionableness of class as a category of analysis. Here she was referring to Marxism and its notion of class tensions as central to social conflict, or class struggle as the primary motor of historical change. Related to this is the third factor she discusses: 'the development of postmodernity itself'.[89] In this connection she mentions Marxism's character as 'a quintessentially modern meta-narrative of progress' (a reference to its materialist conception of history or historical materialism as a universalist theory of global change) and how it has fallen foul of postmodernism's questioning also of absolute truths. A postmodernist suspicion of metanarratives/metahistory may explain scholars' relative disinterest in class, but I doubt that it explains first-year students' lack of awareness of or interest in it. The liberal ideology of classlessness may have more explanatory power, as well as the equally absurd notion that we now live in a post-ideological age. Arguably, students' lack of enthusiasm also for studying capitalism/socialism has much to do with the suspicion of 'ideologies', at least those they recognize as such – not liberalism, given its pose as a non-ideology, but the traditional leftist ideologies. (This does not generally apply to feminism, however, nor necessarily to anarchism since it appears to be enjoying a resurgence of popularity in various parts of the world.)

No doubt there are various reasons for what often seems to be a strange silence in scholarship on matters of class position and difference. Among them Weedon mentions the sorry record of the so-called 'socialist' bloc; and (in relation to Britain) the postwar increase in social mobility and 'the demise of popular forms of working-class identification which were long promoted by the labour movement and other working-class organizations'.[90] (Would 'decline' have been a better word to use than 'demise'?) We could argue about the relative importance of such reasons, but the issue serves, once again, to remind us of just how *presentist* scholarship is: how in History both theoretical/methodological approaches and even the topics chosen for analysis and past people studied are reflective of current concerns and mindsets. A postmodernist suspicion of metahistory or of ideological dogmas should not prevent us, however, from paying sufficient attention to issues of class. Ignoring class differences is out of step with postmodernism's wariness of totalistic, homogenized representations of peoples and societies, past and present. Nor should this suspicion of metanarratives or metahistory encourage us to consign Marxism in its entirety to the 'dustbin of history'. Even Derrida, the father of 'deconstruction', did not do that, as his affirmation of the importance of the legacy of that 'quasi-paternal figure', Karl Marx, has illustrated. This was in *Specters of Marx* cited on p. 138, which was one of his last published works. As Weedon observed, socialism's failures in the former socialist bloc 'mean neither that class has ceased to matter . . . nor do they mean that Marxist theory has no further explanatory power'.[91]

With respect to postmodernism's central concern with difference, Weedon notes a tendency not only to theorize difference, but to celebrate it – without, however, taking full account of the 'material social relations of inequality' that produce differences.[92] This has been a common criticism voiced by those concerned with the central focus in poststructuralism upon language/discourse. The well-known American feminist activist and law professor, Catharine MacKinnon, once described the postmodernist approach to the relation between theory and practice as 'discourse unto death' where 'theory begets no practice, only more text' – as if we can 'deconstruct power relations by shifting their markers around' in our heads.[93] Her general point was that feminist theory should arise from practice, not practice from theory; nor theory from other abstractions. If theory is built out of the diverse experiences and political practices of different women, she observed, feminism would not be subject to criticism for essentializing women, or positing universals based in reality upon the exclusion of all but white middle-class women. As MacKinnon says, 'if a [gender] theory is not true of, and does not work for, women of color, it is not really true of, and will not work for, any women.'[94]

I could take issue with this sort of theory/practice binarism, and in fact will do so in Chapter 4. However, an example MacKinnon offers of theorizing from abstractions is when critics of feminism's failure to take account of racialized and, less often, class-based oppressions themselves dismiss the oppression of the 'white woman'. This abstracted white woman, MacKinnon observes, 'is not poor, not battered, not raped (not really), not molested as a child, not pregnant as a teenager, not prostituted, not coerced into pornography, not a welfare mother, and not economically exploited. She doesn't work.'[95] Here MacKinnon was contesting the hierarchy of oppression put forward by some American activists or scholars who are primarily concerned with racialized oppression, a hierarchy in which 'mere' sex/gender oppression (or that alone, uncombined with other oppressions) has sometimes been trivialized. This is not unlike the habit white American and other radical feminists once had of treating sexual oppression as 'originary': the primary (most fundamental and, by extension, most serious and important) form of oppression from which others flowed. Some socialist feminists, on the other hand, had privileged class over gender oppression, which led Adrienne Rich to critique the 'fruitless game of hierarchies of oppression' in terms similar to MacKinnon's, dismissing the claim that '"bourgeois feminists" are despicable creatures of privilege whose oppression is meaningless beside the oppression of black, Third World, or working-class women or men'.[96] To recognize the privilege that stems from whiteness is not quite the same thing as seeing *the* white woman as entirely 'privileged' in the day to day course of her life, since she may be subject to multiple oppressions of class, sexuality and/or age or 'merely' to a severe expression of sexual oppression.

A justifiable wariness of the essentialism and universalism that can be implied in usage of the category of 'Woman', moreover, does not mean that we cannot speak of systematic, shared women's oppression at all. For MacKinnon:

to speak of social treatment 'as a woman' is . . . not to invoke any abstract essence or homogeneous generic or ideal type, not to posit anything, far less a universal anything, but to refer to this diverse and pervasive concrete reality of social meanings and practices such that, in the words of Richard Rorty, 'a woman is not yet the name of a way of being human . . . .'.[97]

Being treated 'as a woman' in discriminatory terms will differ depending upon how one is racialized, too (different sexist representations in pornography of black and white women is an example MacKinnon mentions), but this does not rule out a shared experience of oppression on the basis of one's 'womanhood'. For example, domestic violence and rape may be subject to different cultural ways of seeing and dealing with them, but they still occur across lines of culture, race/ethnicity, class and religion. Hence, in our histories of women, or histories of gender/sexuality, or histories of racism, we need to take account of the complex or multiple ways in which such categories of differentiation 'intersect' each other, while also recognizing shared oppressions.

In effect, other scholars have been criticizing theorizing from abstractions in other terms. Chilla Bulbeck notes that third world women tend to 'resist the lure of . . . post-discourses' because these 'focus on words rather than things'; they 'focus at least as much attention on discussions of rape and poverty as the experience of those raped or poor'.[98] She acknowledges, however, that some postmodernists are well aware of the inseparability of dominant discourses and relations of power:

> Their focus is not on the so-called 'real' conditions of poverty or exploitation, which they claim we can never know anyway, refracted as they are through writings or other representations of them. Rather, postmodernism explores violence and power in language, the conditions by which some aspects and voices are repressed while others are expressed.[99]

This is an issue I shall address in Chapter 4 in connection with a development called 'practice theory' and its impact upon a new, revisionist style of history. This sort of theory has been centrally concerned with the problem of whether poststructuralism is too narrowly concerned with language/discourse to account fully for the 'material' everyday lives and experiences of people and for self-willed human practice or 'agency'. Though poststructuralists have often been highly critical of structural (material/economic) determinism in Marxism, practice theorists sometimes suggest that the linguistic turn has brought with it its own narrow determinism. The issue is not unconnected with the problems involved in negotiating difference in works of history – it certainly is connected with the essentialist and binaristic logic of difference which I have critiqued here – but it has a particular relevance to constructs of subjectivity and therefore to Chapter 4. There I shall include discussion of whether this critique of the linguistic turn and its necessarily negative effects on the discipline of history is warranted.

Suggestions for further reading

Once again, readers would be very useful. Those most relevant to this chapter are:

- Bill Ashcroft, Gareth Griffiths and Helen Tiffin (eds), *The Post-Colonial Studies Reader*, London and New York: Routledge, 1995 (Part VIII is on feminism and postcolonialism, six essays, including ones by widely known authors, Chandra Talpade Mohanty, Trinh T. Minh-ha and Gayatri Chakravorty Spivak)
- Sneja Gunew (ed.), *A Reader in Feminist Knowledge*, London: Routledge, 1991 (Part 1 comprises essays by Australian Indigenous women on feminism, as well as one by African American feminist, bell hooks/Gloria Watkins)
- Reina Lewis and Sara Mills (eds), *Feminist Postcolonial Theory: A Reader*, Edinburgh: Edinburgh University Press, 2003 (contains many essays, including ones discussed in this chapter by Ien Ang and Mohanty; others by Audre Lord, Natalie Zemon Davis, Spivak, Angela Davis, hooks, Fatima Mernissi, Rey Chow, etc.)
- Sue Morgan (ed.), *The Feminist History Reader*, London and New York: Routledge, 2006 (especially Part III: 'Searching for the subject: lesbian history', and Part IV: 'Centres of difference: decolonising subjects, rethinking boundaries'); another work on feminist history is Joan Scott (ed.), *Feminism and History*, Oxford University Press, 1996

For good overviews of postcolonial or difference feminisms, see:

- Chilla Bulbeck, *Re-Orienting Western Feminism: Women's Diversity in a Postcolonial World*, Cambridge: Cambridge University Press, 1998
- Chris Weedon, *Feminism, Theory and the Politics of Difference*, Oxford, UK and Malden, USA: Blackwell Publishers, 1999

Otherwise, influential theorists and/or historians that I have referred to, for example Edward Said and postcolonial historian, Dipesh Chakrabarty, as well as Joan Scott on differentiation really should be consulted.

Chapter 4

The 'positioned' subject

[W]hen we speak today of a divided subject, it is never to acknowledge his simple contradictions, his double postulations etc.; it is a *diffraction* which is intended, a dispersion of energy in which there remains neither a central core nor a structure of meaning: I am not contradictory, I am dispersed. (author's emphasis)

(Roland Barthes by Roland Barthes)[1]

'Experience' is one of the [empiricist] foundations that has been reintroduced into historical writing in the wake of the critique of empiricism; unlike 'brute fact' or 'simple reality', its connotations are more varied and elusive. It has recently emerged as a critical term in debates among historians about the limits of interpretation and especially about the uses and limits of poststructuralist theory for history.

(Joan Scott, 'The Evidence of Experience')[2]

I

All six of the principles pinpointed in Chapter 1, that many authors see to be consistent with a non-modernist, sceptical, reinvigorated practice of History, have a bearing upon the question of how we represent an historical subject's identity. However, in this chapter I will concentrate on the fifth point: 'a rejection of humanistic views of the centred/essentialized and static or fixed Self'. This is the notion of a core self derived in part from the Christian soul, but more the product of modern Western individualism. In postmodernism, on the other hand, the Self (or individual subjectivity) is seen to be discursively constituted in an ongoing process. In various contexts in earlier chapters I have addressed critiques of essentialist identity – transnational, national, group and, on occasion, individual identity – in relation to culture/nationality, race/ethnicity, sex/gender, or sexuality. But, here the focus will be more on the individual, particularly the political subjectivity of the individual, and also more concerned than earlier with sex/gender and sexuality. As in former chapters, I will be drawing substantially upon feminist theory, which over the years has increasingly featured a central concern with subjectivity and thus has much to contribute to the discussion. However, like in my introduction I will begin by referring particularly to Roland Barthes. In connection with history/historiography, it may be Barthes' notion of history's 'reality effect' that is most often discussed, yet another area in which he has been influential and which is no less important is human subjectivity. The above quote from his so-called 'autobiography', '*R.B.*' or *Roland Barthes by Roland Barthes*, illustrates why, with its reference to the 'divided' or 'dispersed' (otherwise, often termed the 'fragmented') subject or Self. It should be noted that this concept of the acentric or fragmented Self (or multiple selves), is related to a polemic most often associated particularly with Barthes or Foucault, concerning the 'death of the author' or subject.

My remark about how Barthes is usually discussed in connection with his critique of history's 'reality effect' perhaps begs the question of what bearing a critique of the Christian-humanist centred Self has specifically on the practice of history. First, its relevance to the literary and history genre of biography is obvious. Yet we historians often have the occasion to pronounce upon who or what our historical subjects (essentially) were. We may be encouraged in this if our subjects happened to represent their own selves as unitary – structuring their lives and characters in terms of an unchanging core or centre. But the question is, do we merely take such constructs as given, in the manner, arguably, of much conventional biography? The subject said s/he was this or that, so who are we to argue the point? Who are we to question the authority or truth of his/her experience and understanding of his or her Self? But perhaps we should rather be suspending the classic empiricist concern with subjects' accuracy or truthfulness by, as I put it in Chapter 1, enquiring instead into the 'positionalities' they performed.

I shall divide the following discussion of identity/subjectivity into a number of sections beginning with an explication of the concept of the decentred Self and related category of 'experience'.

Experience, as Joan Scott reveals above, is one of history's foundational empiricist categories of analysis, one that even some historians with poststructuralist sympathies have been loathe to dispense with in the wake of the linguistic turn. As with Chapter 3, the latter part of the chapter will be devoted to a consideration of what some have seen to be the 'limits of poststructuralist theory for history', as Scott put it, with particular reference to perceived limits of the postmodernist conception of subjectivity. Apart from discussing the ambivalence with which critiques of centred identities and, by extension, traditional identity politics have been received in some quarters, here I will include consideration of an issue that is inseparable both from difference/differentiation and identity/subjectivity, as I noted above: the critique of linguistic turn historiography for failing to take full account of human practice or 'agency' both at the individual and collective levels. This debate has hinged upon a critique of the poststructuralist notion that the formation of subjectivity takes place within language/discourse for being too deterministic; and also represents a reaction against the poststructuralist critique of humanism's independent-thinking, self-originated and self-willed, individualistic subject.

II

> The coming into being of the notion of 'author' constitutes the privileged moment of *individualization* [writer's emphasis] in the history of ideas, knowledge, literature, philosophy, and the sciences
> . . . .
> I think that, as our society changes . . . the author function will disappear . . . . All discourses . . . would then develop in the anonymity of a murmur. We would no longer hear the questions that have been rehashed for so long: Who really spoke? Is it really he and not someone else? With what authenticity or originality? And what part of his deepest self did he express in his discourse? Instead, there would be other questions, like these: What are the modes of existence of the discourse? Where has it been used, how can it circulate, and who can appropriate it for himself? What are the places in it where there is room for possible subjects? Who can assume these various subject positions? And behind all these questions, we would hear hardly anything but the stirring of an indifference: What difference does it make who is speaking?
>
> (Foucault, 'What is an Author?')[3]

I noted above that the postmodernist concept of the acentric Self is inseparable from a polemic most often associated particularly with Barthes or Foucault – re the 'death of the subject/author'. In the above lines drawn from the beginning and end of Foucault's well-known critique of the modern author function, 'the-man-and-his-work-criticism' comes under fire for (among other things) its humanist-individualistic assumption of the original, independent genius of the author; its belief that a 'work' or body of works could reveal an author's 'deepest self' ('deep' being the hermeneutic expression of a Self's essential being, as if layer upon layer could be peeled away to reveal a 'core'); and its concern with the authenticity lent a work by a proper name, the name of an 'Author'. Foucault points out that this was a departure from the days in Europe when the real or imagined ancientness of anonymous stories, epics or plays was 'a sufficient guarantee of their status', their truth or authenticity. We also see in these passages from 'What is an Author?' the post/structuralist ideas that one takes up a subject position in or through discourse; and that, in writing, one merely participates in existing discourses. It is through participation in existing discourses that one's consciousness and identity(s) are formed, moreover. Even Marx and Freud, two examples of authors Foucault calls 'founders of discursivity', were not the solitary originators of the discourses now named after them suffixed by an 'ism'. However 'original' (or perhaps 'creative') they were, comparatively speaking, even they were formed by the world around them, and could not be other than intertextual in their writing.

The same can be said of one more 'founder of discursivity', Foucault himself, who followed Barthes in employing the concept of the death of the author. Barthes, too, drew for inspiration upon the thinking of others in his notion of a 'dispersed' subject: a subject with multiple selves rather than merely being 'doubled' in the sense of being contradictory (one side of the self warring with another, we might say). Barthes made it clear that the inspiration for a re-thinking of subjectivity came from both within and outside of the traditions of Western thought – from the Western genre of auto-biography and literary criticism,[4] for example, and also Eastern (e.g. Buddhist) thinking. The latter can be seen both in his 'anti-autobiography', *Roland Barthes by Roland Barthes,* and in his work on Japan: *Empire of Signs.*[5]

Since the same can be said of a number of Western theorists who had preceded Barthes (Nietzsche and Heidegger, to name but two), the concept of the Self/subjectivity that goes by the name of 'post-modern' is, broadly speaking, far from new. This notwithstanding, the similarities between some Eastern religio-philosophical tradi-tions and Western postmodernist thinking is an issue that has not been addressed in Western postmodernist scholarship as often as it might have been. Apart from simple eurocentrism, perhaps we can partly blame the 'difference' focus of contemporary scholarship for this in the sense that it tends to occlude investigation into trans-cultural similarities. The similarities or, rather, intertextuality in question include Buddhism's quite unindividualistic perception of a Self that has an 'empty' centre, a Self in flux; and its concept of 'co-dependence' which, in poststructuralism, is paralleled by 'exteriority', the idea that at the level of consciousness one is not unique, not separate from but formed by the world around one. Also pertinent is the practice by Ch'an/Zen masters such as medieval Japan's Dōgen (founder of the Sōtō School of Zen) of a logic of negation or paradox – that first affirms then negates a proposition to avoid what we would now call the 'totalization' or 'closure' of knowledge – which has an interesting similarity to Heidegger's and Derrida's strategy of 'erasure'.[6] Barthes explicitly referred to this sort of strategy on the part of the Ch'an/Zen 'patriarchs' or masters in *Empire of Signs*, whilst echoing Buddhist- or Zen-style ideas in other respects that I will not delve into again here.[7] Suffice it to say that neither in Buddhism nor in poststructuralist or 'high-structuralist' thinking such as is exemplified by Barthes (or Foucault) do we find an acceptance of the self-originated, self-made, self-willed and unitary (structured, essentialized) hero of Western individualistic thought and literature.

As for Barthes and Foucault on the death of the author/subject, the following passage from Barthes' 'The Death of the Author'[8] might be said to 'echo' Foucault's thinking if it had not preceded it. For, in it we find a similar critique of the idea that the author's true self can be discovered in or rather (hermeneutically) 'beneath' the work. Hence, in traditional literary criticism, 'when the author has been found, the text is "explained" – victory to the critic', Barthes jibes, observing that the age of the reign of the Author coincided with that of the literary Critic. We also find the same sort of dismissal of humanist-individualist notions of authorial authenticity and originality:

[W]riting is that neutral, composite, oblique space where our subject slips away, the negative where all identity is lost, starting with the very identity of the body writing . . . .

We know now that a text is not a line of words releasing a single 'theological' meaning (the message of the Author/God) but a multi-dimensional space in which a variety of writings, none of them original, blend and clash. The text is a tissue of quotations drawn from the innumerable centres of culture . . . the writer can only imitate a gesture that is always anterior, never original. His only power is to mix writings, to counter the ones with the others, in such a way as never to rest on any one of them. Did he wish to *express himself* [Barthes' emphasis], he ought at least to know that the inner 'thing' he thinks to 'translate' is itself only a ready-formed dictionary, its words only explainable through other words, and so on indefinitely . . .[9]

Alun Munslow draws upon these ideas on intertextuality versus originality when discussing the 'deconstructively aware' historian who might conclude various things about the history we read and write, including seeing 'the historical text as . . . possessing no original author at all . . . [since] how the narrative is framed depends upon the successive historians through whose hands (and minds) the text has passed'.[10] Another point to note about the putative death of the subject/author is that Barthes and Foucault were suspicious of the assumption found in Cartesian rationalism that the subject is fully conscious of and in control of its agency,[11] extending this to a critique of authorial intentionality. Thus, a commonly encountered theme in poststructural histories or, more broadly, poststructural analyses today concerns how authors are not fully in control of the meaning in their texts. Apart from the question of different readers' interpretations, there is, as I pointed out in an earlier chapter, a 'slippage', 'deferral' or a 'play' of intended meaning in writing: familiar linguistic/rhetorical devices (metaphors and the like) may be utilized that interfere with intended meaning, without authors being fully aware of their doing so.

As opposed to Barthes' conception of the fragmented, dispersed Self, the idea of the self-made and centred Self may seem very 'natural', at least to those of us raised within Anglo-European discursive traditions. (We all want to believe in our originality or complete independence of mind and action.) These traditions include literary/historical genres of self-representational or 'life' writing such as autobiography and biography where, as I have noted, the subject has typically been conceived as possessing an essential Self in a life centred on some particular core meaning. Arguably, although the 'postmodernist' alternative may seem radical, it may be more natural, however, to conceive of individual subjectivity as constructed through language/discourse – as inseparable, that is, from the cultural and political world we are raised in and learn to converse and think within. By extension, it does not seem unnatural to see ourselves as 'in flux' or continually changing as we move through life. I doubt I am alone in pondering at times on both the ways in which I have changed during the course of my life and on the fact that even at one point in time there does not seem to be one central me but rather several: the academic me is rather different from the me I am with my family; different aspects of my character come to the fore in different situations; different contexts may elicit different positionalities.

However one wants to put this basic point, it alludes to the 'postmodern' conception of acentric, multiple selves in flux. Further, I may like to think that I am entirely self-made, but doubtless the ways in which my intellect, politics and life have taken shape have been as much the result of influences working upon me as the effect of my own will or the choices I make, drawing upon available options. Yet this is not the picture we derive from many autobiographies or biographies, especially those traditionally focussed upon the 'great man' or, now more often, the great woman whose greatness rests upon his/her uniqueness, separateness from (ability to 'rise above') the world, originality and 'free' will.

Barthes was not unlike another famed literary theorist of his generation, Paul de Man, according to whom authors of autobiography create a single unitary/centred Self in the very act of writing.[12] Although this might bring to mind some authors of unusually inventive 'memoirs' who have been embroiled in literary scandals ('Helen Demidenko' and Norma Khouri in Australia, James Frey in the United States), the critique by de Man, Barthes and others of the fictiveness of self-representational writing was considerably more far-reaching. Since the 1970s there has been a huge critical literature on self-representational writing (or 'life-writing' which includes biographies) that includes works by leading post/structuralist theorists such as Barthes, de Man and Derrida. As the titles of such works often suggest, their focus has been on the 'art

of self-invention' or the 'fictions of self-representation' that are
intrinsic to the genre(s).[13] It is often pointed out that in the modernist-
humanist genre of autobiography, the unified Self that is created is
in possession of a subjectivity that is at its 'core' unique and
apparently separable from the world around it; it is usually centred,
moreover, on some fixed essence, perhaps a special character trait
or strength that has led to its/his greatness and is said to account for
the individual's 'destiny'. This may be worldly success or a dramatic
death, but whatever it is this essence somehow remains the same in
a linear continuity from the virtual beginning to the end of the life.
The narrativizing of a life-story, moreover, normally takes place
toward the end of a life, so the Self/life that is being centred upon
some essence is teleological: the product of hindsight or the contexts
of its narration.

Naturally, the critical literature on life-writing has targeted
biographies, too, whether they be literary or historical, for much
the same reasons. This is where the postmodernist critique has a
special pertinence to history writing, as I noted, whether we happen
to be writing biographies or merely commenting upon the
biographical details (lives and identities) of some historical subject
in another type of history text. In biography criticism one of my
personal favourites is an essay by Jean-Michel Raynaud, 'What's
What in Biography', where at one point Raynaud asks:

> What happens when various objects left by a person during
> his/her life are taken as able to stand for the entire life? Are
> said to entail the meaning of this life? Is life reducible to a
> meaning? Is a life a text? Is a life a story?[14]

Rather than representing the truth of the life – as is claimed by the
pretensions to 'definitiveness'/closure of each successive biography
of a person – the most that can be said, say, of the most recent
biography of Arthur Rimbaud is that if his 'life had been a story it
would be plausible for it to have been this story'.

In answer to the question Raynaud posed concerning whether a
life is reducible to a single story or meaning, he observes that one
thing that happens in biography is that the life:

> is always presented as the struggle of a subject, the main
> character, against an anti-subject ... for example, a rival,
> society, illness, and at least death. The subject wants to carry

on an action which will give it (*sic*) a certain object of value, fame, success, and so on.

He also points out that, in fact, biographies are not content with telling 'the' story of a *life*, for they do not really finish with the death of the hero:

> The last words at least always indicate the repercussions, the consequences of such a life, of which this actual biography is an illustration in itself. As if to a story telling the triumph of death over a man was added a story telling triumph of an individual over death. Actually, it goes beyond that. All biographies that you can read deal with the same story of which the hero is not one particular individual, but the Individual as such manifested as being the powerful agent acting on everything, on groups, on events, on history. Biography is therefore the story which reveals the Individual, the essential myth of our European society . . . . Biography asserts the survival of the Individual. The 'Soul' cannot die.[15]

Conventional autobiographies and biographies have indeed perpetuated the individualistic 'great man' myth. However, it should be acknowledged that this is not necessarily applicable to sub-genres of self-writing – the sort of sub-genre that has been termed 'critical' or 'out-law' or 'resistance' autobiography. As is pointed out in more than one essay in *De/Colonizing the Subject: The Politics of Gender in Women's Autobiography* edited by Sidonie Smith and Julia Watson, self-representational writing by women or other marginalized groups around the world may, in effect, subvert the bourgeois individualistic genre of autobiography. They may do so, for example, by constructing a collective authorial voice, where the author speaks both as an individual and as representative of/for an oppositional group.[16]

Barthes' critique of autobiography's teleologies and essentialized selves was perhaps at its most incisive in his own 'autobiography': *Roland Barthes by Roland Barthes*. This *anti*-autobiography features none of the usual features of an autobiography or memoir – no linear continuity in the self/life under construction, no teleology, no centred meaning. Here his 'fragmented' Self or selves unfolded in textual fragments, snapshots and scraps of prose, that were not in chronological order but arbitrarily organized under 'a series of names, topics, and concepts', as Paul Jay observes. Jay suggests that this deliberately (some might say, 'ridiculously') reduced representation of the life and self of 'R.B.' reveals how:

> Barthes's work eschews both memory and biography, and insists that writing autobiography is a thoroughly creative activity. He treats of the distance between the biographical and the written self by affirming it, by deconstructing 'Barthes' into a group of fragments . . .[17]

Writing in the third person to accentuate the distance between the text's subject and its author, Barthes himself spoke of his fragmented text and Self/selves in the following passage (in a 'scrap' of over two pages, which I will abbreviate further):

> To write by fragments: the fragments are then so many stones on the perimeter of a circle: I spread myself around: my whole little universe in crumbs; at the center, what?
>
> His first, or nearly first text (1942) consists of fragments; this choice is then justified . . . 'because incoherence is preferable to a distorting order'. Since then, as a matter of fact, he has never stopped writing in brief bursts . . . .
>
> Liking to find, to write [only] *beginnings*, he tends to multiply this pleasure; that is why he writes fragments; so many fragments, so many beginnings, so many pleasures (but he doesn't like the ends: the risk of the rhetorical clausule is too great: the fear of not being able to resist the *last word*).[18]

We should also note the oblique references to the normally single origin in life-narratives, which he prefers to multiply to escape their 'distorted order'; and his suspicion of 'ends' or teleological closures. His preferred structural 'incoherence' also includes the equation of the scattered 'crumbs' of his writing with a similarly 'dispersed' or decentred Self/selves and life. Clearly, this represents quite a contrast with conventional autobiographies or memoirs that are, invariably, legitimized by reference to how they represent a whole life or 'the essential truth of [a] life'.[19]

Barthes also alludes in this passage to 'im-mediate' writing: writing unmediated by time and, by extension, teleological representations of a life and Self. Elsewhere in 'R.B.' he mentions this in connection with both the European surrealist liking for the practice and the Japanese short poem of *haiku*. Like with the composition of haiku, his textual fragments from which he constructed, arbitrarily and in disorder, his own life/Self represented for Barthes 'an immediate delight'. The 'germ of [such] a fragment', he said, could strike him anywhere or anytime, whereupon he would take out his notebook and jot it down. Doubtless, Barthes was thinking of the emphasis on the 'now' or moment at hand in Zen (which he mentioned directly after his comments on disliking 'ends' and conclusions: the 'last word'). Elsewhere in the text, however, he also observed that a book that might 'report a thousand "incidents" but would refuse ever to draw a line of meaning from them' would be 'a book of haiku'. [20] He appeared to be drawing a parallel between a book of haiku and his own life-'story', since neither sought to ascribe a 'line' or linear core of meaning to a text (or life, or Self). To this end, or rather to the avoidance of such an 'end' (telos), he says that at certain moments in the process of writing he felt called upon to 'disorder' or decentre the structure of the book 'in order to halt, to deflect, to divide this descent of discourse toward a destiny of the subject': '*Cut! Resume the story in another way* . . .' was his 'call to order' or, rather, 'to disorder'. [21]

A final point about Barthes' rather playful 'autobiography' concerns whether the target of his critique was only conventional Western self-representational *writing*. Jay emphasizes this when (in the quote above) he speaks of Barthes' work as eschewing memory and biography; as insisting on the thoroughly creative nature of autobiographical writing; and as devoted to emphasizing 'the distance between the biographical and the written self'. We might expect a literary critic (Jay or perhaps Barthes himself) to focus upon writing conventions (and a poststructuralist, too, citing Derrida), but I would think that Barthes' critique was also directed more broadly at Western ways of writing-speaking-thinking of the centred, fixed Self. Certainly, a Buddhist approach would be to doubt our ability to apprehend in consciousness, real individual identity. In any case, in penning an anti-autobiography – or, rather, publishing one composed of fragments penned at different times in his life that were not arranged in any 'rational' order – Barthes obviously did have in mind particular conventions of *fictional* Western writing that purported to be realist. For, according to Barthes, encapsulating the entire life (or Self/selves) of a subject in a text and, further, reducing it to one story, one destiny, one central feature and meaning was a fiction; it represented merely a 'reality effect' in histories of a life.

We can see why now the concept of positionality or subject position is often preferred to the concept of 'identity', fraught as the latter is with essentialist, teleological baggage. The term 'positionality' is more suggestive of the active, ongoing process whereby a human subject is both positioned by the world and exercises choice by taking up (and discarding) positions in response to that. A concern with the performance of fragmented and fluctuating subject positions demands, moreover, that rather than asking ourselves what an historical subject's 'real' identity was – as if that were inseparable from language/discourse, thus singular and fixed – we consider the different discursive-political context(s) in which, and apparent ends to which, the subject *spoke to* the truth of his/her experience and essential identity.

This is a lesson I myself learned through my research into the subjectivity of two Japanese women. In the first and third decades of the twentieth century, respectively, they were both charged with high treason for conspiring to assassinate the reigning emperor, and found guilty. Of particular interest to me was the second of the two, Kaneko Fumiko, not just because there is good reason to doubt her guilt (an exaggeration of which, I believe, was part of her resistance), but because she wrote at the request of a judge an extended prison memoir that was designed to explain how she came to her current resistant identity of 'nihilistic egoism'. (This was influenced by Nietzsche and Max Stirner, and roughly equivalent to individualistic anarchism elsewhere). Even the highly unusual circumstances in which she penned her autobiography had not prevented biographers and other scholars from simply repeating her *prison-life* story (*sic*) in positivist fashion, when what it demands is reflection upon the teleological nature of the narrative: its inseparability from the immediate context of the writing, which was prison due to a charge of treason.[22] I became convinced that one needs to read such a text in light of the apparent (political) ends to which its author reduced or centred her life-experience and subjectivity. This particular 'texted' life and Self was centred upon social oppression and the resultant political identity of a nihilistic egoist, but to my mind similar reading strategies should be applied to any such texts – any memoirs or life-stories, that is, not just prison or other resistance self-writing.

III

If one means by experience the common-sense notion of having lived through something, for example, the experience of the

> Holocaust or of rape victims, it retains an important role. But the nature of this role should be specified and its implications assessed. For example, it might be argued that experience provides a basis for a subject-position that, especially in certain cases (such as that of victims), should be respected and attended to, and it may even give a prima facie claim to knowledge. But experience in and of itself neither authenticates nor invalidates an argument or point of view, and it cannot be invoked to silence others – either those having or those not having it.
>
> (Dominick LaCapra, *History and Reading*)[23]

If the postmodernist approach to individual subjectivity is to doubt that it can be captured in a text or, more broadly, in discourse, we might expect the empiricist category of 'experience' to be seen as problematic, too. After all, a subject's personal experience has often been seen to represent both the basis of 'true' (self-) knowledge of a subject on the part of the subject him/herself and the authentication of it on the part of the historian/scholar. Another important reason for scepticism about the empiricist approach to experience is that it has often been seen as the ground upon which consciousness and identity are formed. What usually accompanies such a view, moreover, is the notion of a singular, unified identity, this being the product of a similarly totalized and essentialized life-experience. Today's scepticism about the uses and abuses of 'experience' is attested to by deconstructionist historian, Dominick LaCapra, who nevertheless follows the above passage with the caution that, 'One should not peremptorily dismiss the concept of experience or the need to come to terms with it'. Yet the question for sceptically minded historians is how we *can* act upon the recognition that 'experience in and of itself neither authenticates nor invalidates an argument or point of view', as LaCapra puts it, while simultaneously respecting 'the common-sense notion of having lived through something' such as an act, incident or sustained practice of violence or oppression. I shall return to this question at the end of this section, after having discussed in more detail the postmodernist critique of the notion of 'experience'.

As we saw at the beginning of the chapter, in Joan Scott's influential essay on 'The Evidence of Experience' (first published in 1991 and often reprinted since then) she notes that 'experience' is a foundational empiricist category in the discipline of history. In the following passage she indicates why it should be treated with caution:

[E]xperience . . . establishes the prior existence of individuals. When it is defined as internal, it is an expression of an individual's being or consciousness; when external, it is the material on which consciousness then acts. Talking about experience in these ways leads us to take the existence of individuals for granted (experience is something people have) rather than to ask how conceptions of selves (of subjects and their identities) are produced. It operates within an ideological construction that not only makes individuals the starting point of knowledge, but that also naturalizes categories such as man, woman, black, white, heterosexual, and homosexual by treating them as given characteristics of individuals.[24]

To begin 'unpacking' this passage: first, when people, historical subjects and historians alike, speak of experience as part of a person's internal make-up, part of his/her 'being or consciousness' or identity, it means that in terms of causation the person's present (consciousness) is apparently determined by his/her past (lived experience on which basis consciousness arises) in a linear fashion. This makes a common sort of sense – a bad car accident might well lead one to fear driving – but isn't it also the case that when we ascribe meaning to past experience in the present, it is often our present acting upon and determining our constructions of the past?

Scott's reference to experience as the 'material' acted upon by consciousness is also significant since lived experience is often treated as part of a material reality that is external to the individual: 'lived' experience is 'something people have', as she says, a material possession that, once again, causes consciousness or identity. And, as such, for historians it can more easily count as (material) 'evidence' and thus 'truth'. As Scott asks, 'what could be truer, after all, than a subject's own account of what he or she has lived through?' Her reference is also to materialist causation associated particularly with Marxism, so she may have had Marxist social historians in mind when speaking of how lived experience has been seen as the 'material' that acts upon consciousness/identity. A Marxist who does privilege materialist over 'idealist' causation (determination by ideas/consciousness) would doubtless be suspicious of the poststructuralist emphasis upon linguistic or discursive determination as just a new idealism ('new' to distinguish it from the idealism of liberals and other conservatives who often distanced themselves from Marxism in such terms).

Scott also cautions us not to 'take the existence of *individuals* [my emphasis] for granted'. What she means by this or the apparently strange remark that experience 'establishes the prior existence of individuals' is partly that if, at the level of consciousness, individuals are formed from material or lived experience, the experience actually precedes consciousness and identity. Is it not often the case that an occurrence – let's say, being subject to some form of 'discrimination' – can only be defined as such (as 'an occurrence', an 'experience' and, further, as an 'experience of discrimination'), through a prior understanding of what constitutes 'discrimination'? In other words, it is through individual consciousness, which is itself formed through discourse, that something comes to count as an event or 'an experience'. In Scott's poststructuralist vision the common-sensical view of causation is thereby inverted.

This common-sense vision of causation, of consciousness arising out of an *individual's* prior experience, also hinges upon what Raynaud referred to as 'the essential myth of our European society' – concerning 'the Individual as such manifested as being the powerful agent acting on everything, on groups, on events, on history' (e.g. the 'great man' as 'maker of history'). Similarly, Scott is questioning the 'ideological' emphasis in individualism upon the 'interiority' of the Subject (the individual as 'the starting point of knowledge') when she warns us not to take the *prior* existence of the *individual* for granted. For, at the level of consciousness 'individuals' do not exist separate from, and prior to, language/discourse and knowledge but come to awareness, generally, and also to a sense of Self through them.

To draw upon my own personal experience, I might ask myself: Was my becoming a women's liberationist in the 1970s the result of my being a 'natural' feminist from the 'beginning' – for example, in my youthful frustration at being treated as society expected a girl to be treated? Can I really claim that I was 'a feminist' at the tender age of seven or so? Or was it more the case that reading Germaine Greer and otherwise becoming aware of feminist thinking in my twenties encouraged me to rethink my background and attribute a feminist meaning to that frustration? Thus, in our histories of others or 'our'-selves we should rather be asking 'how conceptions of selves (of subjects and their identities) are produced': in what sort of discursive contexts, that is, do subjects come to read certain things as formative experiences in the constitution of their ('individual') identities?

To relate this to my discussion above of the postmodernist vision of the acentric or multiple Self/selves in flux, what if I were to decide today to write an autobiography, a history of my life and self? Surely the meaning(s) I accord these and my past experience would differ now from how I saw them when in my teens, twenties or thirties. While my commitment to feminist politics may explain a lot about my life, does it explain it all? I might be tempted now to centre my identity on feminism, claiming that I was a 'natural' feminist virtually from the day I was born, and attribute meaning to my life experience in terms of that, but what if I were to 'find God' tomorrow and that reminded me that I was an avid Christian in my Sunday School days? Then I would have to rewrite the whole thing! Imagine the situation of my biographer, too, if s/he had taken my first reading of my past ideas-experience-life-Self at face value, only to unearth after the publication of her work, my revised autobiography.

Scott mentioned another problem with the individualistic construction of experience: namely, that it treats categories such as man, woman, black, white, heterosexual and homosexual as natural rather than discursive. That is, it *naturalizes* them. These essentialist categories I will discuss in more detail in the section below, where I look at the issue of identity politics and resistance to post-structuralist critiques of essentialized identity on the part of its adherents. With regard to 'experience', however, Scott notes how, for orthodox historians who treat experience as 'evidence' and thus a foundation for certain self-'knowledge' of a subject, or our knowledge of her or him, the identities of those whose experience they are documenting become 'self-evident'.[25] To take the example of homosexuality, with which Scott begins her discussion of 'experience', its difference is thereby naturalized: homosexual difference or resistance is treated as existing 'outside its discursive construction'. This means that it is as if (what is now regarded as) 'homosexuality', or sexuality in general, has not been subject to cultural and other variations and historical change. I shall quote Scott at length on the example she discusses of histories that 'document the "hidden" world of homosexuality', seeking to render visible the impact upon homosexuals' lives of this world's being silenced (say, with 'closeting') and otherwise repressed:

> [T]he project of making experience visible precludes critical examination of the workings of the ideological system itself, its

categories of representation (homosexual/heterosexual, man/
woman, black/white as fixed immutable categories), its premises
about what these categories mean and how they operate, and
of its notions of subjects, origin, and cause. Homosexual
practices are seen as the result of desire, conceived as a natural
force operating outside or in opposition to social regulation. In
these stories homosexuality is presented as a repressed desire
(experience denied), made to seem invisible, abnormal, and
silenced by a 'society' that legislates heterosexuality as the only
normal ['natural'] practice .... Resistance and agency are
presented as driven by uncontainable desire; emancipation is a
teleological story in which desire ultimately overcomes social
control and becomes visible. History is a chronology that makes
experience visible, but in which categories appear as nonetheless
ahistorical: desire, homosexuality, heterosexuality, femininity,
masculinity, sex, and even sexual practices become so many
fixed entities being played out over time, but not themselves
historicized.[26]

One of Scott's central points is that the causation in said
narratives is back to front, for ('natural') desire and experience
precede their discursive construction as the (teleological) origins of
identity – as in the often-heard claim that one is born a homosexual,
it is not the product of environment or choice. (Partly due to the
influence of poststructuralists such as Judith Butler, advocates of
queer politics today often do not accept such a vision.) Another key
point is that investigating the different historical constructions of
sexual practices and identity would both be a more critical form of
history and of more utility for resistance to ideologies and institutions
built upon a repressive heteronormativity believed to be 'natural'
or timeless. Hence, she concludes that rather than treating 'the
evidence of experience' as 'evidence for the [immutable] fact of
difference', we would do better to investigate how difference comes
to be – 'how difference is established, how it operates, how and in
what ways it constitutes subjects who see and act in the world'; and
also how it is subject to change. That way we come to a clearer
realization that categories such as homosexual or woman/femininity
are just that, linguistic/discursive categories, and that they and the
meanings attributed to them are not the product of nature but rather
of society and, certainly, 'history'. To see that, one need only be
aware of how they have differed in different societies (and social
classes, too) and have also changed over time.

In this essay on the empiricist category of 'experience' Scott recommends that historians treat any category of representation or analysis as 'contextual, contested, and contingent'.[27] Those she mentions are class, race, gender, relations of production, biology ('nature', too, of course), identity, subjectivity, agency, experience and also culture. And let us not forget others such as 'difference'. We should be asking: how the foundational status of such terms has been achieved in formal knowledges such as history and with what epistemological and political effects; what it means when we research the past in such terms and when individuals speak of themselves in such terms; and what the relation is between the use of such categories today and their use in the past. To that we must of course add: *if* they then existed: 'homosexual' being a good case in point, one I mentioned in Chapter 3. If we are, for example, researching the life, actions, writings of some particular historical subject who, we find, engaged in same-sex practices, do we invest him or her with what we now take to be a 'homosexual' *identity*, centring his or her life and subjectivity on this? Investigating the history of the concepts we use, and our subjects use, would help us see how they are subject to change, 'contextual', as Scott says, or 'contingent'.

In this manner the historian's relationship to the aspect of the past s/he investigates can also be more clearly articulated. (This, as Scott points out, is partly what Foucault meant by history as 'genealogy'.) However, taking the coming into play of such concepts and identities as historical events that demand explanation does not mean that we do *only* that; we also need to consider their socio-political effects and how they condition human behaviour.[28] (The whole world is not, in fact, 'a text', as critics of poststructuralism are often heard to complain.) For example, what, in some particular time, place, class, religion and so on did it mean to be treated by the world as a 'woman'? What were the forces that opened up a space for individuals to embrace or resist such a category, and the notions of feminine subjectivity and social roles associated with it? Scott concludes that there is no reason why we should not be able to 'make visible [our] assignment of subject positions' in a way that does not replicate 'the imposition of a categorical (and universal) subject status (*the* worker, *the* peasant, *the* woman, *the* black) that has masked the operations of difference in the organization of social life.'[29] In short, we should neither be accepting universalized (timeless, ahistorical) identity or other categories, nor failing to acknowledge the historical character of the ones we ourselves employ.

Gabrielle Spiegel comments on Scott's 'impeccable consistency' in her poststructuralist view of experience as 'a linguistic event'.[30] In this Scott pursues a '(post)structuralist logic to the end', she says. Scott is consistent also in her belief that historians' attempts to reinvigorate experience as a central category of historical analysis represents a re-essentialization of the Subject or Self. The question, then, is whether Scott's poststructuralist approach does expose the supposed 'limits of poststructuralist theory for history' (or, indeed for feminism), as its critics have claimed, while preferring to see experience as the basis of knowledge that lies outside discourse, grounded in 'the bodily and material conditions' of everyday life.[31] Personally, I agree with Scott and LaCapra that we cannot take experience as self-evident or straightforward and use it to establish incontrovertible truths. Although even poststructuralists should not 'peremptorily dismiss' the category of experience, as LaCapra put it, nor should it be envisioned as anything other than an *interpretation* of a subject's 'lived reality'. It is 'at once always an interpretation *and* in need of interpretation', as Scott says, and also 'always contested, and always therefore political'.[32] If historians continue to take as their project the mere reconstruction of knowledge, the unquestioned truth of which is established by a subject's experience, *it would indeed seem to preclude analysis of how that knowledge is produced*, which is what Scott advocates. Such an analysis would represent a 'nonfoundational history' that does not base itself on or replicate 'naturalized categories'; one that does not, moreover, rest upon empiricist claims as to the 'neutrality' or impartiality of the historian. After all, the decision of which categories to historicize or deconstruct (or leave unexamined) is itself a political decision, inseparable from 'the historian's . . . stake in the production of knowledge'.[33] For a historian to treat the *category* of 'homosexual' as natural/ timeless and fail to deconstruct it is as much a political act, we might say, as treating same-sex desire and practices as 'unnatural' in heteronormative terms.

I noted at the outset that a central question that arises in connection with 'experience' is how we can act upon LaCapra's recommendations for sceptically minded historians. How can we, that is, recognize that 'experience in and of itself neither authenticates nor invalidates an argument or point of view', while simultaneously respecting the common-sense idea of a historical subject's having 'lived through something' such as an act, incident or sustained practice of violence or oppression. Like LaCapra, I used the example of a rape victim in Chapter 1 where I noted that she (where the victim is a woman) will not necessarily interpret the experience in a certain way: she might, through an awareness of feminist standpoints on sexual violence, come to see it first as 'rape' and then the product of 'patriarchy', and hence a vindication of feminism and perhaps important in the formation of her feminist identity. Alternatively, she might believe that it did not constitute 'rape', perhaps because the man physically forcing her to comply (by 'right') was a husband or boyfriend. Or she might not see herself as a 'victim' because her own 'immodesty' in dress or behaviour led to her being targeted justifiably (since males are unable to control their 'natural' impulses when unreasonably provoked) and mend her ways accordingly. Then again, she might believe this at first, but years later become acquainted with feminist discourse on the issue and change her mind about the experience.

What if we were writing a feminist history, analysing the texts and self-representations of a woman who had had such an experience, and who interpreted it in the second way? Do we as historians fail to 'respect' our subject if we disagree with her account of the experience? Whether or not we judge it to be 'true' rather depends upon our own standpoints. 'Evidence', moreover, will not help us with the quandary raised by this example, since the facticity of the incident, its actual occurrence, is not in doubt; the question is rather one of meaning or whose interpretation of it we judge to be sound. A postmodernist might recommend that we deconstruct the subject's account, including her usage of the word 'rape' (if it was used), treating it as we would any category of representation or analysis as 'contextual, contested, and contingent'. Of course this would still be intrinsically connected with our own feminist politics. For, why else would we do this if not to make a point about the political uses and effects of male-serving discourses about rape? This returns us to the issue discussed in Chapter 2, where I emphasized that many feminists, whether poststructuralist or not, would see no need to deny that our histories are presentist and political. So why should we feel a need to accept the experientially based truth claims of this imaginary subject when she denied that the experience was a 'rape'?

What would be more to the point in a postmodernist feminist history would be reading 'the complex and changing discursive processes by which identities are ascribed, resisted, or embraced', as Scott says[34]; and subjects' experience understood. In my own research project on Kaneko Fumiko the truth of her representations of her experience, identity, life was beside the point, even if she was probably quite 'truthful' about the 'facts' or events that had occurred in her life. (I did spend rather a lot of time cross-checking her prison life-story with details given by her parents and other witnesses in their trial testimonies.) I could have focused on the issue of whether her interpretation of events, rather than that of her mother or father, represents 'the' truth, but what was more to the point was how her interpretation conditioned her resistance. (This was through an embracement of a political identity that represented for her the absolute antithesis of Japan's imperialist state, unequal society and authoritarian patriarchal family structure.)

Concerning 'truth', the historian, as LaCapra says, may grant a subject's account the status of 'truth' just 'on the face of it' or treat it as plausible. Yet, still it should be acknowledged that, unless we write relativist histories that simply counterpose one story to another being very careful not to make or imply judgements about the truth of either one, neither LaCapra's approach nor the discursive focus recommended by Scott will allow us to suspend the question of the truth of experience (or its presentation as such) entirely. Nor will a focus upon mere events enable us to treat the 'fact(s)' of an occurrence as if this can be entirely divorced from interpretation, whether it be the subject's or our own.

All one can ask, perhaps, is that we be self-reflexive about our standpoints and readings, both about them and about how even the most sceptical of histories will still involve some recourse to reality- or truth-effects. Even a focus on the self-representations of a subject will still involve claims on our part, however implicitly, that our readings of them are convincing because plausible, if not final. Furthermore, we can either pretend that we are not putting forward our own (self-consciously feminist or other) interpretations of past discourses or processes of representation, or acknowledge them and engage in what LaCapra calls a 'dialogic' approach. This involves a self-reflexive dialogue both between ourselves and our historical subjects and between ourselves and other interpreters of the past. This is part of the paradoxical, 'pastiche' nature even of histories inspired by radical doubt about the certainties and absolutes of empiricist history – the fact, that is, that even epistemologically sceptical histories cannot completely transcend them. Derrida would say that we have no option but to work within existing languages, logics, discursive systems (or Hayden White, standard narrative emplotments), but that does not mean that we do so unthinkingly. Yet such systems are not 'set in stone'. That they are subject to transformation over time through human agency is a 'fact' or 'certainty' that any good historian could justifiably attest to.

IV — categories - sexuality

> In recent years, the new gender politics has offered numerous challenges from transgendered and transsexual peoples to established feminist and lesbian/gay frameworks . . . . the Left . . . have been under pressure to rethink the political sphere in terms of its gendered and sexual presuppositions. The suggestion that butch, femme, and transgendered lives are not essential referents for a refashioning of political life, and for a more just and equitable society, fails to acknowledge the violence that the otherwise gendered suffer in the public world and fails as well to recognize that embodiment denotes a contested set of norms governing who will count as a viable subject [or even 'human'] within the sphere of politics . . . embodiment is not thinkable without a relation to a norm, or a set of norms.
>
> (Judith Butler, *Undoing Gender*)[35]

I shall return to the issue of an empiricist naturalization of conventional categories of identity (including 'man' and 'woman', and 'homosexual' and 'heterosexual') after first commenting briefly on what might be regarded as a relatively new sub-branch of feminist/gender studies: the study (including history) of sexualities. Foucault's substantial work, *The History of Sexuality*,[36] had a marked impact upon its introduction and development, as has the increasing popularity of the 'queen of Queer Theory', Judith Butler, and Queer Theory more generally. Some have questioned whether the study of sexualities should properly be subsumed under gender studies, as Butler has noted whilst critiquing the notion sometimes found in queer studies that 'gender' is the preserve of feminist studies and 'sex/sexuality' the property of queer studies[37] – as if the two categories are separable. It is mostly Butler's critique of the standard binarisms typically brought to bear in constructs of sex-gender-sexuality that will be discussed in this section, a critique that drew on Foucault in various ways. A central one concerns gender as a 'regulatory' social norm and gender constructs as both repressive and 'productive' (productive of resistance, for example).

Another aspect of Foucault's work that has been influential was his insistence in *The History of Sexuality* that 'homosexual' was a category that only came into existence in Europe in the latter part of the nineteenth century. This was the point at which, in law and medical discourse, same-sex acts began to be pathologized and seen to constitute an individual's sexual or core identity.[38] Though same-sex desire and practice had of course existed before that time and been documented and condemned in religious and civil law as sinful, it was in modern times, Foucault argued, that 'homosexual' came into being to refer to 'a personage, a past, a case history' or a whole 'species' of persons, whose identity was now centred on this aspect of their sexual practice, even if they were not exclusively 'homosexual'. That homosexuality became an identity only in modern times was not just the case, moreover, in Europe; elsewhere, say, in East Asia there were similar developments due to the influence of European imperialism where, once again, male same-sex practices were criminalized for the first time. This basic point about homosexual as a modern category of identity is broadly accepted in the study of sexualities, though Annamarie Jagose notes that there is no consensus on the exact time of emergence of European 'homosexuality'. Some have dated the emergence of an urban homosexual subculture in England, for example, back to the 'molly houses' from around 1700 where homosexual practices among men began to be seen as the basis of a sense of community and identity – the molly culture developing its own language and distinctive ways of dressing and behaving.[39]

For Joan Scott, as noted, one of the central problems with the standard empiricist categories of experience and identity is that they are naturalized. That is, linguistic or social/historical categories such as man, woman, black, white, heterosexual, and homosexual are taken as prediscursive, thus as given, fixed or timeless. The postmodernist position is that, rather than their being the product of 'nature', they are linguistic constructs, the product of a binaristic logic of difference where one category only makes sense or comes to have a certain meaning by being (hierarchically) opposed to another. I have already commented on how in different contexts, different people have been defined as 'black' or white'. Moreover, the fact that people of indigenous descent in, say, Africa or Australia might define themselves as black despite being in possession of light-coloured skin (or South Asians not see themselves as 'black' whatever their skin-colour) well illustrates the point that blackness or whiteness is more a cultural or political category than the product of genes or 'nature'. Even recourse to 'biology' will not help us prove that constructs of race are natural, moreover, when there are no genetic markers that can be found in the human body that signal whiteness alone, or blackness etc. A person with an Eastern European heritage may find that others from Asia or Africa have the closest DNA or genetic match to themselves. Even in scientific thinking, in short, we find the idea that 'race' is not a scientific but rather a historical, social construct.

Similarly, many feminist and queer theorists problematize the conventional idea that differences between man and woman/male and female are essentially biological. Hence, in the first of a series of influential books, *Gender Trouble* (1999), Judith Butler asked, 'Can we refer to a "given" sex or a "given" gender without first inquiring into how sex and/or gender is given, and through what means? And what is "sex" anyway? Is it natural, anatomical, chromosomal, or hormonal . . .?'[40] Further, she asked how we are to 'assess the scientific discourses which purport to establish such "facts" for us'. Anatomy, chromosomes and hormones can contradict each other 'scientifically', by refusing to fall neatly together into the dichotomy of male or female demanded by conventional discourse or 'society' (or, rather, many societies, since historically some have allowed for a 'third sex').[41] With anatomy, as is well known, if at a birth parents and doctors cannot announce with confidence 'It's a girl!', perhaps simply because a large clitoris looks too much like a penis, soon the scalpels will be wielded to excise the offending body-part to return the infant to its 'true' sex (and identity), chromosomes being brought to bear in this case to define an essential femaleness. But what of the confusion wrought by another infant, this time a 'male' because of a penis but with a womb, too, or still another with a penis but no Y-chromosome? On what basis, therefore, would we categorize a historical subject – let's say a person who apparently had the surface bodily markers of a 'male' but cross-dressed and apparently believed s/he was female – as 'really' male or 'really' female?

Transgressions of gender, Butler points out in her work, *Undoing Gender*, invite social 'punishments' that include:

> the surgical correction of intersexed persons, the medical and psychiatric pathologization and criminalization in several countries including the United States of 'gender dysphoric' people, the harassment of gender-troubled persons on the street or in the workplace, employment discrimination, and violence.[42]

With surgical normalization – being 'submitted . . . to the knife of the norm', as Butler nicely puts it – we find the ideality of gender being 'quite literally incised in the flesh'. This is one illustration of why it is common in feminist theory for writers to reject mind-body dualisms with respect to gender constructs – since gender is not just about ideas and how they affect roles, behaviour, or the social 'performance' of a prescribed gender – and to speak of how gender is imprinted on the body itself. (There are many historical examples that reveal how bodies themselves have been marked and transformed with the signs of gender, through corsetry or 'tightlacing', male castration and circumcision, 'FGM: female genital mutilation', female footbinding, and the like.) In this quote Butler comments on the zeal with which medical, psychiatric, legal or other powers want to subject people with gender/sex that is considered aberrant to 'regulation'. For, without this, they cannot be 'culturally intelligible' (they cannot 'exist').[43] Citing the case of children born with 'irregular primary sexual characteristics', she notes the irony that they are seen to need surgical correction 'in order to fit in, feel more comfortable, achieve normality', yet 'the physical and psychic costs of the surgery' can be terrible. This sort of 'regulatory enforcement of gender' has often resulted in 'bodies in pain, bearing the marks of violence and suffering'.

Butler has exhibited a particular concern with the effects upon 'intersex' people of conventional gender binarisms, which is one reason for her popularity in Queer Theory and queer culture (mostly in Anglophone countries). More generally, her style of critiquing the conventional binaristic conflation of sex, gender and sexuality – male/masculine (to be truly so, one must of course be heterosexual) and female/feminine/heterosexual – is often seen to be a more incisive challenge to the institutions of heterosexism and thus have more liberatory potential. She is known particularly for the challenge she mounted to the conventional Second Wave feminist distinction between 'sex' as a natural/biological category and 'gender' as a social-historical construct. Hence, according to *Gender Trouble*:

> Gender ought not to be conceived merely as the cultural inscription of meaning on a pregiven sex (a juridical conception); gender must also designate the very apparatus of production whereby the sexes themselves are established. As a result, gender is not to culture as sex is to nature; gender is also the

discursive/cultural means by which 'sexed nature' or 'a natural sex' is produced and established as 'prediscursive', prior to culture, a politically neutral surface *on which* culture acts.[44]

Butler was not the first to question the sex-gender distinction, however, as she herself illustrates in an extended discussion of French feminist, Monique Wittig. Wittig took up Simone de Beauvoir's famous statement in *The Second Sex* that 'One is not born a woman, but rather *becomes* one' (meaning merely that gender-identification is a process and that 'gender' is something socially acquired) and ran with it, so to speak, taking the proposition further to argue that 'there is no distinction between sex and gender'. As Butler puts it, discussing Wittig's position: 'the category of "sex" is itself a *gendered* category, fully politically invested, naturalized but not natural.'[45]

The concept of 'performativity', too, which again is usually associated with Butler, was partly inspired by Wittig's work. In their usage of the term it refers to sex-gender as an activity, something one acts out in line with or in contravention to conventional sex-gender constructs, rather than something one is or has. Similarly, Witting also put forward 'the idea of the co-extensivity of gender with the regulatory discourse of heterosexuality',[46] which was influenced by Foucault's substantial work on the history of sexuality(s) as well. Butler comments in the following passage on gender as a regulatory social norm:

> The notion that there might be a 'truth' of sex, as Foucault ironically terms it, is produced precisely through the regulatory practices that generate coherent identities through the matrix of coherent gender norms. The heterosexualization of desire requires and institutes the production of discrete and asymmetrical oppositions between 'feminine' and 'masculine', where these are understood as expressive attributes of 'male' and 'female'.[47]

One historical illustration of this, or rather of how sex, gender and sexuality have been treated as co-extensive in Western thinking, but not always elsewhere, can be found in the history of the Philippines. Its premodern world of religion exhibited significant cultural and temporal differences from European Christendom in its visions of at least some sex/gender roles and identity. Carolyn Brewer has discussed how, when missionaries arrived there in the sixteenth century they did not know what to make of the facts, first that women had a leading role in the native animist religions as shamans, and second that occasionally 'men' who played a similar shamanic role did so in feminine garb, acting also in a feminine manner.[48] The missionaries came from a culture where there were Biblical injunctions that men dress as men and women as women and that strictly demarcated their roles in religion, work, the family, etc.; hence, the question in their minds was could these individuals really be 'men'. Surely these 'effeminates' must have been anatomically deficient, or else they were practitioners of the so-called 'deadly sin' (homosexuality), or both? What the missionaries were doing, in short, was conflating 'biological' sex, with 'matching' gender roles and behaviours, and those in turn with sexuality.

I don't know that they ever did discover whether the 'men' had anything 'lacking', but, interestingly, as it turned out it was not unusual for them to be the husbands of the female priestesses. It seems that this case did not represent a 'third sex', which is what Brewer concludes, though there were cases in Asia of belief not in just two sexes but rather three. The formula in the Philippines, with regard to these individuals at least, seems to have been male+feminine+heterosexual: merely a case of men taking on what were perceived to be women's roles and therefore dressing and acting feminine ('performing' gender). Apparently, this did not, moreover, have anything to do with sexual preference. Whatever the precise meanings were that were involved in this cultural practice, clearly, we would not get very far understanding them looking through the lenses of the binaristic Western conflation of biological maleness with a gender performance of masculinity and, in turn, a necessary heterosexuality.

This poststructuralist critique of sex-gender as a regulatory norm, co-extensive with compulsory heterosexuality, partly represents a critique of conventional feminism's unthinking heterosexism in its adherence to a (biology) sex and (culture) gender distinction. Thus, in this Butler-style critique we again find conventional discursive categories such as 'man' and 'woman' being challenged for their essentialism and consequent norm-based 'universalizing' and marginalizing properties. It is on different grounds, however, to those discussed earlier in connection with the postcolonial feminist critique. There the concern was mostly with how, purportedly, when 'Western, white, middle-class' Second Wave feminists spoke of 'woman's' problems and needs, or even of the ideal of a global sisterhood of women, it was the problems, needs and solidarity of Western, white, middle-class women they had in mind. With the critique popularized particularly by Judith Butler, however, the identity category of 'woman' – not only 'woman' (and 'man') but 'male' and 'female', 'hetero- /homo-sexual' – began to be treated with suspicion because it essentialized and universalized 'woman' once again, but this time on biologist grounds of sexual difference and heteronormativity.

V – subjectivity

> Considering that it is as subject one comes to voice, then the post-modernist focus on the critique of identity appears at first glance to threaten and close down the possibility that this discourse and practice will allow those who have suffered the crippling effects of colonization and domination to gain or regain a hearing. Even if this sense of threat and the fear it evokes are based on a misunderstanding of the postmodernist political project, they nevertheless shape responses. It never surprises me when black folks respond to the critique of essentialism, especially when it denies the validity of identity politics by saying, 'Yeah, it's easy to give up identity, when you got one.' Should we not be suspicious of postmodern critiques of the 'subject' when they surface at a historical moment when many subjugated people feel themselves coming to voice for the first time.
>
> (bell hooks, 'Postmodern Blackness')[49]

The poststructuralist vision of subjectivity has been the focus of much scholarly and activist resistance. Clearly, for some, more is at stake than a merely 'abstract', epistemological critique of the empiricist category of experience in debates surrounding 'the uses and limits of poststructuralist theory', as Scott put it. To understand the problem this raises for traditional identity politics, we need first to understand that the question of how we treat representations of (the 'truth' of) experience is dependent upon how we view human subjectivity. If we see that as discursively produced, and thus subject to change in an ongoing process – 'the Self' thus becoming no longer singular, unitary and essentialized but 'fragmented/ dispersed' and multiple – it becomes more difficult to speak in the ways scholars habitually do of 'the' (womanly, or homosexual, or black) identity of the individual social or historical subject. In turn, if the subjectivity of the historical subject is not envisioned as centred or fixed but 'dispersed' and in flux, then what is also ruled out is the possibility of our treating her/his life as if it were a story emplotted from beginning to end in some particular mode or structured teleologically around an intrinsic meaning.

However, the widespread political suspicion that greeted the critique of essentialized identities (built upon personal experience) is understandable, given the fact that much has been achieved by various social movements under the banner of identity politics. The black civil rights movement in North America was built upon pride in being black, just as Indigenous movements and the women's and gay liberation movements in various places exploded into action galvanized partly by pride in an identity as Indigenous, women or gay. 'Black', 'Indian', 'Aboriginal', 'woman' and 'gay' (or 'queer') had been 'dirty words' before their appropriation and re-valorization by such movements.

For many feminists then it seemed ironic that just when a hard battle was being fought and some concessions won, suddenly the category of 'woman' was no longer in vogue. This was not just at the governmental level (to cite the example of Australia), where politicians began to speak of 'family' rather than 'women's' issues (and reduce or dispense with funding to 'women's' bureaus or groups accordingly), but even among feminists. On the one hand, there was the challenge mounted in postcolonial feminism to the universalism of the Second Wave usage of the term, 'Woman', as well as the critique in some poststructuralist feminism of the narrow biologism and heteronormativity upon which binarisms of female/male and woman/man were being based, even in feminism. On the other hand, there was also the fact that since the 1980s 'gender studies' has tended to displace 'women's studies' (more markedly, perhaps, in the United Kingdom, Canada and Australia than in the United States)[50] with university departments, centres or programmes of women's studies being renamed accordingly. To some it seemed that 'woman/women' were becoming invisible once again. In 2001, in a comparative study of interdisciplinary feminist studies degrees and programmes, sociologist Elizabeth Bird (University of Bristol) cited one of her respondents, an unnamed pioneer of women's studies in the United States, who had observed of the trend toward 'gender' studies: 'What worries me as an old feminist is that it may represent the old problem, the problem we had from day one, that nobody likes the word woman.'[51]

The problem for many 'old feminists' (and, from what I have seen in feminism classes, some young ones, too) is, what would a 'feminism' be that dismissed the possibility of solidarity among 'women' on the grounds of their many differences? Are political projects by and *for* 'women' necessarily suspect on the grounds of essentialism – the marginalisation of the 'Other' woman or biologist notions of sexual difference – because they cannot represent all women or can only represent those deemed socially to be 'real' women 'biologically'? An often-heard opinion of the critique of the conventional sex/gender distinction mounted by Judith Butler and Queer Theory and the emphasis on gender as performative is that it is more liberatory, but the question is: For whom? For intersex and transgender people, no doubt, but how about women: say, lesbians in queer groups or movements? How would they counter sexism if/when it occurs (as in the days of Gay Liberation that was deserted in many places by lesbian-feminists who felt they would find a more congenial home in Women's Liberation) if they cannot speak of their experience/oppression and needs as *women*?

In fact, the problem would not be insurmountable since even within queer theoretical terms a critique of being *treated* as conventional sexism does 'women' is possible. Nevertheless, even if it is likely that 'moving beyond the male/female binary will free us from unnecessary gender discrimination currently present in many aspects of social life', as American queer-feminist scholar Kathy Rudy has claimed, she agrees with others of like mind that there are still androcentric and phallocratic tendencies in queer communities. Suzanna Walters, Shane Phelan, Biddy Martin and Pat Califia are those she mentions, who she says have taken up a queer 'identity' (*sic*). Queer must be feminist, too, she insists, or else queer theory/studies will simply end up as 'another fight among boys'.[52] She herself suggests that she has not left her 'woman-identified-woman' identity behind her, nor indeed her commitment to traditional identity politics, but clearly she positions herself in terms that are multiple: queer, woman and feminist.

Similar doubts about the political effects on black identity of poststructuralist critiques of essentialized identity have been voiced by the well-known African-American feminist and cultural critic, bell hooks. In *Yearning: Race, Gender and Cultural Politics*, in the essay quoted above entitled 'Postmodern Blackness', she warned that:

The postmodern critique of 'identity', though relevant for renewed black liberation struggle, is often posed in ways that are problematic. Given a pervasive politic of white supremacy which seeks to prevent the formation of radical black subjectivity, we cannot cavalierly dismiss a concern with identity politics. Any critic exploring the radical potential of postmodernism as it relates to racial difference and racial domination would need to consider the implications of a critique of identity for oppressed groups.[53]

This includes the historian as critic. For example, we need to ensure that, in taking heed of the postmodern critique of identity and altering the ways we speak about it and experience, we do not help to undermine the (ongoing) 'formation of a radical black subjectivity', or a woman's/feminist or 'subaltern'/underclass subjectivity. After all, no one could deny the benefits for marginalized groups of the social history research since the 1970s, even if most of it has accepted empiricist-humanist notions of identity. As the authors of *Telling The Truth About History* observe, in the United States, for example, this:

> has lifted from obscurity the lives of those who had been swept to the sidelines in the metahistory of progress. It has also pierced the veil of those hidden systems which regulated the flow of opportunities and rewards in the United States, demonstrating how their functioning influenced the personal outcomes of success and failure. Those disinherited from the American heritage had at last found advocates at the bar of historical justice.[54]

Arguably, another 'truth' of (social) history is that it has helped the 'oppressed groups' mentioned by hooks to sustain or develop further a pride in their collective identities and determination to resist.

How, then, can postmodernist histories do better, that is if they also seek to step up to 'the bar of historical justice'? If we look to cultural critics such as bell hooks for inspiration, we should note that she does not adhere to conventional notions of identity; in fact, she sees it as 'crucial' that essentialist identity politics be revised so that identity is seen as 'a stage in a process wherein one constructs radical black identity'. She has no quarrel with postmodernist critiques of 'static notions of black identity' because 'they urge transformation of our sense of who we can be and still be black'; indeed, she observes that an acceptance of such critiques does not rule out the possibility of retaining a commitment either to black identity or to black liberation struggle.[55] One can 'be' black (and/or a woman or queer) if one affirms 'the connection between identity and politics' by utilizing the concept of 'positionality', she concludes.

On positionality, hooks cites Linda Alcoff on the 'identity crisis' in feminism concerning how identity politics and positionality can be combined to 'conceive of the subject as nonessentialized and emergent from a historical experience'.[56] Put simply, positionality refers to how we may be positioned by the world as black and/or other objects (woman, queer, etc.), that is, objectified as such in discriminatory representations (and it won't get us anywhere to forget that!), but we lay claim to a radical subjectivity when we also position ourselves, as we resist, as we take up and act upon political subject positions. These do not, however, remain fixed or unchanging, but rather are shifting, perhaps politically strategic and temporary. They are also multiple – as in the case of, say, a now gay or transsexual man who once identified himself as heterosexual; or a black queer woman activist who takes up and acts upon her subject positions as pressing social issues emerge, continually reproducing herself discursively and through political action. In certain contexts or amidst action on particular issues, this may involve the strategic use of an essentialist identity. The same applies to the historical subjects we study who may essentialize their identities for strategic political purposes, whether fully consciously or not.

For hooks, then, although the postmodernist critique of essentialist identity has its political dangers, it need not occasion a 'crisis' in black identity; it can rather serve to reinvigorate the liberation struggle. As she expresses it, 'for African-Americans concerned with reformulating outmoded notions of identity', it can be useful to the extent that it allows more space for contesting 'constricting notion[s] of blackness' that are imposed from both the outside and from within.[57] A view of subject-*positions* as decentred and fluid would hinge upon an individual's or group's internal 'multiplicity' over time and even at one point in time. In other words, its focus would be upon 'difference', not stereotypical notions of blackness, in two senses: with regard to how black experience and black subjectivity is internally differentiated, and also with regard to how the conventionally binaristic 'politics of difference' or 'Otherness' is inseparable from 'the politics of racism'.[58]

My reference above to 'strategic essentialism' is suggestive of Gayatri Spivak's discussion of its use by historians, specifically the Subaltern Studies group. In her influential essay 'Subaltern Studies: Deconstructing Historiography' (1985), Spivak observed that the group's pairing of an anti-humanist critique with the Marxian term 'consciousness' was confusing. Though the group did not 'wittingly engage with the poststructuralist understanding of "consciousness"', she recommended a reading of their works that would 'see them as *strategically* adhering to the essentialist notion of consciousness' because it would naturally 'fall prey to an anti-humanist critique'.[59] Or, we might say, it would naturally fall prey to a self-reflexive contradiction or paradox. For example, one thing that offset the Subaltern historians' appearance of positing the 'definitive accessibility of subaltern consciousness' (or any totalistic representation of 'it') was the way in which they situated it 'in the place of a difference rather than an identity'.[60] This opened the door to 'deconstructive gestures' on the part of the group, for example the recognition that any reconstruction ('retrieval') of subaltern consciousness could represent no more than a subaltern subject-*effect*. That which appears to operate as a 'subject', she explained:

> may be part of an immense discontinuous network . . . of strands that may be termed politics, ideology, economics, history, sexuality, language, and so on . . . . Different knottings and configurations of these strands, determined by heterogeneous determinations which are themselves dependent upon myriad circumstances, produce the effect of an operating subject.[61]

Spivak saw the way in which these historians departed from the empiricist (or 'positivist') assumption that we can access and 'know' subaltern consciousness as founded on an acceptance of 'it' as fluid and internally differentiated (though even this sort of language suggests that 'it' is some '*thing* to be disclosed', a thing that exists prior to its conceptualization as a structured whole). She points out, furthermore, that a 'continuist and homogenist deliberative consciousness symptomatically requires a continuous and homogeneous cause for this effect and thus posits a sovereign and determining subject.'

Put simply, the lesson for historians in this example is that, unless it is for temporary, strategic and self-reflexive purposes, we should not be speaking of 'the' self-consciousness of the subaltern, or their identity or will in singular holistic terms. (In this case, we should desist from conceptualizing insurgency as the result of the single cause of a single collective 'will' rather than as different responses to different 'crises'.) Nor should we be utilizing categories or concepts suggestive of the bourgeois-humanist myth of the independent, self-creating individualistic subject: the subaltern (or anyone else) as 'the' subject or maker or motor of history. If the Subaltern group appeared to do that, it was a 'strategic use of positivistic essentialism in a scrupulously visible political interest', Spivak concludes – one that was in line with the 'critical force' of the anti-humanism of Marx as well as Nietzsche, Foucault, Barthes and Derrida, and therefore self-reflexive about its essentialist moments.

Still, to return to my initial point, it is understandable that critiques of the essentialized 'sovereign' subject of humanism would come to be treated with suspicion on political grounds. As bell hooks noted in the passage that headed this section: 'Should we not be suspicious of postmodern critiques of the "subject" when they surface at a historical moment when many subjugated people feel themselves coming to voice for the first time?' In her wariness of the effects of this on identity politics in liberation movements, she was expressing similar concerns to those voiced by the historians and other scholars discussed in the next section. Unlike Spivak who challenged the notion that 'the' subaltern can 'speak' (in an authentically 'original' voice) and argued that the Subaltern group's subaltern 'subject of history' was merely a subject-*effect*, in their view one of the central failings of poststructuralism is that it allows insufficient space for human action and agency.

VI

A *self* does not amount to much, but no self is an island; each exists in a fabric of relations that is now more complex and mobile than ever before. Young or old, man or woman, rich or poor, a person is always located at 'nodal points' of specific communication circuits, however tiny these may be. Or better: one is always located at a post through which various kinds of messages pass. No one, not even the least privileged among us, is ever entirely powerless over the messages that traverse and position him at the post of sender, addressee, or referent. One's mobility in relation to these language game effects (language games, of course, are what this is all about) is tolerable, at least within certain limits (and the limits are vague); it is even solicited by regulatory mechanisms, and in

> particular by the self-adjustments the system undertakes in order
> to improve its performance. It may even be said that the system
> can and must encourage such movement to the extent that it
> combats its own entropy; the novelty of an unexpected 'move', with
> its correlative displacement of a partner or group of partners, can
> supply the system with that increased performativity it forever
> demands and consumes. (author's emphasis)
>
> (Jean-François Lyotard, *The Postmodern Condition*)[62]

Lyotard goes on to saythat he is not claiming that this is true of the
'*entirety* of social relations'. It seems nevertheless to be a rather
mechanistic picture of our determination by social 'systems', even
if we are not 'entirely powerless over the messages that traverse
and position us' and we do have 'tolerable' mobility. This passage
may help explain why 'practice theory' has had an impact on some
historians – specifically, those who are concerned that linguistic
turn historiography cannot account sufficiently for human practice
or agency. In the 2005 work edited and introduced by American
historian Gabrielle Spiegel, *Practicing History: New Directions in Historical
Writing after the Linguistic Turn*, she describes 'practice theory' as the
modification by a number of 'loosely grouped' historians of 'the
semiotic model of culture that informed "linguistic turn" historical
writing'.[63] The fact that this revisionist trend among historians does
not necessarily imply an outright rejection of central poststructuralist
principles is illustrated by Spiegel's inclusion of essays by defenders
of the linguistic turn (including Scott on experience).

Spiegel reminds us that this model hinged on the belief that the
world and what we know of it have a 'fundamentally linguistic
character': practitioners of linguistic turn scholarship all work
from the premise that language is prior to the world it shapes, our
experience of 'reality' being a social construct or effect of the
linguistic systems we are raised and cannot do other than work
within.[64] She also reminds us that for historians engaged in the
debate that arose in response to the 'semiotic challenge', what were
at stake were concepts central to traditional historiographical
practice – not only empiricist history's 'notions of evidence, "truth",
and objectivity' but also 'causality, change, authorial intent, stability
of meaning, human agency, and social determination'. (Note that
I have covered all but one so far, 'agency', so it would seem that
we are in agreement. I would, however, note the omission of the
essentialized Self, or identity more broadly.)

Spiegel implies that in 'practice theory' it is particularly problems connected with the last two concepts that have inspired revisionism in historians: human agency and social determination. For, critics of the challenge posed by a succession of structuralists, Geertzian semioticians (e.g. 'ethnographic' and other cultural historians), post-structuralists and deconstructionists have exhibited 'a growing sense of dissatisfaction with its overly systematic account of the operation of language in the domain of human endeavours of all kinds'.[65] As I have indicated, the model is seen to be *too narrow in its 'structural' (linguistic) determinism*. In the following passage Spiegel illustrates this point:

> [T]he semiotic challenge . . . is currently undergoing a process of alteration, at least with respect to the ways in which those who accept its basic premise of the social/linguistic construction of the world construe its relevance to, and operation in, the past understood both as an object of study and a subject of practice. We need, then to examine the current status of the debate over the 'linguistic turn' by looking at a range of historians who seek to integrate some of its most important principles and yet to refashion them in a way more congenial to historians' traditional concerns with the role of historical actors in shaping the worlds they inherit, inhabit, and inform.

Indeed, a model that could not account for human agency would be more deterministic than the 'metahistory' of Marxism. It should be acknowledged, however, this has often been criticized for a narrow materialist (economic) determinism that is not suggested by Marx's own 'dialectical' emphasis on people as both the creatures and creators of the worlds they inhabit. As I noted in Chapter 3, there has been a longstanding tendency among its critics, whether they be liberals (i.e. conservatives) or postmodernists, to reduce the whole of Marxist scholarship to its crude ('base determines super-structure' model) orthodox varieties.

British labour historian, Gareth Stedman Jones, seems to be a trifle reductionist in this regard in an essay in *Practicing History*. Here he characterizes Marxism in its entirety as adhering to the 'determination of thought by social being' (when a dialectical approach would have the determination going both ways); and explains the new interest in the linguistic turn from the late 1970s as deriving from its transcendence of the then common perception of language as a mere 'reflection of reality'.[66] Stedman Jones notes that the new approach seemed to offer social historians:

> new ways of connecting social and intellectual history free from the problems embodied in the Marxian notion of ideology, whose effect was always [*sic*] to turn thought into a derivative second order entity, the product of a set of practices belonging to a 'superstructure' whose meaning was ultimately to be deciphered by reference to the ('material' or 'economic') 'base'.

This is not the place to resurrect old debates about Marxism, though one should at least acknowledge that the more sophisticated streams of Marxism ('Hegelian'/'Western' or even 'structuralist/Althusserian') have not, or in the latter case, not consistently, been advocates of this sort of narrow materialist determinism.[67]

What is of particular interest in this essay by Stedman Jones entitled 'The Deterministic Fix' is his suggestion that old habits on the part of formerly Marxist or Marxist-influenced social historians have been holding back the development of linguistic turn historiography. It would seem that 'the undead residue of historical materialism' that Stedman Jones finds in many works that go by the name of the new discursive/linguistic history is the product of 'Foucauldian baggage' that is no less deterministic than Marxism, and indeed was influenced by it. (Strangely, he refers particularly to structuralist Althusserian Marxism in this regard, in which thought/language was part of material reality not a mere reflection of it; but to continue . . . .) Foucault's theory, he argues, was 'built upon a crude functionalist [i.e. Marxist-like] notion of social control' in which discursive positions are linked 'unilaterally to relations of power' and individuals are treated as mere 'assignees of subject positions within discursive practices' without a recognition of how these practices change due to the 'changing utterances and activities of these same individuals'.[68] In short, Stedman Jones criticizes Foucault (and his influence on practitioners of linguistic turn historiography) for replacing the Marxist emphasis on modes and relations of production with an equally materialist 'relations of *power*' approach that, in its social (structural/ist) determinism, could still not account adequately for human agency.

British sociologist Anthony Giddens, in another essay included in *Practicing History*, expresses the same problem when he notes that in functionalism and structuralism – whether the determination be by socio-economic structures (in Marxism), that is, or structures of power or linguistic/discursive 'systems' (*a la* Lyotard) – structure has 'primacy over action, and the constraining qualities of structure are strongly accentuated'.[69] One is reminded of how in feminist scholarship since the 1980s there has been a widely generalized reaction against so-called 'victim feminism'. Thus, in feminist history, too, (as in postcolonial or, more broadly, social history) 'agency' became a 'buzz-word', a way of suggesting that too much emphasis on women's 'oppression' through the systemic/ structural constraints found in 'patriarchy' rendered invisible the myriad ways in which women have always managed to circumvent or resist patriarchal constraints. It was often insisted also that women, too, are agents of, or 'make history'. On the other hand, as Mary Spongberg points out, women's historians began to refute the 'ahistoricity' found particularly in radical feminist theory[70] – for example, in its tendency to speak of the system/structure of 'patriarchy' in universalist terms (at least once the golden days of pre-historical or ancient 'matriarchies' had gone), as if it had always and everywhere existed, or there had only ever been one single form of it.

I might note in passing that Spiegel sees social historians as comparatively insignificant in the shift from the late 1970s to linguistic turn historiography (that involved a semiotic approach focussed upon 'textuality' inspired by the influence upon intellectual and then cultural historians of 'French' and literary theory as well as Geertzian anthropology).[71] After that time, however, social historians have had 'a highly visible role' in historiographical debates, as historians turn away from 'the literary phase in the reception of French theory' back to an interest in social and sociological theory. (Hence, her inclusion in her book of essays both by Giddens and the scholar whose theory of practice he drew upon: radical French sociologist, Pierre Bourdieu). What this suggests to Spiegel is that:

> the deepest challenge posed by the 'linguistic turn' was to the practice of social history and discloses the extent to which the rise of cultural history . . . was governed by discontents arising from the then dominant practice of social history, Marxist and non-Marxist alike.

In light of these developments, it is perhaps to be expected that the current movement away from structuralist and post-structuralist readings of history and historiography is similarly governed by the needs and goals of social history, albeit of a kind quite different from that which preceded the 'linguistic turn'.

If social historians were slow to take up a linguistic/discursive approach, as Spiegel says, and then their reception of linguistic turn historiography was 'incomplete', as Stedman Jones argues, it does suggest that it was more problematic for them than for other historians. For example, intellectual historians traditionally concerned with the 'history of ideas' could gravitate more easily to a focus on language/discourse. This explains Spiegel's suggestion that although revisionist social history today might still involve an 'appropriation' of a linguistic model, it more often represents a more conscious 'retreat from positions staked out during the high tide of "linguistic turn" historiography'.

As to why this might be the case, of course a central concern of social historians has always been to rectify the exclusions of conventional history: to write woman, the subaltern, people 'of colour', all of those seen in traditional political or intellectual history to be insignificant, into the pages of history. Also, as Spongberg observes:

> Social history as it emerged in the post-war period focused upon people's collective control over their experience, with class-consciousness and working-class culture being the ultimate expression of human agency. Central to this new understanding of history was the sense that oppressed groups 'made' themselves, that they evolved out of their own distinctive culture.[72]

She follows with a reference to E. P. Thompson's often-cited quip (explaining his title of *The Making of the English Working Class*) that the working class was 'present at its own making'. However, just when social history had really begun to make its influence felt, the linguistic turn came along apparently threatening to turn the clock back to the days when ordinary people played no part in the grand narratives of nation-building, and the 'ignorant masses' in particular were unable to rise above their social conditioning (if peasants, for example, unable to see beyond parochialism to develop a real class consciousness in order to effect significant social change, e.g. revolution). Spivak's dismissal of subalterns as the 'subjects of history' could conceivably be read in that way, though to do so would overlook her rejection of the bourgeois-humanist myth of pure self-determination for anyone as well as her acceptance of the importance of subaltern or women's action and resistance.

We again find the claim that 'what tends to get lost in the language of structure is the efficacy of human action – or "agency"' in another essay in *Practicing History*, this time by American Professor of History and Political Science, William Sewell. He claims in his 'A Theory of Structure: Duality, Agency and Transformation' that:

> Structures tend to appear in social scientific discourse as impervious to human agency, to exist apart from, but nevertheless to determine the essential shape of, the strivings and motivated transactions that constitute the experienced surface of social life. A social science trapped in an unexamined metaphor of structure tends to reduce actors to cleverly programmed automatons.[73]

If linguistic turn historiography is indeed informed by such a metaphor, it is difficult to see how it could account either for human agency or historical change. As Marx put it (or as my memory of Marx has it), humans make history but in circumstances not of their own choosing.

However, the question that presents itself is whether a consistent linguistic approach to history *need* be overly deterministic. Does such an approach necessarily reduce people to 'automatons' trapped in this case in pre-existing systems of language or discourse? Literary critic and theorist of history, Elizabeth Deeds Ermarth, insists in her essay on 'Agency in the Discursive Condition' that in this era of postmodernity, 'personal agency takes on new and different kinds of importance' because it 'provides for an assertion of personal uniqueness that is far more complex and creative than what Cartesian philosophy once asserted'.[74] This is a personal uniqueness that I construct rather than receive (from God, for example) on a changing day-to-day basis, drawing in my own way upon the multiple potentials I share with those around me. Postmodern subjectivity, she explains, is 'individual in its sequence, not in some irreducible core' (as the centred Self of Christianity or modernist humanism would have it): it is not essentialized and static, but rather like 'a moving nexus or intersection'. Its 'uniqueness lies in its trajectory' which cannot be anticipated because within this trajectory 'an unpredictable series of specifications are made from among the available languages'.

The term she coins for this new, postmodern subjectivity is 'anthematic' meaning a very complex pattern – an interlaced design 'where themes or patterns arrive and depart from various posting places, recurring and recrossing without exact repetition, and yet providing a kind of open system of rythmic iteration and patterning.' Her metaphor is reminiscent of Spivak on p. 184 on the 'subaltern subject-effect' or Lyotard on our being located at 'posts' or 'nodal points' of communication networks on pp. 185–6. However, one does not receive from Ermarth the impression that in the 'postmodern condition' agency is beyond the reach of linguistically determined 'automatons' even if, as she argues, 'the problem of agency has to be re-thought from the ground up, beginning with functional recognition that practice takes place in the discursive condition'. Indeed, one wonders how such a 'rethinking' could be otherwise – unless, that is, thought is prior or external to discourse. But, how can we think or conceptualize anything, if not through learned language/concepts?

In answer to the question of what a history would be that had left traditional history's founding, modernist (rationalist, free willed and unitary/essentialist) subject behind, Ermarth again returns us to the theme of 'difference' when she observes that:

> Where the political agendas of modernity reduced, even sublimated or denied differences in order to produce a putatively common world, the political agendas of post-modernity treat difference as constitutive and irreducible. That shift of emphasis forecloses on all the endless wars for possession of Truth. It constrains all activity to the play of systems wherein all definition is differential and internal to a [linguistic/discursive] system, and thus no basis for truth claims.[75]

She recognizes that postmodernism – for example, this sort of 'relativizing' of truth or the critique of how modernist essentialism has to date informed identity politics – raises difficulties for the '*modern* [my emphasis] political problem of collective action'. (Such difficulties have often been emphasized by those who denounce postmodernity from a modernist standpoint, as she says, though arguably this is not the case with an ambivalent critic such as bell hooks.) Yet Ermarth also insists that a linguistic approach hardly rules out attention to collective action: we cannot do other than 'act under collective obligation because the bases of all practice are the discursive systems or "languages", including the language we call "History".' The individual's negotiation of available languages might be 'original, or conventional, or a bit of both'; the only thing it cannot be is divorced from 'collective enterprise'.

If, then, we were to seek to reinvent our historiographical practice in the postmodern terms recommended by Ermarth we would have to rethink historical subjectivity, practice and agency in a number of ways:

1   rejecting the conventional binarism between language (or discourse or theory) and action or practice, since practice is linguistic or discursive;
2   recognizing the 'anthematic', fluid complexity of individual subjectivity; and
3   departing from the modernist individualistic myth where personal uniqueness (originality and greatness) hinged upon detachment from the world or the transcendence of it.

I might be inclined to quarrel with Ermarth's emphasis on 'personal uniqueness' or her suggestion that the individual's negotiation of available discourses can be 'original'. Perhaps it is just a case of the limitations of language (we need to find better words that are not suggestive of the humanist myth of the independent, self-made individual). Instead of 'originality', perhaps it is an unusually *creative* form of intertextuality that is indicated. However, I accept her general point about the individual's being subject to a collective, discursive immersion in the world but also able to engage with it in a creative manner (the degree of creativity varying considerably).

Finally, to return to Ermarth's point concerning difference, this must be seen as 'constitutive' of the subject, a reference to what Scott calls 'processes of differentiation': how constructs of difference form us in the sense of our both being subject to them and renegotiating them. Difference for both is also '*irreducible*'. This I take to mean that our object should no longer be to try to 'iron out' difference through, say, a liberal-humanist strategy of inclusion. As I noted in Chapter 3, the differentiation Joan Scott refers to (in 'After History?')

in connection with the essentialized identity of individuals, groups or nations is one of two aspects of processes of discursive production, the other being homogenization.[76]

In the poststructuralist style of history posited by Ermarth and Scott difference and identity, moreover, should no longer rest on the empiricist pillar of one's own 'experience' and consequent 'truths'. For, this represents a claim to realism or a 'reality effect' that rests upon the binaristic separation of a 'real', 'material' world of experience from the world of language, discourse or representation (for example, of identities) that followed it, was determined by it and thus was somehow exterior to it.

For Scott, as we have seen, experience is not prediscursive. It is rather:

> a linguistic event (it doesn't happen outside established meanings), but neither is it confined to a fixed order of meaning. Since discourse is by definition shared, experience is collective as well as individual. Experience can confirm what is already known (we see what we have learned to see) and upset what has been taken for granted (when different meanings are in conflict we readjust our vision to take account of the conflict or to resolve it – that is what is meant by 'learning from experience', though not everyone learns the same lesson or learns it at the same time or in the same way). Experience is a subject's history. Language is the site of history's enactment. Historical explanation cannot, therefore, separate the two.[77]

In formulations such as these, a discursive approach to subjectivity does not rule out a recognition of human agency. Scott explicitly denies that it does just as she denies that it represents 'a new form of linguistic determinism'. To say that experience cannot be divorced from discourse is not to overlook 'conflicts among discursive systems, contradictions within any one of them, multiple meanings possible for the concepts they deploy'. To say that subjects have agency in the manner that Scott does, moreover, is not to reintroduce the self-creating subject of humanism or 'subject of history'. The danger of this is arguably greater among the so-called 'materialist' critics of poststructuralism who – in their justifiable desire to prove that the underclasses are no more 'automatons' than anyone else – could be seen to be returning, paradoxically, to the bourgeois-individualist paradigm of the self-willed, 'self-made man' even when their focus is more on collective than individual action. Interestingly, one hears an echo of that great 'materialist', Marx, on humans making history but in circumstances not of their own choosing in (the 'impeccably consistent' poststructuralist) Scott's remark that people are 'subjects whose agency is created through situations and statuses conferred upon them'; the conditions they find themselves in do 'enable choices, although they are not unlimited'. Does this make Scott as 'deterministic' as Marx, one might ask, or does it just make both (and Spivak and Lyotard, too) cognizant of the fact that 'no [hu]man is an island'?

A final 'footnote' concerns how we continually confront in discourse a theoretical detachment from each other of things that can have no independent existence. This may be 'just for the purpose of analysis', but arguably the analysis will be skewed while linguistic categories such as practice/experience and discourse (or 'material reality' and language/discourse) are treated as separate and opposed to each other. The way in which critiques of post-structuralism's linguistic approach have often been expressed is that this focus upon discourse/representation (as if the whole world were 'a text') rules out or diverts our attention from 'real', 'material' processes, past and present, and problems or the 'realities' faced by people in their everyday lives. I mentioned the examples in Chapter 3 of Catharine MacKinnon, for whom postmodernism represents 'discourse unto death' or the danger of it for feminism ('theory begets no practice, only more text'); and Chris Weedon, who observed that postmodernism's emphasis on difference has led to a tendency to celebrate it without taking account of the 'material social relations of inequality'. There may be a certain justice in both critiques, yet it is hard to see how political practice can be anything other than theorized or discursive from the outset (rather than MacKinnon's ideal of theory arising out of practice); and we might also wonder at Weedon's reference to social relations (of inequality or anything else) as 'material'. Perhaps the latter was a slip of the tongue, since Weedon would doubtless accept that social relations are discursive – and discourse, 'material'.

As a practical example of the inseparability of relations of in-equality from discourse, we could consider the workings of (liberal-individualistic) capitalism. Its 'material' abuses are frequently defended in terms of the needs of the owners (of the 'means of production', to use a Marxist phrase), which, in turn, are represented as synonymous with those of 'the nation'. The rights of capitalists to individual profit take precedence over other 'material' considerations such as workers' safety and quality of life or over the needs of the environment. Through individual workplace agreements (very topical in Australia in 2006, for example) traditional union memberships and protections are being whittled away, while the rights of employers alone to set the terms of employment with only minimal government intervention are being shored up, once again in traditional style, by the language of economic individualism. To make such observations, however, is not to take a new 'idealist' as opposed to 'materialist' position – linguistic versus economic determinism – but rather to try to transcend this binarism by asking whether material practices are separable from discourse. The real world (of oppression or social inequality) does not precede language in the sense that ideological justifications of material practices always tag along after the event. But, nor do material practices necessarily originate in ideology in the narrow sense of, say, the starting point of an introduction of individual workplace agreements being only economic individualism and not also the material interests it is tied to. It may sound idealist when one makes the general point that individuals are raised, learn to think and also act within linguistic/discursive or semiotic/symbolic systems, but the process is more complex. One could again use the Marxist term, 'dialectical', to suggest that causation or determination goes both ways or, to put it another way, ideology/discourse and practice are intricately intertwined as part of 'material reality' or everyday life.

VII

Such critiques from social or other historians about 'the limits of poststructuralism for history' may seem partly justified. Perhaps these critics have in mind particular works of linguistic turn historiography that do feature a central concern with language: for example, a concern with the 'poetics' of, or rhetorical gestures in, some particular texts: their 'emplotments, slippages or play of meaning, metaphorical displacements, logic paradoxes', and so on and so forth. I doubt, however, that either a poststructuralist history approach centred, say, on 'processes of differentiation' and subject positions as discursively produced of the type outlined by Scott or Ermarth, or even the above sort of history focussed on rhetoric and figuration can justifiably be taken as representative of poststructuralism's supposed belief that *the world* is 'a text'. This is an idea often attributed by critics to Derrida's (in)famous remark in *Of Grammatology* that there is 'no outside-text' or 'nothing outside the text', meaning simply that a text cannot be collapsed into a purported referent or ('material') reality outside the text.[78] Language is 'self-referential'; texts refer to a multitude of other 'texts'. A history text, for example, may give the impression that it is a merely objective description, reflection, or reconstruction of reality (the 'reality effect' of empiricist history wherein there appears to be no mediation between the two). Yet history texts are as intertextual as any others, or dependent upon other 'texts' for their interpretations, reinterpretations and revisions: primary sources and other histories, history and other theory, political ideologies, narratives of various descriptions, conventional emplotments. (The list is potentially end-less.) However, as I have noted, this is not the same thing as claiming nihilistically that the world is a text and that there is no reality out there to try to capture in a text.

Another common criticism of poststructuralism is that 'anything goes', due to its suspicion of certainties, truth claims, final words – or, indeed, the omniscient or at least authoritative style of narration or analysis in conventional histories. I addressed this issue in Chapter 2. Derrida, we might note, denied in *Of Grammatology* that any interpretation of a text is possible or permissible; his 'decon-struction' is a very refined form of analysis or method of interpreting texts that demands 'a highly developed self-consciousness and self-reflexivity', as Curthoys and Docker observe.[79] Ideally, decon-structionist or poststructuralist historians, if they are consistent, should be no less rigorous in their scholarship than others – no less inclined, for example, even to bury themselves in libraries or even in the archives, where that is required by their research projects, trying to immerse themselves imaginatively in the worlds of their subjects. Ideally, to the extent that the postmodernist historian can follow his or her own prescriptions for historiographical praxis, s/he should be more rigorous.

To my mind there is no reason why postmodernism and even social history have to be seen as mutually exclusive or antagonistic. Why should an acceptance of subject positions as discursively pro-duced or of experience as a discursive construction rule out sufficient attention to agency? After all, it is subjects' engagement with established discourse, their ability to accept, revise or resist it that is at issue. Arguably, to cite Stedman Jones again (who was criti-cizing Foucault's works but defending linguistic turn historiography),

individuals are not merely assigned subject positions within discursive practices; these practices change partly due to the 'changing
utterances and activities of these same individuals'. The same goes
for the postmodernist critique of essentialist identities, whether of
individuals, groups or nations: this is not necessarily antagonistic
to radical politics, but can rather help to reinvigorate liberation
movements (as many believe it has in the queer movement). By
extension, many new histories of sexuality(s) could be taken to
exemplify the fact that an acceptance of postmodernist subjectivity
need not undermine but rather serve liberation struggles. As for
social history, when practised by those with a poststructuralist turn
of mind this will of course differ markedly from the social history
of the 1960s or 1970s. However, the question is whether the moral-
political motivations of social history's practitioners, past and
present, differ all that much. One would think that the desired effect
of social history still today, however postmodernist it may be, is
that it contribute to giving voice to those who had been silenced in
traditional metahistories of 'progress', narratives of nation-building,
or stories of the great men who 'made history'. This is another way
of saying that marginalized groups, too, were agentic – even if they
were no more the self-determined 'subjects of history' than those
individuals to whom history-making is usually attributed.

Suggestions for further reading

Like with my suggestions related to Chapter 2, I would recommend
that readers go back to the sources, though none of the following
could be said to be easy reading: Barthes (*Roland Barthes by Roland
Barthes*, and 'The Death of the Author'), Foucault ('What is an
Author?'), Scott (on 'experience': original, complete version of the
essay in *Critical Inquiry*, Summer 1991, vol. 17, 773–97), and Judith
Butler. Butler's book, *Undoing Gender*, 2004, seems more accessible
than earlier ones, however. Autobiography (or life-writing) critique
can be 'pretty packed', too, but I believe that it represents a good
point of entry into the poststructuralist discourse on the Self/
subjectivity and the writing of it. Like with all the above, works by
critics such as Paul Jay, Paul Eakin, Sidonie Smith, Derrida and de
Man that I drew upon in this chapter or referred to in references
are listed in the Bibliography. Otherwise, feminist readers I listed
in earlier chapters invariably contain articles on subjectivity (see
the two feminist history ones, in particular). Two further books of

collected essays that are not new but still good, on postmodernism and feminism, are:

- Judith Butler and Joan W. Scott (eds), *Feminists Theorize the Political*, New York and London: Routledge, 1992 (contains one abridged version of Scott's 'experience'); and
- Linda J. Nicholson (ed.), *Feminism/Postmodernism*, New York and London: Routledge, 1990 (Part III is on 'identity and differentiation')

Apart from works by Judith Butler, other works of queer theory and scholarship (some included in references and the bibliography) often contain good discussions of identity issues. Two edited collections are:

- Robert J. Corber and Stephen Valocchi (eds), *Queer Studies: An Interdisciplinary Reader*, Malden, US and Oxford, UK: Blackwell Publishing, 2003
- Katherine O'Donnell and Michael O'Rourke (eds), *Queer Masculinities, 1550–1800: Siting Same-Sex Desire in the Early Modern World*, New York: Palgrave Macmillan, 2005

Chapter 5

Reflections

Rather than attempting to sum up all that has gone before and offer a 'final word' on the subject of sceptical history, I thought I would append a 'conclusion' that reflects upon the problems that plagued me during the writing of the book. This suggests the first question to be confronted. Given that I so often emphasized the need for self-reflexivity in works of history, was I myself reflective enough throughout the book? Before addressing that question, however, let me reiterate how in Chapter 1, though I was loathe to be too definitive about principles of practice, I did nevertheless isolate six commonly mentioned guidelines: briefly, concerning self-reflexivity, leaving arguments open, discontinuities, difference (or, rather, discourses of differentiation), a view of the Self as acentric, multiply positioned and in flux, and sustained (if not only an) attention to historiography.

Concerning self-reflexivity, perhaps my desire to end the book in this way is not only indicative of (as Barthes would say) a dislike of ends, rhetorical closure, the last word; but also of an attempt to rectify a lapse. The book may not be a standard history, but rather a discussion of the postmodern critique of history and 'alternative visions', but it still is, in small part, *a history* of history. To that extent, though I did often incorporate a consideration of practical problems associated with the sceptical history I was advocating, perhaps I could have been more self-reflexive. My desire not to complicate the picture further is not, perhaps, a convincing excuse for not, for example, continually interspersing description and explanation with reflections upon associated problems, quandaries or reflexive paradoxes.

One thing is certain – that it is not easy to dispense entirely with familiar rhetorical modes of writing that stem from the empiricist foundations of the discipline. Even for those who are wary of empiricist history's authoritative voice and the role it plays in creating a reality-, truth- and objectivity-effect, it is hard to dispense with the habit of speaking as if one's way of seeing things is the only possible way of seeing them. Our training encourages us to effect ('affect') closure by suppressing interpretative plurality and epistemological doubt – or to try to iron out history's inherent 'wrinkles', in order to speak with authority. In this connection reference to Katherine Kearns' amusing reading of how critiques of postmodernism have been gendered is again apposite. She pointed out that for some critics postmodern-style scepticism and self-reflexive doubt feel too 'feminine'; hence their preference for the more 'masculine' pose of objectivity and authority, their mask of epistemological certainty with regard to what can be 'known' about the past.

Kearns referred to the gendered nature of critiques of theorized history also in connection with demands for 'manly plain language' (the 'plain language of truth'), as we saw in the early chapters. My own desire to write of theory in terms that are more comprehensible than is often the case was/is not tied to achieving a truth-effect. It is not even specific to this book and its intended readership of both academics and tertiary students and, indeed, anyone else with an interest in the subject. I would like to see more works of theory (and not just postmodern theory) being produced that are more accessible. The more obscure and tortuous it is, the more impressive the work, according to some. This I find somewhat ironic when the writer purports to be politically radical, yet seems to be preaching only to the 'converted' or to those with a substantial education in interdisciplinary theory. My hope is that, in writing the book, I did not lose sight of my desire to sit on the fence, straddling 'high' theory and too reduced a rendition of it by recourse to a 'plainer' style of explanation that nevertheless sought to familiarize readers with commonly used theoretical language.

Other general issues include the question of whether I was too arbitrary in devoting special attention to three areas that I see to have a particular bearing on the practice of 'sceptical' history: teleology/presentism, difference/differentiation, and the Self/positionality. I might be tempted to observe that I am 'allowed' in postmodernism to concentrate simply on issues of personal interest to me. However, the fact is that I have long been interested in other aspects of the postmodern critique that I dealt with perhaps too summarily – for example, the emphasis associated most often with

Hayden White on history as essentially a literary, 'fictive' endeavour that draws upon standard emplotments and other narrative/ rhetorical devices. And there may be other important issues that I appear to have overlooked or dealt with too briefly. My decision concerning what to select for special attention, however, was partly based upon a feeling that there is ample material already available that goes into great detail about this and other aspects of the postmodern critique of conventional history (its purported facticity and objectivity, and so on). What is not so readily available, however, is material that focuses in an extended way on the question of how to practise postmodern history; and in this connection these three aspects of the postmodern critique seemed to me to be important and deserving of particular attention.

Ironically, as it turned out, one of the chapters that I had imagined would be the easiest and quickest to write because of my greater familiarity with the central issues proved to be the one I struggled with the most. This was Chapter 2 where, as I noted, I was trying to resolve the contradiction between critiquing (unconscious) teleology, which is everywhere apparent in constructs of the past, origins and tradition, even in the works of those who deny their present-centredness, and defending (conscious) presentism that is politically motivated, say, with respect to writing frankly positioned feminist or other history. Whatever my emphasis there, for example on historians' needing to be more aware of this 'secondary paradox' that troubles the discipline (the inconsistencies of the first group), perhaps what really underpinned my argument is a political suspicion of only some sorts of presentism.

One obvious example is historians who accept and repeat essentialistic and marginalizing nation narratives and associated nationalistic myths, whether in an unthinking or self-aware manner. Similarly, even where androcentric visions of the past *unwittingly* reflect the androcentrism of the present, I have less tolerance for this sort of presentism than for what Joan Scott referred to as an unconscious projection of our (feminist) selves back onto the subjectivities of women in the past. At least the latter has the virtue of a sense of responsibility toward female historical subjects and to going some way toward redressing the traditional exclusions of a patriarchal discipline. In short, this question returns us to the proposition put forward in that chapter that history cannot be other than presentist, in political and other ways, though that need not encourage us to produce histories that make no attempt to historicize the periods, events and subjects in question. Our commitment to a radical, resistant practice of sceptical history need not result in 'irresponsible' histories that are pure fantasy.

Another tension exhibited in the work was between a focus upon 'difference' and upon 'processes of differentiation'. On the one hand, on political grounds I want to recognize difference and support those who identify themselves as 'irreducibly' Other (often amidst a justifiable critique of humanist universals and norms and pluralist notions of inclusion). Yet, I also understand why poststructuralists would want to take a discourse analysis approach, arguing that attention to processes of differentiation is more to the point, partly because of scepticism about racial, cultural or sexual/ gender essentialism. (Self- or inverse-Orientalism was an example I discussed in this connection.) None the less, the second sort of focus on difference or, rather, differentiation will not necessarily or automatically enable us to avoid the conceptual problems attending the first. It would do so only if we were to be selective about whose essentialism we target. It goes without saying that we would want to target it in conservatives, but 'we' (if we are 'white, Western, middle-class') might not feel comfortable criticizing it in black or Indigenous activists. This recalls the issue raised with respect to South Africa, of whether only self-identified 'black' activists/scholars can 'speak for', or 'know', or represent other black people(s) and do so without homogenizing them. The same sort of debate occurred amidst a Second Wave feminist politics of activism and scholarship by women, about women and for women, concerning men who sought to represent women, 'appropriate' their struggle, and so on. These days the dominant trend in feminism is to doubt that women can speak for other women, though invariably it is only white, Western, middle-class women who are subject to such critiques.

On another front, I might ask myself: did I really square a political sympathy for identity and those who defend identity politics with an epistemologically based preference for 'positionality'? Did I really engage with critiques of poststructuralism for focussing only upon discourse/representation and overlooking 'real, material' situations and oppressions? I recall thinking that there was a bit of 'sleight of hand' going on in Elizabeth Deeds Ermarth's defence of a linguistic approach as necessarily having to involve collective action since language forms the basis of all practice; but chose not to comment upon it. Clearly, those who criticize poststructuralism in such terms worry that an attention just to language or discourse will overlook oppressive practices and institutions and possibly undermine a very specific sort of practice: traditional identity politics or identity-based activism. Whatever its pitfalls, say, the potential for authoritarian pressures to conform to such identities, I myself have been known to ask whether Butler-style critiques of linguistic categories such as 'woman/man', 'homo/heterosexual' are not a trifle dangerous at least in the manner of their (common) reception by some postist feminists or self-identified queers. Can't they be read as just a new style of inner-directed personal politics and individualism, especially when combined with an emphasis on 'difference' that seems to rule out even shared positionalities as bases for action? (To wit: 'I'm so unique in my complex, multiple identities that I have nothing in common with the next person.') It remains to be seen whether 'queer' or 'post- or third wave feminism' will prove to be *as* vigorous and effective as the identity politics of former decades.

As to writing our histories, however, paying attention to how subjects are multiply positioned, their subjectivities not fixed but in flux, should serve to illustrate the necessary complexity of the people in the past with whom we engage in dialogues. In contrast to the reductionist methods of former times, now we are expected to consider both how our historical subjects are treated by the world in terms of complex webs of identity markers and also how they respond to such categories either by embracing or resisting them, not for all time but contextually, strategically. Moreover, a recognition that some particular subject whose life, actions, ideas, subjectivity we are investigating was not only a woman but positioned in terms also of class, race, sexuality, relation to colonialism and more need not render our history un-feminist. Not recognizing such 'intersections', on the other hand, could well be taken to signify a politics of homogenization.

Since I feel like I am slipping into the reiteration and 'last word' mode of conventional conclusions, I might end by going back to the book's beginnings. There I dedicated the book especially to undergraduate students, to those who have encouraged my interest in history theory over the years and to those who are or will shortly embark on higher research in history. My hope is that I can contribute to inculcating in the next generation of historians a commitment to turning the discipline into a more consistent mode of 'higher learning', one that does not shy away from the difficult questions concerning history as a 'Knowledge'. I believe that epistemological scepticism is not a dangerous disease nor indicative of murderous impulses but, rather, a marker of the health of a discipline. History will become 'moribund' only when it ceases to question itself.

Notes

Preliminaries

1 Re empiricism versus postmodernism, Callum Brown explains that:

> For traditional scholars, trained in empiricist philosophy, events happened and can be discovered, recorded, and represented by the expertise of the professional social scientist or historian in a textual narrative. For postmodernists, events happened, processes occurred, reality exists, but none of these can be accurately represented ... Postmodernism denies that it is possible to show reality – only versions of it.
>
> (Callum G. Brown, *Postmodernism for Historians*, Harlow, UK: Pearson Longman, 2005, p. 7)

2 Hilary Lawson, *Reflexivity: The post-modern predicament*, London: Hutchinson, 1985, p. 29.

3 Jean-François Lyotard, *The Postmodern Condition: A Report on Knowledge*, Manchester: Manchester University Press, (1986), 2004 reprint.

4 Alun Munslow, *Deconstructing History*, London and New York: Routledge, 1997, p. 187 (Munslow has since revised the work, in 2006).

5 Ibid.

6 For example: Inga Clendinnen, *Ambivalent Conquests: Maya and Spaniard in Yucatan, 1517–1570*, Cambridge, New York and Melbourne: Cambridge University Press, 1987.

7 To cite the example of the department I am a part of (1997–2007, continuing), in past years the School of History at The University of New South Wales has followed common practice in mounting special courses in history theory and method only at advanced levels (pre-honours and honours, third and fourth year). However, now the School offers a special series of extra lectures on historiography for first-year students and above to try to ensure that students are familiarized with it. Like anywhere, individual practice varies with respect to the extent of its incorporation into individual history courses, and this represents an attempt to supplement those that overlook it.

8 Keith Jenkins, *Re-Thinking History*, London and New York: Routledge, 1991; and *Refiguring History*, Routledge, 2003.

9   But for the first (1997), these are books published in 2004–6 that will be referred to shortly.

10 G. E. Elton, *The Practice of History*, London: Fontana Press, 1967 (first published by Sydney University Press in the same year); E. H. Carr, *What is History?*, Penguin Books (first published by Macmillan, 1961), 1977.

11 Alun Munslow, *The Routledge Companion to Historical Studies*, London and New York: Routledge, 2000, p. 7 (revised 2006).

12 The book edited by Gabrielle M. Spiegel, *Practicing History: New Directions in Historical Writing after the Linguistic Turn* (New York and London: Routledge, 2005) represents a collection of essays on 'practice theory' by historians and other scholars, some defending and some critiquing postmodernism.

13 Lawson, op. cit., p. 93.

14 For example, see Keith Windshuttle's *The Killing of History*, Sydney: Macleay Publications, 1994.

15 On reconstructionist history, see Munslow, *Deconstructing History*, (Chapter 3), pp. 35–56.

16 Editor's introduction in Michael T. Gibbons (ed.), *Interpreting Politics*, Oxford and New York: Basil Blackwell, 1987, p. 3.

17 Keith Jenkins and Alun Munslow (eds), *The Nature of History Reader*, London and New York: Routledge, 2004, Part Four entitled 'Endisms'.

18 Jenkins, *Refiguring History*, pp. 2–3.

19 Like Windshuttle, Geoffrey Elton has been one of the more vituperative defenders of traditional history in *Return to Essentials* (Cambridge: Cambridge University Press, 1991).

20 Ann Curthoys and John Docker, *Is History Fiction?*, Sydney: University of New South Wales Press, 2006.

21 This critique by feminist scholar, Rita Felski, will be discussed in Chapter 1: Felski, 'Fin de Siècle, Fin de Sexe: Transsexuality, Postmodernism and the Death of History ', *Literary Theory*, vol. 27, no. 2, 337–49, reproduced in Jenkins and Munslow (eds), *The Nature of History Reader*, Part Four, 'Endisms', Chapter 39, pp. 270–280.

22 Katherine Kearns, *Psychoanalysis, Historiography, and Feminist Theory: The Search for a Critical Method*, Cambridge and New York: Cambridge University Press, 1997, Chapter Four, especially pp. 121 ff.

23 F. R. Ankersmit, 'Historiography and Postmodernism', in Keith Jenkins (ed.), *The Postmodern History Reader*, London and New York: Routledge, 1997, p. 294.

1 History, postmodern critique and alternative visions

1   Jane Austen, *Northanger Abbey*, Middlesex, England: Penguin Books, 1972 (1976 reprint), p. 123. (The speaker is the heroine, Catherine Morland.) I was reminded of this passage by the title of an essay on historiography that I shall be referring to below.

2   Gabrielle Spiegel, 'History, historicism and the social logic of the text in the Middle Ages', in Keith Jenkins (ed.), *The Postmodern History Reader*, London and New York: Routledge, 1997, p. 181.

3 Alun Munslow, *Deconstructing History*, London and New York: Routledge, 1997, p. 189.
4 Spiegel, op. cit.
5 F. R. Ankersmit, 'Historiography and Postmodernism', in Jenkins (ed.), op. cit., p. 284.
6 Ibid., p. 282.
7 Ibid., p. 284.
8 Munslow, loc. cit., p. 185.
9 Ibid.
10 Ibid., p. 187.
11 Callum G. Brown, *Postmodernism for Historians*, Harlow, UK: Pearson Longman, 2005, Glossary, p. 183.
12 Roland Barthes, 'The Discourse of History', excerpt (Section III: 'Signification') reproduced in Jenkins (ed.), op. cit., p. 121.
13 Ibid., p. 122.
14 Munslow, op. cit., p. 188 (defining 'referentiality').
15 Brown, op. cit., p. 65.
16 Ibid.
17 Barthes, op. cit., p. 121
18 Ibid, pp. 121, 120.
19 Cited in ibid., p. 121.
20 Munslow, op. cit., pp. 6–7.
21 Keith Jenkins and Alun Munslow (eds), *The Nature of History Reader*, London and New York: Routledge, 2004, (Introduction), p. 12.
22 Gertrude Himmelfarb, 'Telling it as you like it: postmodernist history and the flight from fact', in Jenkins (ed.), op. cit. p. 162.
23 Barthes, op. cit., p. 123.
24 Hayden White's major works include *Metahistory: The Historical Imagination in the Nineteenth Century*, Baltimore MD: Johns Hopkins University Press, 1973; *Tropics of Discourse: Essays in Cultural Criticism*, 1978 (same publisher); and *The Content of the Form: Narrative Discourse and Historical Representation*, 1987 (same publisher).
25 Hilary Lawson, *Reflexivity: The Post-Modern Predicament*, London: Hutchinson, 1985, p. 100.
26 Ibid.
27 White, *The Content of the Form*, p. 44.
28 Munslow, op. cit., p. 189.
29 Fredric Jameson, *The Prison-House of Language: A Critical Account of Structuralism and Russian Formalism*, Princeton NJ: Princeton University Press, 1972, p. 145.
30 June Phillipp was not quite so well known, perhaps, as Greg Dening or Inga Clendinnen in the 1980s or since, but her essay, 'Traditional Historical Narrative and Action-Oriented (or Ethnographic) History', is representative of the thinking of the time and ethnographic school of thought in history: *Historical Studies*, April 1983, vol. 2, La Trobe University, Melbourne, pp. 339–52.
31 Dominick LaCapra, *History and Reading: Tocqueville, Foucault, French Studies*, Toronto: University of Toronto Press (Melbourne University Press reprint), 2000, p. 65.
32 Himmelfarb, op. cit., p. 159.

33 Ibid., p. 162.
34 Alun Munslow and Robert A. Rosenstone (eds), *Experiments in Rethinking History*, London and New York: Routledge, 2004.
35 Munslow, 'Introduction: Theory and Practice', in ibid., pp. 7–11.
36 Keith Jenkins, *Refiguring History: New Thoughts on an Old Discipline*, London and New York: Routledge, 2003, p. 6.
37 Lawson, op. cit., p. 9
38 Ibid., p. 93.
39 Ibid., p. 28.
40 Jean-François Lyotard, *The Postmodern Condition: A Report on Knowledge* (Geoff Bennington and Brian Massumi, trans.; foreword by Frederick Jameson), University of Minnesota, 1984, Manchester University Press reprint, 2004.
41 Lawson, op. cit., p. 114.
42 Ibid., pp. 110, 118–19.
43 Jenkins, *Refiguring History*, pp. 2–3.
44 Rita Felski, 'Fin de Siècle, Fin de Sexe: Transsexuality, Postmodernism and the Death of History', *Literary Theory*, vol. 27, no. 2, 337–49, reproduced in Jenkins and Munslow (eds), *The Nature of History Reader*, Part Four, 'Endisms', Chapter 39, pp. 270–80.
45 Felski was discussing poststructuralist feminists at this point (p. 277).
46 Ibid., p. 278.
47 Jenkins, *Refiguring History*, p. 2.
48 Joan Scott, 'After History?', abridged version in Jenkins and Munslow (eds), *The Nature of History Reader*, Part Four: 'Endisms', Chapter 38, p. 261.
49 Katherine Kearns, *Psychoanalysis, Historiography, and Feminist Theory: The Search for Critical Method* (Cambridge: Cambridge University Press, 1997, pp. 31 ff.).
50 Hans Kellner, 'Language and Historical Representation', in Jenkins (ed.), op. cit., p. 137.
51 Kearns, op. cit., p. 166.
52 Ibid.
53 Ibid., pp. 166–7
54 Kellner, op. cit., p. 136.
55 Foucault's 'Nietzsche, Genealogy, History' cited in Scott, p. 264.
56 Scott, ibid.
57 Ibid., p. 263.
58 Ibid., p. 264.
59 Ibid., p. 265.
60 Ibid., p. 266.
61 Ibid., pp. 266–7.
62 I have discussed Barthes' *Empire of Signs* (about Japan) and his critique of autobiography and the centred Self in 'Takuboku's "Poetic Diary" and Barthes' Anti-Autobiography: (Postmodernist?) Fragmented Selves in Fragments of a Life', *Japanese Studies*, 1999, vol. 19, no. 2, 183–99. On Barthes on the 'fragmented/scattered' Self, cf. Paul Jay, *Being in the Text: Self-Representation from Wordsworth to Roland Barthes*, Ithaca and London: Cornell University Press, 1984, pp. 161–83.
63 Jameson, op. cit., p. 130

64 Joan W. Scott, 'Experience', in Judith Butler and Joan Scott (eds), *Feminists Theorize the Political*, New York and London: Routledge, 1992, pp. 22–40.
65 Ibid., p. 24.
66 Ibid., p. 33.
67 Ibid.
68 Examples of two major works are Scott's earlier explication of 'gender' as opposed to women's history, *Gender and the Politics of History*, New York: Columbia University Press, 1988; and her more later work on feminism in France, *Only Paradoxes to Offer: French Feminists and the Rights of Man*, Cambridge, MA and London: Harvard University Press, 1996.
69 Elton was still publishing defences of empiricist, reconstructionist, objectivist history in the 1990s. For example: G. E. Elton, *Return to Essentials*, 1991, Cambridge: Cambridge University Press.
70 Gertrude Himmelfarb, op. cit., p. 169.
71 Kearns, op. cit., p. 165.
72 Ibid., p. 136
73 Ibid., p. 166.

2 Reinventing the wheel: the present-past nexus

1 Gertrude Himmelfarb, *The New History and the Old: Critical Essays and Reappraisals*, Cambridge, Mas. and London: The Belknap Press of Harvard University Press, 1987, p. 16 (essay first published in 1984).
2 Ellen Somekawa and Elizabeth Smith, 'Theorizing the Writing of History or "I Can't Think Why It Should Be So Dull, For A Great Deal Of It Must Be Invention",' *Journal of Social History*, 1988, vol. 22, no. 1, 156.
3 Joan Scott, 'After History?', abridged version in Keith Jenkins and Alun Munslow (eds), *The Nature of History Reader*, London and New York: Routledge, 2004, Part Four: 'Endisms', Chap. 38, p. 267.
4 Keith Jenkins, *Re-thinking History*, London and New York: Routledge, 1991, p. 40.
5 Somekawa and Smith, loc. cit.
6 Ibid., p.155.
7 A 2006 work on historiography (Ann Curthoys and John Docker, *Is History Fiction?*, Sydney: University of New South Wales Press) contains chapters entitled 'Anti-Postmodernism and the Holocaust' and 'History Wars' that address well-known debates over whether postmodernist relativism is unconcerned about facticity (since one interpretation is 'as good' as another) thereby leaving 'the door open [even] to fascist or racist views of history' (p. 211). The first discusses the Holocaust debate to which authors such as Saul Friedländer, Hayden White, Dominick LaCapra and Martin Jay contributed; the second addresses similar debates connected with Japanese, Australian and other history.
8 Somekawa and Smith, op. cit., p. 154
9 Alun Munslow, *Deconstructing History*, London and New York: Routledge, 1997, Chapter 8: 'Hayden White and deconstructionist history', p. 159.

10 Somekawa and Smith, op. cit., p. 158.
11 Acton cited in Curthoys and Docker, op. cit., p. 81.
12 Dominick LaCapra, *History and Reading: Tocqueville, Foucault, French Studies*, Toronto: University of Toronto Press (Melbourne University Press reprint), 2000, p. 60.
13 Somekawa and Smith, op. cit., pp.157–8.
14 Munslow, *Deconstructing History*, p. 160.
15 Jenkins, *Re-thinking History*, p. 17.
16 Cf. note 7 above (on 'history wars' in various places, discussed in Curthoys and Docker, especially Chapter 11, pp. 220–37).
17 Jenkins, *Re-thinking History*, pp. 17–18.
18 On this issue, a classic essay from 1975 by American historian of Japan, John Dower, is still well worth reading. Focussed upon the ultimately tragic career of an early 20th century Canadian historian, E. H. Norman, it discusses the effects on the field of state-sponsored 'modernization theory' that arose in the wake of McCarthyism from about 1960: see the introduction in John Dower (ed.), *Origins of the Modern Japanese State: Selected Writings of E. H. Norman*, New York: Pantheon Books, 1975.
19 From 1979, for example, ongoing debate followed an article by reconstructionist, narrative historian, Lawrence Stone, who believed that 'structural' or 'ethnographic' history (sometimes termed 'semiotic' history or the history of meaning, influenced by anthropology and literary theory) represented a return to traditional narrative: a 'new, old history'. This was hotly contested by various historians, including the 'Melbourne Group/School' of ethnographic history (comprising Greg Dening, Inga Clendinnen, Rhys Isaac, June Philipp, *et al.*). Cf. Lawrence Stone, 'The Revival of Narrative: Reflections on a New Old History', *Past and Present*, 1979 (Nov), vol. 85, 3–24; and June Philipp, 'Traditional Historical Narrative and Action-Oriented (or Ethnographic) History', *Historical Studies* (Australia), 1983 (Apr), vol. 2, 339–52.
20 Alun Munslow and Robert A. Rosenstone (eds), *Experiments in Rethinking History*, London and New York: Routledge, 2004.
21 Herman Ooms, *Tokugawa Ideology: Early Constructs, 1570–1680*, Princeton, NJ: Princeton University Press, 1985, (Chapter One, 'Introduction: Beginnings'), p. 5.
22 Ibid., pp. 5–6.
23 Eric Hobsbawm and Terence Ranger (eds), *The Invention of Tradition*, UK: Cambridge University Press, 1983 (Canto Edition 1992), p. 14.
24 David Cannadine, 'The Context, Performance and Meaning of Ritual: The British Monarchy and the "Invention of Tradition", c. 1820–1977', in ibid., p. 102.
25 Ibid., pp. 107–8.
26 Ibid., pp. 124–5.
27 Ibid., pp. 161–2.
28 Eric Hobsbawm, 'Introduction: Inventing Traditions', in Hobsbawm and Ranger (eds), in ibid., p. 9.
29 Ibid., p. 283.
30 Terence Ranger, 'The Invention of Tradition in Colonial Africa', in ibid., p. 213.

31 Deborah Simonton, *A History of European Women's Work, 1700 to the Present*, London and New York: Routledge, 1998, p. 262.

32 Jeanne Maracek, ' "Am I a Woman in These Matters?" Notes on Sinhala Nationalism and Gender in Sri Lanka', in Tamar Mayer (ed.), *Gender Ironies of Nationalism: Sexing the Nation*, London and New York: Routledge, 2000, p. 141.

33 Ania Loomba, *Colonialism/Postcolonialism*, New York and London: Routledge, 1998 (Section on Spivak from Chapter 3), p. 235.

34 Mina Roces, 'Gender, Nation and the Politics of Dress in Twentieth-Century Philippines', *Gender and History*, 2005 (Aug), vol. 17, no. 2, 1–24.

35 Cited in Cynthia Steele, '"A Woman Fell into the River": Negotiating Female Subjects in Contemporary Mayan Theatre', in Diana Taylor and Juan Villegas (eds), *Negotiating Performance: Gender, Sexuality and Theatricality in Latin/o America*, Durham NC: Duke University Press, 1994, p. 242.

36 Ibid., p. 243.

37 Ibid., p. 254.

38 Geoffrey Elton, *Return to Essentials*, Cambridge: Cambridge University Press, 1991, extract (pp. 6–11) in Jenkins and Munslow (eds), *The Nature of History Reader*, p. 22.

39 Curthoys and Docker, op. cit., pp. 128–9 (the said essay appeared in Michael Oakeshott, *Rationalism in Politics and Other Essays*, 1962, London: Methuen).

40 Oakeshott's words, cited in ibid., p. 129.

41 In Jacques Derrida, *Writing and Difference* (Alan Bass, trans.), London: Routledge, 1990, pp. 278–93.

42 Ibid., pp. 278–9.

43 Callum G. Brown, *Postmodernism for Historians*, Harlow, UK: Pearson Longman, 2005, pp. 76–7.

44 Derrida, op. cit., p. 279.

45 Munslow, *Deconstructing History*, p. 170.

46 For a non-orthodox view of Shinto, see Helen Hardacre's *Shinto and the State, 1868–1988*, 1989, Princeton: Princeton University Press; and 'Creating State Shinto: The Great Promulgation Campaign and the New Religions', *Journal of Japanese Studies*, 1986 (Winter), vol. 12, no. 1, 29–63; and also Kuroda's seminal article on the subject referred to below. Much of the following discussion of Shinto is derived from or partly influenced by their works. A collection whose editors are aware of such critiques of ancient 'Shinto' as anachronism is John Breen and Mark Teeuwen (eds), *Shinto in History: Ways of the Kami*, Surrey: Curzon Press, 2000. The critical quality of essays in the work is somewhat uneven, however.

47 Carol Gluck, *Japan's Modern Myths: Ideology in the Late Meiji Period*, 1985, Princeton: Princeton University Press (Chapter 7: 'End of an Era'), pp. 213–27.

48 Kuroda Toshio, 'Shinto in the History of Japanese Religion', *Journal of Japanese Studies*, 1981, vol. 7, no. 1, 1–21.

49 Ibid.

50 Tonomura Hitomi, *Community and Commerce in Late Medieval Japan: The Corporate Villages of Tokuchin-ho*, Stanford, Calif.: Stanford University Press, 1992.

51 Hobsbawm and Ranger (eds), op. cit., p. 303.
52 Joshua A. Fogel (ed.), *The Teleology of the Modern Nation-State: Japan and China*, Philadelphia, PA: University of Pennsylvania Press, 2005, p. 7.
53 Hobsbawm, op.cit., (Introduction), p. 2.
54 Elton, op. cit., pp. 22–3.
55 Scott, op. cit., p. 267.
56 Ibid., p. 266.
57 Himmelfarb, loc. cit.
58 Scott, op. cit., p. 268.
59 Ibid.
60 Himmelfarb, op. cit., pp. 16, 22, 26.
61 Geoffrey Elton, *The Practice of History*, London: Fontana Paperbacks, 1989 (first Fontana edition, 1969; first published by Sydney University Press, 1967).
62 Ibid., p. 20.
63 Gertrude Himmelfarb, 'Telling It as You Like It: Postmodern History and the Flight from Fact' (first published in 1992), in Keith Jenkins (ed.), *The Postmodern History Reader*, London and New York: Routledge, 1997, pp. 158–74.
64 Judith Allen, 'Evidence and Silence: Feminism and the Limits of History', in Carole Pateman and Elizabeth Gross (eds), *Feminist Challenges: Social and Political Theory*, Sydney, London, Boston MA: Allen & Unwin, 1986, pp. 173–89.
65 Elton, *Return to Essentials*, p. 22.
66 Curthoys and Docker, 'Chapter I: Herodotus and World History', in op. cit., p. 30.
67 Ibid., 'Chapter VI: History, Science and Art', pp. 74–5.
68 Ibid., pp. 75–6.
69 Greg Dening, *History's Anthropology: The Death of William Gooch*, Lanham, New York and London: University Press of America, 1988, pp. 1 and 9.
70 Curthoys and Docker, op. cit., pp. 201–2.
71 Dening, *History's Anthropology*, p. 1.
72 Ibid.
73 Ibid., p. 100.
74 Ibid., p. 9.
75 See Jenkins, 'Chapter 3: Beginning Again, On Disobedient Dispositions', in *Refiguring History*, London and New York: Routledge, 2003, pp. 59 ff.
76 Greg Dening, 'Writing, Rewriting the Beach: an Essay', in Alun Munslow and Robert A. Rosenstone (eds), op. cit., pp. 30–55.
77 Munslow and Rosenstone, ibid., p. 13.
78 Ibid., p. 14.
79 Greg Dening, *Mr Bligh's Bad Language: Passion, Power and Theatre on the Bounty*, Cambridge, New York and Oakleigh, Victoria (Australia): Cambridge University Press, 1992, p. 366.
80 Ibid., p. 367.
81 Robin Bisha, 'Reconstructing the Voice of a Noblewoman of the time of Peter the Great: Daria Mikhailovna Menshikova', in Munslow and Rosenstone (eds), op. cit., pp. 183–94.
82 Ibid., p. 184.

83 Judith P. Zinsser, 'A prologue for La Dame d'Esprit: The biography of the marquise Du Châtelet', in ibid., pp. 195–208.
84 Ibid., p. 201.
85 Ibid., p. 202.
86 LaCapra, op. cit., pp. 64 ff.
87 Ibid., pp. 65, 67.
88 Ibid., p. 68.

3 Negotiating 'difference'

1 Dipesh Chakrabarty, Extract from *Provincializing Europe: Postcolonial Thought and Historical Difference* (Princeton, NJ: Princeton University Press, 2000, pp. 3–11) in Keith Jenkins and Alun Munslow (eds), *The Nature of History Reader*, London, and New York: Routledge, 2004, this passage, p. 193.
2 Chris Weedon, *Feminism, Theory and the Politics of Difference*, Oxford UK and Malden, US: Blackwell Publishers, 1999, p. 100.
3 Chris Weedon, *Feminist Practice & Poststructuralist Theory*, Oxford and Cambridge, Mas.: Blackwell, 1987, p. 25.
4 Weedon, *Politics of Difference*, p. 119.
5 Michel Foucault, 'The Life of Infamous Men', in Meaghan Morris and Paul Patton (eds), *Michel Foucault: Power, Truth, Strategy*, Sydney: Feral Publications, 1979, p. 85.
6 Ibid., p. 86.
7 Weedon, *Politics of Difference*, p. 116.
8 On 'comrade love' in Japan see Gregory M. Pflugfelder, *Cartographies of Desire: Male-Male Sexuality in Japanese Discourse, 1600–1950*, Berkeley, California: University of California Press, 1999.
9 Weedon, *Practice and Poststructuralist Theory*, p. 165.
10 Ann Curthoys and John Docker, *Is History Fiction?*, Sydney: University of New South Wales Press Ltd, 2006, pp. 198–9.
11 Bill Ashcroft, Gareth Griffiths and Helen Tiffin (eds), *The Post-Colonial Studies Reader*, London and New York: Routledge, 1995, p. 8.
12 Linda Gordon, 'What's New in Women's History?', in Sneja Gunew (ed.), *A Reader in Feminist Knowledge*, London: Routledge, 1991, p. 80 (essay first published in 1986).
13 Jean-Paul Sartre's Preface to Frantz Fanon's *The Wretched of the Earth*, 1961 (pp. 25–6), cited in Weedon, *Politics of Difference*, p. 187.
14 Ibid.
15 Chakrabarty, op. cit., p. 192.
16 Marx cited in Edward Said, *Orientalism*, London: Penguin Books, 1978, p. 154.
17 Aijaz Ahmad, Extract from 'Jameson's Rhetoric of Otherness and the "National Allegory"' (*Social Text*, 17, Fall 1987), reproduced in Ashcroft *et al.* (eds), op. cit., p. 77.
18 Ibid., p. 78.
19 Ibid., p. 79.
20 Ibid., p. 82.
21 Dipesh Chakrabarty, 'Minority histories, subaltern pasts', *Postcolonial Studies*, 1998, vol. 1, no. 1, 15.
22 Ibid., p. 16.

23 Weedon, *Practice and Poststructuralist Theory*, p. 148.

24 Amitav Ghosh and Dipesh Chakrabarty, 'A Correspondence on *Provincializing Europe*', *Radical History Review*, Spring 2002, Issue 83, 154–5.

25 On this see my 'Resistance to Difference: Sexual Equality and its Lawful and Out-Law (Anarchist) Advocates in Imperial Japan,' *Intersections*, 2002 (March), Issue 7, 1–11: Murdoch University, Western Australia, e-journal: http://wwwsshe.murdoch.edu.au/intersections/.

26 Gordon, op. cit., p. 79.

27 Elizabeth Gross [Grosz], 'Conclusion: What Is Feminist Theory?', in Carole Pateman and Elizabeth Gross (eds), *Feminist Challenges: Social and Political Theory*, Sydney, London and Boston: Allen & Unwin, 1986, pp. 191–2.

28 Bonnie G. Smith, *The Gender of History: Men, Women, and Historical Practice*, Cambridge, MA and London: Harvard University Press, 1998, p. 1.

29 Ibid.

30 As I indicated in Chapters 1 and 2, the gendering of the discipline itself in masculine terms (in various ways: its 'Oepidal' underpinnings, demands for 'manly' plain language, objectivism also as 'manly', and so on) has also been discussed by Katherine Kearns: *Psychoanalysis, Historiography, and Feminist Theory*, Cambridge: Cambridge University Press, 1997.

31 Mary Spongberg, *Writing Women's History since the Renaissance*, Basingstoke, UK and New York: Palgrave Macmillan, 2002, pp. 186–7.

32 Julia Kristeva, 'Women's Time', *Signs: Journal of Women in Culture and Society*, 1981 (Autumn), vol. 7, no. 1, 13–35 (translated and with an introduction by Alice Jardine and Harry Blake; this issue includes an equally well-known piece by Hélène Cixous, 'Castration and Decapitation', which is also well worth reading, partly because of its humour).

33 Ibid., p. 16.

34 Ibid., p. 17.

35 Joan Kelly-Gadol, 'The Social Relations of the Sexes: Methodological Implications of Women's History', in Sandra Harding (ed.), *Feminism and Methodology: Social Science Issues*, Indiana University Press, 1987, pp. 16–17.

36 Reina Lewis, *Gendering Orientalism: Race, Femininity and Representation*, London and New York: Routledge, 1996, p. 7.

37 Spongberg, op. cit., p. 182.

38 The difference between Zemon Davis's approach and that of Kelly-Gadol is discussed in Curthoys and Docker, op. cit., pp. 171–2.

39 Smith, op. cit., p. 2.

40 Joan Wallach Scott, *Gender and the Politics of History*, New York: Columbia University Press, 1988, p. 197.

41 Gross [Grosz], op. cit., p. 204.

42 Sidonie Smith, *The Poetics of Women's Autobiography: Marginality and the Fictions of Self-Representation*, Bloomington MD and Indianapolis IN: Indiana University Press, 1987, p. 18.

43 It should be noted, however, that in her book, *Undoing Gender* (New York and London: Routledge, 2004, p. 178), Butler acknowledges that, for Irigaray, sexual difference is not 'foundational . . . . not a given . . . a basis

on which to build feminism', but rather 'a *question* that prompts a feminist inquiry', a 'question for our times'.

44　Weedon, *Practice and Poststructuralist Theory*, p. 65.
45　Ibid., p. 150.
46　Lyndal Roper, *Oedipus and the Devil: Witchcraft, Sexuality and Religion in Early Modern Europe*, London and New York: Routledge, 1994 (Chap. 10: 'Oedipus and the Devil'), p. 229.
47　Ibid., p. 233.
48　Ien Ang, Chapter Five: 'I'm a feminist but . . . "Other" Women and Postnational Feminism', in Barbara Caine and Rosemary Pringle (eds), *Transitions: New Australian Feminisms*, NSW: Allen & Unwin, 1995, p. 73.
49　Aileen Moreton-Robinson, *Talkin' Up to the White Woman: Aboriginal Women and Feminism*, Brisbane: University of Queensland Press, 2000, p. 110.
50　Ibid., pp. 110–11.
51　Ien Ang, op. cit., p. 57.
52　Ibid., pp. 57–8.
53　Chandra Talpade Mohanty, 'Cartographies of Struggle: Third World Women and the Politics of Feminism', in Mohanty, Ann Russo and Lourdes Torres (eds), *Third World Women and the Politics of Feminism*, Bloomington IN: Indiana University Press, 1991, p. 4.
54　Ibid., pp. 5–6.
55　Yvonne Corcoran-Nantes, 'Female Consciousness or Feminist Consciousness? Women's Consciousness-Raising in Community-Based Struggles in Brazil', in Bonnie G. Smith (ed.), *Global Feminisms Since 1945*, London and New York: Routledge, 2000, pp. 81–100.
56　Mohanty, op. cit., p. 7.
57　Ibid., p. 4.
58　Ibid., p. 7.
59　Ien Ang, op. cit., p. 73.
60　See Pat O'Shane, 'Is There any Relevance in the Women's Movement for Aboriginal Women?', *Refractory Girl*, 1976 (September), vol. 12, 31–4.
61　Shireen Hassim and Cherryl Walker, 'Women's Studies and the Women's Movement in South Africa: Defining a Relationship', *Women's Studies International Forum*, 1993, vol. 16, no. 5, 523.
62　Ibid., p. 528.
63　Ibid., p. 529.
64　Joan W. Scott, 'Experience', in Judith Butler and Joan W. Scott (eds), *Feminists Theorize the Political*, New York and London: Routledge, 1992, p. 37.
65　Hassim and Walker, op. cit., p. 530.
66　Scott, 'Experience', p. 26.
67　Ibid., p. 33.
68　Lewis, op. cit., p. 3.
69　Ibid., p. 4.
70　Jacques Derrida, *Specters of Marx: The State of the Debt, the Work of Mourning, and the New International*, New York and London: Routledge, 1994, pp. 13–14.

71 Chilla Bulbeck, *Re-Orienting Western Feminisms: Women's Diversity in a Postcolonial World*, Cambridge, Cambridge University Press, 1998, p. 221. (Here she was citing Indrani Ganguly's 'Some Thoughts on Feminism and Racism', *Connect!*, Newsletter of the Australian Sociological Women's Association, 1995, vol. 3, no. 2, p. 4.)

72 Ibid.

73 Iwabuchi Koichi, 'Complicit Exoticism: Japan and Its Other', *Continuum*, 1994, vol. 8, no. 2, 49–82.

74 Ibid., pp. 66–70.

75 Ibid., p. 53.

76 Ibid., pp. 50–3.

77 Ibid., pp. 52–3.

78 Ibid., p. 78.

79 Edward W. Said, *Representations of the Intellectual: The 1993 Reith Lectures*, London: Vintage Random House, 1994, x and p. 9.

80 Ibid., xi, and pp. 10, 15.

81 Rita Felski, 'Fin de Siècle, Fin de Sexe: Transsexuality, Postmodernism and the Death of History', reproduced in Jenkins and Munslow (eds), *The Nature of History Reader*, (Chapter 39), p. 277.

82 Weedon, *Politics of Difference*, pp. 131–2.

83 Corcoran-Nantes, op. cit., p. 98.

84 Reina Lewis and Sara Mills (eds), *Feminist Postcolonial Theory: A Reader*, Edinburgh: Edinburgh University Press, 2003.

85 Felski, loc. cit.

86 Morwenna Griffiths, *Feminisms and the Self: The Web of Identity*, London and New York: Routledge, 1995.

87 I have discussed this issue in relation to the self-representations of Japanese anarchist women of the early twentieth century, for example in 'Anarcho-Feminist Discourse in Prewar Japan: Ito Noe's Autobiographical Social Criticism', *Anarchist Studies* (UK), 2001, vol. 9, 97–125 (particularly Section VI), pp. 115 ff.

88 Merry E. Wiesner-Hanks, *Christianity and Sexuality in the Early Modern World: Regulating Desire, Reforming Practice*, New York and London: Routledge, 2000.

89 Weedon, *Politics of Difference*, p. 133.

90 Ibid., p. 132.

91 Ibid.

92 Ibid., p. 133.

93 Catharine A. MacKinnon, 'From Practice to Theory, or What Is a White Woman Anyway?', *Yale Journal of Law and Feminism*, Fall 1991, vol. 4, no. 1, 13.

94 Ibid., p. 18.

95 Ibid., pp. 18–19.

96 Adrienne Rich (*On Lies, Secrets and Silence: Selected Prose 1966–1978*, London: Virago, 1984, p. 289) cited in Bulbeck, op. cit., pp. 9–10.

97 MacKinnon, op. cit., p. 16.

98 Bulbeck, op. cit., p. 14.

99 Ibid., p. 15.

4 The 'positioned' subject

1 Richard Howard (trans.), *Roland Barthes by Roland Barthes*, London and Basingstoke: Macmillan (first published in French in 1975), 1977, p. 144.
2 Joan Scott, 'The Evidence of Experience', in Gabrielle M. Spiegel (ed.), *Practicing History: New Directions in Historical Writing after the Linguistic Turn*, New York and London: Routledge, 2005, p. 204 (the original, full version of this essay was in *Critical Inquiry*, Summer 1991, vol. 17, 773–97).
3 Michel Foucault, 'What is an Author?', in Paul Rabinow (ed.), *The Foucault Reader*, London: Penguin Books, 1984, pp. 101, 119–20.
4 In Paul Jay's study of Western self-representational 'life' writing (*Being in the Text: Self-Representation from Wordsworth to Roland Barthes*, Ithaca and London: Cornell University Press, 1984), Barthes' style of autobiography critique in his 'anti-autobiography', *Roland Barthes by Roland Barthes*, is seen to follow trends in that direction represented, for example, by Nietzsche and Carlyle (who indulged in a 'retailoring' of the subject) and then Paul Valéry and Barthes (who both posited a 'fragmented' subject).
5 Roland Barthes, *Empire of Signs*, New York: Hill and Wang, 1982 (first published in French in 1970).
6 During a 1984 visit to Japan Derrida apparently disagreed with the view of Japanese postmodernists such as Karatani Kōjin and Asada Akira (and a number of non-Japanese Derridean or other scholars such as Steve Odin, Robert Magiola and David Dilworth) that 'deconstruction' had long existed in Buddhism, most particularly Dōgen's (Sōtō School) Zen. The issue is discussed in Steve Odin, 'Derrida and the Decentred Universe of Ch'an/Zen Buddhism', in Charles Wei-hsun Fu and Steven Heine (eds), *Japan in Traditional and Postmodern Perspectives*, New York: State University of New York, 1995, pp. 1–23. On Dōgen's paradoxical logic, see Abe Masao, 'The Idea of Purity in Mahayana Buddhism', in William R. LaFleur (ed.), *Zen and Western Thought*, Honolulu: University of Hawaii Press, 1985, pp. 216–22.
7 On Barthes and Zen, see my 'Takuboku's "Poetic Diary" and Barthes's Anti-autobiography: (Postmodernist?) Fragmented Selves in Fragments of a Life', *Japanese Studies* (Australia), 1999, vol. 19, no. 2, 183–99.
8 Roland Barthes, 'The Death of the Author', in Stephen Heath (ed., trans.), *Image, Music, Text/Roland Barthes*, London: Fontana Press, 1977, pp. 143–8.
9 Ibid., pp. 142, 146.
10 Alun Munslow, *Deconstructing History*, London and New York: Routledge, 1997, p. 116.
11 Morwenna Griffiths, *Feminisms and the Self: The Web of Identity*, London and New York: Routledge, 1995, p. 179.
12 Paul de Man, 'Autobiography as De-facement', *Modern Language Notes*, 1979, vol. 94, no. 5, 919–30.
13 To cite a few examples, Jacques Derrida, *The Ear of the Other*, New York: Schocken Books, 1985; Paul John Eakin, *Fictions in Autobiography: Studies in the Art of Self-Invention*, Princeton: Princeton University Press, 1985; Sidonie Smith, *A Poetics of Women's Autobiography: Marginality and the Fictions of Self-Representation*, Bloomington: Indiana University Press, 1987 (and her later works).

14 Jean-Michel Raynaud, 'What's What in Biography', in James Walter (ed.), *Reading Life Histories: Griffith Papers on Biography*, Institute for Modern Biography, Brisbane: Griffith University, 1981, p. 93.

15 Ibid.

16 Sidonie Smith and Julia Watson (eds), *De/Colonizing the Subject: The Politics of Gender in Women's Autobiography*, Minneapolis: University of Minnesota Press, 1992 (cf. essays by Caren Kaplan and John Beverley, for example). I have also addressed the differences in resistant sub-genres of life-writing in my 'Death as Life: Political Metaphor in the Testimonial Prison Literature of Kanno Suga', *Bulletin of Concerned Asian Scholars* (US), 1997, vol. 29, no. 4, 3–12; and 'Anarcho-Feminist Discourse in Prewar Japan; Ito Noe's Autobiographical Social Criticism', *Anarchist Studies* (UK), 2001, vol. 9, 97–125.

17 Paul Jay, 'Being in the Text: Autobiography and the Problem of the Subject', *Modern Language Notes*, December 1979, vol. 94, no. 5, 1055.

18 *Roland Barthes by Roland Barthes*, pp. 92–5.

19 A good example was a television interview with the above-mentioned James Frey who, despite the media furore over the degree of inventiveness in his 'non-fictional' 'memoir', *A Million Little Pieces* (Doubleday, 2003), 'still stands by it' on the grounds of its essential truth.

20 *Roland Barthes by Roland Barthes*, p. 151.

21 Cited in Jay, 'Problem of the Subject', p. 1,055.

22 On this prison memoir see Hélène Bowen Raddeker, 'The Past Through Telescopic Sights – Reading the Prison-Life-Story of Kaneko Fumiko', *Japan Forum* (UK), Autumn 1995, vol. 7, no. 2, 155–69; and *Treacherous Women of Imperial Japan: Patriarchal Fictions, Patricidal Fantasies*, London and New York: Routledge, 1997.

23 Dominick LaCapra, *History and Reading: Tocqueville, Foucault, French Studies*, Melbourne: Melbourne University Press, 2000, pp. 60–1.

24 Scott, 'The Evidence of Experience', in Spiegel (ed.), op. cit., p. 205.

25 Ibid., p. 202.

26 Ibid., p. 203.

27 Ibid., p. 213.

28 Ibid., p. 211.

29 Ibid. Scott was discussing essays by Spivak on the Subaltern Studies group, 'A Literary Representation of the Subaltern' and 'Subaltern Studies; Deconstructing Historiography', in Gayatri Chakravorty Spivak, *In Other Worlds: Essays in Cultural Politics*, New York, 1987.

30 Gabrielle M. Spiegel, 'Introduction', in Spiegel (ed.), op. cit., p. 18.

31 Ibid., p. 19.

32 Scott, in Spiegel (ed.), op. cit., p. 213.

33 Ibid., p. 214.

34 Joan W. Scott, 'Experience', in Judith Butler and Joan Scott (eds), *Feminists Theorize the Political*, New York and London: Routledge, 1992. p. 33.

35 Judith Butler, *Undoing Gender*, New York and London: Routledge, 2004, p. 28.

36 Michel Foucault, *The History of Sexuality, Volumes 1 to 3*, New York: Pantheon, 1978–86.

37 Butler, op. cit., p. 181.
38 Annamarie Jagose, *Queer Theory*, Carlton South, Melbourne: Melbourne University Press, 1996, p. 11.
39 Ibid., pp. 11–12.
40 Judith Butler, *Gender Trouble: Feminism and the Subversion of Identity*, New York and London: Routledge, 1999, p. 10.
41 See, for example, Carolyn Brewer, *'Baylan, Asog*, Transvestism and Sodomy: Gender, Sexuality and the Sacred in Early Colonial Philippines, *Intersections*, May 1999, Issue 2, 1–20 (http://wwwsshe.murdoch.edu.au/intersections/).
42 Butler, *Undoing Gender*, p. 55.
43 Ibid., pp. 52–3.
44 Butler, *Gender Trouble*, p. 11.
45 Ibid., pp. 141, 143.
46 Rosi Braidotti, *Metamorphoses: Towards a Materialist Theory of Becoming*, Oxford: Polity Press and Blackwell Publishers, 2002, p. 36.
47 Butler, *Gender Trouble*, pp. 23–4.
48 Brewer, op. cit.
49 bell hooks, 'Postmodern Blackness', in hooks, *Yearning: Race, Gender, and Cultural Politics*, Boston: South End Press, 1990, p. 28.
50 Elizabeth Bird, 'Disciplining the Interdisciplinary: Radicalism and the Academic Curriculum', *British Journal of Sociology of Education*, 2001, vol. 22, no. 4, 476.
51 Ibid., p. 475.
52 Kathy Rudy, 'Radical Feminism, Lesbian Separatism, and Queer Theory', *Feminist Studies*, Spring 2001, vol. 27, no. 1, especially pp. 218–21.
53 hooks, 'Postmodern Blackness', p. 26.
54 Joyce Appleby, Lynn Hunt and Margaret Jacob, *Telling the Truth about History*, New York and London: W.W. Norton and Company, 1994, p. 154.
55 hooks, 'Radical Black Subjectivity', in *Yearning*, op. cit., p. 20.
56 Alcoff's 'Cultural Feminism versus Post-Structuralism: The Identity Crisis in Feminist Theory', cited in ibid.
57 hooks, 'Postmodern Blackness', p. 28.
58 Ibid., p. 26.
59 Gayatri Chakravorty Spivak, 'Subaltern Studies: Deconstructing Historiography' (first published in 1985), in Donna Landry and Gerald Maclean (eds), *The Spivak Reader: Selected Works of Gayatri Chakravorty Spivak*, New York and London: Routledge, 1996, p. 216.
60 Ibid., p. 213.
61 Ibid.
62 Jean-François Lyotard, *The Postmodern Condition: A Report on Knowledge*, Manchester: Manchester University Press, 1984 (first published in French in 1979), p. 15.
63 Spiegel (ed.), op. cit., pp. 1–2.
64 Ibid., p. 3.
65 Ibid.

66 Gareth Stedman Jones, 'The Deterministic Fix: Some Obstacles to the Further Development of the Linguistic Approach to History in the 1990s', in Spiegel (ed.), op. cit., p. 63.

67 Among others, Alfred Schmidt (aligned with the 'critical' Marxism of the Frankfurt School) once criticized Althusserian Marxism in similar terms, however: *History and Structure: An Essay on Hegelian-Marxist and Structuralist Theories of Marxism* (Jeffrey Herf, trans.), Cambridge, MA and London: The MIT Press, 1981.

68 Stedman Jones, op. cit., p. 67.

69 Anthony Giddens, 'The Constitution of Society: Outline of the Theory of Structuration', in Spiegel (ed.), op. cit., p. 123.

70 Mary Spongberg, *Writing Women's History since the Renaissance*, Basingstoke, UK and New York, Palgrave Macmillan, 2002 p. 192.

71 Spiegel, op. cit., p. 4.

72 Spongberg, op. cit., p. 193.

73 William H. Sewell, Jr, 'A Theory of Structure: Duality, Agency and Transformation', in Spiegel (ed.), op. cit., pp. 143–65.

74 Elizabeth Deeds Ermarth, 'Agency in the Discursive Condition', in Spiegel (ed.), ibid., p. 105.

75 Ibid., p. 108.

76 Joan Scott, 'After History?' (1996), in Keith Jenkins and Alun Munslow (eds), *The Nature of History Reader*, London and New York: Routledge, 2004, p. 266.

77 Joan Scott, 'The Evidence of Experience', in Spiegel (ed.), op. cit., p. 212.

78 Ann Curthoys and John Docker, *Is History Fiction?*, Sydney: University of New South Wales Press, 2006, p. 148.

79 Ibid., pp. 146–8.

Bibliography

Readers, edited collections, reference works

Appleby, Joyce *et al.* (eds), *Knowledge and Postmodernism in Historical Perspective*, New York and London: Routledge, 1994.

Ashcroft, Bill, Griffiths, Gareth and Tiffin, Helen (eds), *The Post-Colonial Studies Reader*, London and New York: Routledge, 1995.

Brown, Callum G., *Postmodernism for Historians*, Harlow, UK: Pearson Longman, 2005.

Butler, Judith and Scott, Joan (eds), *Feminists Theorize the Political*, New York and London: Routledge, 1992.

Gibbons, Michael (ed.), *Interpreting Politics*, Oxford and New York, Basil Blackwell, 1987.

Gunew, Sneja (ed.), *A Reader in Feminist Knowledge*, London: Routledge, 1991.

Harding, Sandra (ed.), *Feminism and Methodology: Social Science Issues*, Bloomington: IN: Indiana University Press, 1987.

Jenkins, Keith (ed.), *The Postmodern History Reader*, London and New York: Routledge, 1997.

—— and Munslow, Alun (eds), *The Nature of History Reader*, London and New York: Routledge, 2004.

Landry, Donna and Maclean, Gerald (eds), *The Spivak Reader: Selected Works of Gayatri Chakravorty Spivak*, New York and London: Routledge, 1996.

Lewis, Reina and Mills, Sara (eds), *Feminist Postcolonial Theory: A Reader*, Edinburgh: Edinburgh University Press, 2003.

Mayer Tamar (ed.), *Gender Ironies of Nationalism: Sexing the Nation*, London and New York: Routledge, 2000.

Mohanty, Chandra Talpade, Russo, Ann and Torres Lourdes (eds), *Third World Women and the Politics of Feminism*, Bloomington IN: Indiana University Press, 1991.

Morgan, Sue (ed.), *The Feminist History Reader*, London and New York: Routledge, 2006.

Munslow, Alun, *The Routledge Companion to Historical Studies*, London and New York: Routledge, 2000 (revised 2006).

—— and Rosenstone, Robert A., (eds), *Experiments in Rethinking History*, London and New York: Routledge, 2004.

Pateman, Carole and Gross, Elizabeth (eds), *Feminist Challenges: Social and Political Theory*, Sydney, London and Boston: Allen & Unwin, 1986.

Rabinow, Paul (ed.), *The Foucault Reader*, London: Penguin Books, 1984.

Smith, Bonnie G. (ed.), *Global Feminisms Since 1945*, London and New York: Routledge, 2000.

Spiegel, Gabrielle M., *Practicing History: New Directions in Historical Writing after the Linguistic Turn*, New York and London: Routledge, 2005.

Weed, Elizabeth and Schor, Naomi (ed.), *Feminism Meets Queer Theory*, Bloomington, IN: Indiana University Press, 1997.

Feminism: critiques, history, historiography, interdisciplinary theory

Allen, Judith, 'Evidence and Silence: Feminism and the Limits of History', in Carole Pateman and Elizabeth Gross (eds), *Feminist Challenges: Social and Political Theory*, Sydney, London, Boston: Allen & Unwin, 1986, pp. 173–89.

Ang, Ien, 'I'm a feminist but . . . "Other" Women and Postnational Feminism', in Barbara Caine and Rosemary Pringle (eds), *Transitions: New Australian Feminisms*, NSW: Allen & Unwin, 1995, pp. 57–73.

Appleby, Joyce, Hunt, Lynn and Jacob, Margaret, *Telling the Truth about History*, New York and London: W.W. Norton & Company, 1994.

Bisha, Robin, 'Reconstructing the Voice of a Noblewoman of the Time of Peter the Great: Daria Mikhailovna Menshikova', in Alun Munslow and Robert A. Rosenstone (eds), *Experiments in Rethinking History*, New York and London: Routledge, 2004, pp. 183–94.

Bowen Raddeker, Hélène, 'The Past Through Telescopic Sights – Reading the Prison-Life-Story of Kaneko Fumiko', *Japan Forum* (UK), Autumn 1995, vol. 7, no. 2, 155–69.

—— 'Death as Life: Political Metaphor in the Testimonial Prison Literature of Kanno Suga', *Bulletin of Concerned Asian Scholars* (US), 1997, vol. 29, no. 4, 3–12.

—— *Treacherous Women of Imperial Japan: Patriarchal Fictions, Patricidal Fantasies*, London and New York: Routledge, 1997.

—— 'Takuboku's "Poetic Diary" and Barthes' Anti-autobiography: (Postmodernist?) Fragmented Selves in Fragments of a Life', *Japanese Studies*, (Australia) 1999, vol. 19, no. 2, 183–99.

—— 'Anarcho-Feminist Discourse in Prewar Japan: Ito Noe's Auto-biographical Social Criticism', *Anarchist Studies* (UK), 2001, vol. 9, 97–125.

—— 'Resistance to Difference: Sexual Equality and its Law-ful and Out-Law (Anarchist) Advocates in Imperial Japan', *Intersections*, March 2002. Issue 7, 1–11 (http://wwwsshe.murdoch.edu.au/intersections/).

—— 'Difference between the Waves versus the "Eternal Return": Today's Students of Feminism', *Outskirts*, May 2006, vol. 14 (www.chloe.uwa.edu. au/outskirts/).

Braidotti, Rosi, *Metamorphoses: towards a Materialist Theory of Becoming*, Oxford: Polity Press and Blackwell Publishers, 2002.

Brewer, Carolyn, '*Baylan, Asog*, Transvestism and Sodomy: Gender, Sexuality and the Sacred in Early Colonial Philippines', *Intersections*, May 1999, Issue 2, 1–20 (http://wwwsshe.murdoch.edu.au/intersections/).

Bulbeck, Chilla, *Re-Orienting Western Feminisms: Women's Diversity in a Postcolonial World*, Cambridge: Cambridge University Press, 1998

Butler, Judith, *Gender Trouble: Feminism and the Subversion of Identity*, New York and London: Routledge, 1999.

—— *Undoing Gender*, New York and London: Routledge, 2004.

Corcoran-Nantes, Yvonne, 'Female Consciousness or Feminist Consciousness? Women's Consciousness-Raising in Community-Based Struggles in Brazil', in Bonnie G. Smith (ed.), *Global Feminisms Since 1945*, London and New York: Routledge, 2000, pp. 81–100.

Ermarth, Elizabeth Deeds, 'Beyond the "Subject"', in Keith Jenkins and Alun Munslow, *The Nature of History Reader*, London and New York: Routledge, 2004 (in Part Four, 'Endisms'), pp. 281–95.

—— 'Agency in the Discursive Condition', in Gabrielle M. Spiegel (ed.), *Practicing History: New Directions in Historical Writing after the Linguistic Turn*, New York and London: Routledge, 2005, pp. 99–110.

Felski, Rita, 'Fin de Siècle, Fin de Sexe: Transsexuality, Postmodernism and the Death of History', *Literary Theory*, vol. 27, no. 2, pp. 337–49, reproduced in Jenkins and Munslow (eds), *The Nature of History Reader*, Part Four, 'Endisms', Chapter 39, pp. 270–80.

Gordon, Linda, 'What's New in Women's History?', in Sneja Gunew (ed.), *A Reader in Feminist Knowledge*, London: Routledge, 1991, pp. 73–82.

Griffiths, Morwenna, *Feminisms and the Self: The Web of Identity*, London and New York: Routledge, 1995.

Hassim, Shireen and Walker, Cherryl, 'Women's Studies and the Women's Movement in South Africa: Defining a Relationship', *Women's Studies International Forum*, 1993, vol. 16, no. 5, 523–34.

hooks, bell, *Yearning: Race, Gender, and Cultural Politics*, Boston: South End Press, 1990.

Irigaray, Luce, *This Sex which Is Not One*, (Catherine Porter, trans.), Ithaca: Cornell University Press, 1985.

—— *An Ethics of Sexual Difference* (Carolyn Burke and Gillian C. Gill, trans.), Ithaca: Cornell University Press, 1993.

Jagose, Annamarie, *Queer Theory*, Carlton South, Melbourne: Melbourne University Press, 1996.

Kearns, Katherine, *Psychoanalysis, Historiography, and Feminist Theory: The Search for a Critical Method*, Cambridge: Cambridge University Press, 1997.

Kristeva, Julia, 'Women's Time' (translated and with an introduction by Alice Jardine and Harry Blake), *Signs: Journal of Women in Culture and Society*, 1981 (Autumn), vol. 7, no. 1, 13–35.

Lewis, Reina, *Gendering Orientalism: Race, Femininity and Representation*, London and New York: Routledge, 1996.

Loomba, Ania, *Colonialism/Postcolonialism*, New York and London: Routledge, 1998.

MacKinnon, Catharine A., 'From Practice to Theory, or What Is a White Woman Anyway?', *Yale Journal of Law and Feminism*, Fall 1991, vol. 4, no. 1, 13–22.

Maracek, Jeanne '"Am I a Woman in These Matters?" Notes on Sinhala Nationalism and Gender in Sri Lanka', in Tamar Mayer (ed.), *Gender Ironies of Nationalism: Sexing the Nation*, London and New York: Routledge, 2000, pp. 139–60.

Moreton-Robinson, Aileen, *Talkin' Up to the White Woman: Aboriginal Women and Feminism*, Brisbane: University of Queensland Press, 2000.

O'Shane, Pat, 'Is There Any Relevance in the Women's Movement for Aboriginal Women?', *Refractory Girl*, 1976 (September), vol. 12, 31–4.

Roces, Mina, 'Gender, Nation and the Politics of Dress in Twentieth-Century Philippines', *Gender and History*, 2005 (Aug.), vol. 17, no. 2, 1–24.

Roper, Lyndal, *Oedipus and the Devil: Witchcraft, Sexuality and Religion in Early Modern Europe*, London and New York: Routledge, 1994.

Rudy, Kathy, 'Radical Feminism, Lesbian Separatism, and Queer Theory', *Feminist Studies*, Spring 2001, vol. 27, no. 1, 191–222.

Scott, Joan Wallach, *Gender and the Politics of History*, New York: Columbia University Press, 1988.

—— *Only Paradoxes to Offer: French Feminists and the Rights of Man*, Cambridge Mas. and London: Harvard University Press, 1996.

—— 'The Evidence of Experience', in Gabrielle M. Spiegel (ed.), *Practicing History: New Directions in Historical Writing after the Linguistic Turn*, New York and London: Routledge, 2005, pp. 199–216 (a different abridged version than the above; first published in *Critical Inquiry*, Summer 1991, vol. 17, 773–97).

—— 'Experience', in Judith Butler and Joan W. Scott (eds), *Feminists Theorize the Political*, New York and London: Routledge, 1992, pp. 22–40.

—— 'After History?', abridged version in Keith Jenkins and Alun Munslow (eds), *The Nature of History Reader*, London and New York: Routledge, 2004, Part Four: 'Endisms', Chapter 38, pp. 259–70.

Simonton, Deborah, *A History of European Women's Work, 1700 to the Present*, London and New York: Routledge, 1998.

Smith, Bonnie G., *The Gender of History: Men, Women, and Historical Practice*, Cambridge, Mas. and London: Harvard University Press, 1998.

Smith, Sidonie, *A Poetics of Women's Autobiography: Marginality and the Fictions of Self-Representation*, Bloomington, IN: Indiana University Press, 1987.

—— and Julia Watson (eds), *De/Colonizing the Subject: The Politics of Gender in Women's Autobiography*, Minneapolis: University of Minnesota Press, 1992.

Somekawa, Ellen and Smith, Elizabeth, 'Theorizing the Writing of History or "I Can't Think Why It Should Be so Dull, for a Great Deal of It Must Be Invention"', *Journal of Social History*, 1988, vol. 22, no. 1, 149–61.

Spivak, Gayatri Chakravorty, 'Can the Subaltern Speak?', in Bill Ashcroft, Gareth Griffiths and Helen Tiffin (eds), *The Post-Colonial Studies Reader*, London and New York: Routledge, 1995 (essay first published 1988), pp. 24–8.

—— 'Subaltern Studies: Deconstructing Historiography' (first published in 1985), in Donna Landry and Gerald Maclean (eds), *The Spivak Reader: Selected Works of Gayatri Chakravorty Spivak*, New York and London: Routledge, 1996, pp. 203–35.

Spongberg, Mary, *Writing Women's History since the Renaissance*, Basingstoke, UK and New York: Palgrave Macmillan, 2002.

Steele, Cynthia, '"A Woman Fell into the River": Negotiating Female Subjects in Contemporary Mayan Theatre', in Diana Taylor and Juan Villegas (eds), *Negotiating Performance: Gender, Sexuality and Theatricality in Latin/o America*, Durham: Duke University Press, 1994, pp. 239–56.

Weedon, Chris, *Feminist Practice and Poststructuralist Theory*, Oxford and Cambridge, Mas.: Blackwell, 1987.

—— *Feminism, Theory and the Politics of Difference*, Oxford, UK and Malden US: Blackwell Publishers, 1999.

Wiesner-Hanks, Merry E., *Sexuality and Religion in Early Modern Europe*, London and New York: Routledge, 1994.

—— *Christianity and Sexuality in the Early Modern World: Regulating Desire, Reforming Practice*, New York and London: Routledge, 2000.

——Judith P. Zinsser, 'A Prologue for La Dame d'Esprit: The Biography of the Marquise Du Châtelet', in Alun Munslow and Robert A. Rosenstone, (eds), *Experiments in Rethinking History*, London and New York: Routledge, 2004, pp. 195–208.

Other works: history, historiography, interdisciplinary theory

Abe Masao, 'The Idea of Purity in Mahayana Buddhism', in William R. LaFleur (ed.), *Zen and Western Thought*, Honolulu: University of Hawaii Press, 1985, pp. 216–22.

Ahmad, Aijaz, Extract from 'Jameson's Rhetoric of Otherness and the "National Allegory"' (*Social Text*, 17, Fall 1987), reproduced in Ashcroft, Bill, Griffiths, Gareth and Tiffin, Helen (eds), *The Post-Colonial Studies Reader*, London and New York: Routledge, 1995, pp. 77–82.

Ankersmit, F. R., 'Historiography and Postmodernism', in Keith Jenkins (ed.), *The Postmodern History Reader*, London and New York: Routledge, 1997, pp. 277–97.

Austen, Jane, *Northanger Abbey*, Middlesex England: Penguin Books, 1972 (1976 reprint).

Barthes, Roland, *Roland Barthes by Roland Barthes* (Richard Howard, trans.), London and Basingstoke: Macmillan, 1977.

—— 'The Death of the Author', in Stephen Heath (ed., trans.), *Image, Music, Text/Roland Barthes*, London: Fontana Press, 1977, pp. 143–8.

—— *Empire of Signs*, New York: Hill and Wang, 1982.

—— 'The Discourse of History', excerpt (Section III: 'Signification') reproduced in Keith Jenkins (ed.), *The Postmodern History Reader*. London and New York: Routledge, 1997, pp. 120–3.

Breen, John and Teeuwen, Mark (eds), *Shinto in History: Ways of the Kami*, Surrey: Curzon Press, 2000.

Chakrabarty, Dipesh, 'Minority histories, subaltern pasts', *Postcolonial Studies*, 1998, vol. 1, no. 1, 15–29.

—— *Provincializing Europe: Postcolonial Thought and Historical Difference* (Princeton: Princeton University Press, 2000.

Clendinnen, Inga, *Ambivalent Conquests: Maya and Spaniard in Yucatan, 1517–1570*, Cambridge, New York and Melbourne: Cambridge University Press, 1987.

Curthoys, Ann and Docker, John, *Is History Fiction?*, Sydney: University of New South Wales Press, 2006.

Dening, Greg, *The Bounty: An Ethnographic History*, Melbourne: Melbourne University Press Monograph Series, 1988.

—— *History's Anthropology: The Death of William Gooch*, Lanham, New York and London: University Press of America, 1988.

—— *Mr Bligh's Bad Language: Passion, Power and Theatre on the Bounty*, Cambridge, New York, and Oakleigh, Victoria (Australia): Cambridge University Press, 1992.

—— 'Writing, Rewriting the Beach: an Essay', in Alun Munslow and Robert A. Rosenstone (eds), *Experiments in Rethinking History*, London and New York: Routledge, 2004, pp. 30–55

Derrida, Jacques, *The Ear of the Other*, New York: Schocken Books, 1985.

—— *Writing and Difference* (Alan Bass, trans.), London: Routledge, 1990.

—— *Specters of Marx: The State of the Debt, the Work of Mourning, and the New International*, New York and London: Routledge, 1994.

Dower, John (ed.), *Origins of the Modern Japanese State: Selected Writings of E .H. Norman*, New York: Pantheon Books, 1975 (Introduction).

Eakin, Paul John, *Fictions in Autobiography: Studies in the Art of Self-Invention*, Princeton: Princeton University Press, 1985.

Elton, Geoffrey, *The Practice of History*, London: Fontana Paperbacks, 1989 (first published by Sydney University Press, 1967).

—— *Return to Essentials*, Cambridge: Cambridge University Press, 1991.

Fogel, Joshua A. (ed.), *The Teleology of the Modern Nation-State: Japan and China*, Philadelphia: University of Pennsylvania Press, 2005.

Foucault, Michel, *The History of Sexuality, Volumes 1 to 3*, New York: Pantheon, 1978–86.

——— 'The Life of Infamous Men', in Meaghan Morris and Paul Patton (eds), *Michel Foucault: Power, Truth, Strategy*, Sydney: Feral Publications, 1979, pp. 76–91.

——— 'Nietzsche, Genealogy, History', in Paul Rabinow (ed.), *The Foucault Reader*, London: Penguin Books, 1984, pp. 76–100.

——— 'What is an Author?', in Paul Rabinow (ed.), *The Foucault Reader*, London, Penguin Books, 1984, pp. 101–20.

Ghosh, Amitav and Chakrabarty, Dipesh, 'A Correspondence on *Provincializing Europe*, *Radical History Review*, Spring 2002, Issue 83, 146–72.

Giddens, Anthony, 'The Constitution of Society: Outline of the Theory of Structuration', in Gabrielle M. Spiegel (ed.), *Practicing History: New Directions in Historical Writing after the Linguistic Turn*, New York and London: Routledge, 2005, pp. 121–42.

Hardacre, Helen, 'Creating State Shinto: The Great Promulgation Campaign and the New Religions', *Journal of Japanese Studies*, 1986 (Winter), vol. 12, no. 1, 29–63.

——— *Shinto and the State, 1868–1988*, Princeton: Princeton University Press, 1989.

Himmelfarb, Gertrude, *The New History and the Old: Critical Essays and Reappraisals*, Cambridge, Mas. and London: The Belknap Press of Harvard University Press, 1987, p. 16 (essay first published in 1984).

——— 'Telling It as You Like It: Postmodernist History and the Flight from Fact', in Keith Jenkins (ed.), *The Postmodern History Reader*. London and New York: Routledge, 1997, pp. 158–74.

Hobsbawm, Eric and Ranger, Terence (eds), *The Invention of Tradition*, Cambridge: Cambridge University Press, 1983 (Canto Edition 1992).

Iwabuchi, Koichi, 'Complicit Exoticism: Japan and Its Other', *Continuum*, 1994, vol. 8, no. 2, 49–82.

Jameson, Fredric, *The Prison-House of Language: A Critical Account of Structuralism and Russian Formalism*, Princeton: Princeton University Press, 1972.

Jay, Paul, *Being in the Text: Self-Representation from Wordsworth to Roland Barthes*, Ithaca and London: Cornell University Press, 1984.

Jenkins, Keith, *Re-Thinking History*, London and New York: Routledge, 1991.

——— *Refiguring History: New Thoughts on an Old Discipline*, London and New York: Routledge, 2003.

Kellner, Hans, 'Language and Historical Representation', in Keith Jenkins (ed.), *The Postmodern History Reader*, London, New York, Canada: Routledge, 1997, pp. 127–38.

Kuroda, Toshio, 'Shinto in the History of Japanese Religion', *Journal of Japanese Studies*, 1981, vol. 7, no. 1, 1–21.

LaCapra, Dominick, *History and Reading: Tocqueville, Foucault, French Studies*, Toronto: University of Toronto Press (Melbourne University Press reprint), 2000.

LaFleur, William R. (ed.), *Zen and Western Thought*, Honolulu: University of Hawaii Press, 1985.

Lawson, Hilary, *Reflexivity: The Post-Modern Predicament*, London: Hutchinson, 1985.

Lyotard, Jean-François, *The Postmodern Condition: A Report on Knowledge* (Geoff Bennington and Brian Massumi, trans.; foreword by Frederick Jameson), (Manchester: Manchester University Press, copyright 1984 (2004 reprint).

de Man, Paul, 'Autobiography as De-facement', *Modern Language Notes*, 1979, vol. 94, no. 5, 919–30.

May, Reinhard, *Heidegger's Hidden Sources: East Asian Influences on his Work*, (Graham Parkes, trans.), London and New York: Routledge, 1996.

Munslow, Alun, *Deconstructing History*, London and New York: Routledge, 1997.

Odin, Steve, 'Derrida and the Decentred Universe of Ch'an/Zen Buddhism', in Charles Wei-hsun Fu and Steven Heine (eds), *Japan in Traditional and Postmodern Perspectives*, New York: State University of New York, 1995, pp. 1–23.

Ooms, Herman, *Tokugawa Ideology: Early Constructs, 1570–1680*, Princeton, NJ: Princeton University Press, 1985.

Pflugfelder, Gregory M., *Cartographies of Desire: Male-Male Sexuality in Japanese Discourse, 1600–1950*, Berkeley, CA: University of California Press, 1999.

Philipp, June, 'Traditional Historical Narrative and Action-Oriented (or Ethnographic) History', *Historical Studies* (Australia), 1983 (Apr), vol. 2, 339–52.

Raynaud, Jean-Michel, 'What's What in Biography', in James Walter (ed.), *Reading Life Histories: Griffith Papers on Biography*, Institute for Modern Biography, Brisbane: Griffith University, 1981.

Said, Edward W., *Orientalism*, London: Penguin Books, 1978.

—— *Representations of the Intellectual: The 1993 Reith Lectures*, London: Vintage Random House, 1994.

Schmidt, Alfred, *History and Structure: An Essay on Hegelian-Marxist and Structuralist Theories of Marxism* (Jeffrey Herf, trans.), Cambridge, MA: and London, The MIT Press, 1981.

Sewell, William H. Jr, 'A Theory of Structure: Duality, Agency and Transformation', in Gabrielle M. Spiegel (ed.), *Practicing History: New Directions in Historical Writing after the Linguistic Turn*, New York and London: Routledge, 2005, pp. 143–65.

Spiegel, Gabrielle, 'History, Historicism and the Social Logic of the Text in the Middle Ages', in Keith Jenkins (ed.), *The Postmodern History Reader*, London and New York: Routledge, 1997, pp. 260–73.

Stedman Jones, Gareth, 'The Deterministic Fix: Some Obstacles to the Further Development of the Linguistic Approach to History in the 1990s', in Gabrielle M. Spiegel (ed.), *Practicing History: New Directions in Historical Writing after the Linguistic Turn*, New York and London: Routledge, 2005, pp. 62–75.

Stone, Lawrence, 'The Revival of Narrative: Reflections on a New Old History', *Past and Present*, 1979 (Nov.), vol. 85, 3–24.

Tonomura, Hitomi, *Community and Commerce in Late Medieval Japan: The Corporate Villages of Tokuchin-ho*, Stanford: Stanford University Press, 1992.

White, Hayden, *Metahistory: The Historical Imagination in the Nineteenth Century*, Baltimore: Johns Hopkins University Press, 1973.

—— *Tropics of Discourse: Essays in Cultural Criticism*, Baltimore: Johns Hopkins University Press, 1978.

—— *The Content of the Form: Narrative Discourse and Historical Representation*, Baltimore: Johns Hopkins University Press, 1987.

Windshuttle, Keith, *The Killing of History*, Sydney: Macleay Publications, 1994.

Index

abortion, incidence in history 86
Acton, Lord 59
'After History' (J. W. Scott) 44, 47, 54, 82, 193
'Agency in the Discursive Condition' (E. D. Ermarth) 191
Ahmad, Aijaz 109–10
Alcott, Linda 183
Allen, Judith 92–3; and Elton 85, 86, 87, 118
anarchism 102, 163
Ang, Ien 129, 130, 131, 133
Ankersmit, Frank 20–1, 24–5, 57–8, 73
Asiatic Mode of Production, Marx on 109
Austen, Jane 19, 26
Australia: history education 6
author functions, Foucault on 155
authorial authenticity, humanistic-individualistic notion of 156–7
authorial intention *see* intentionality
autobiographies: and Barthes 152, 153, 160–2; conventional 160, 161; and Derrida 75; life-writing 158; modernist-humanist genre 159; and postmodernism 27

Barthes, Roland 12, 15; anti-humanism of 185; 'The Death of the Author' 155, 156; 'The Discourse of History' 22–3;

Empire of Signs 155, 156; and Foucault 155; on 'fragmented' or multiple selves 153, 157–8; on meaning 24–5; on Nietzsche 25, 29, 45; on reality effect 29, 153; *Roland Barthes by Roland Barthes* 152, 153, 155, 160–2; on Self 45, 153; on self-referentiality in language 21; on status of history as distinct knowledge 24; as structuralist 23
Bartholome, Regina 126–8
beginnings/origins 64–5
Beyond Good and Evil (F. Nietzsche) 73
binarisms, and difference 22
biographies 153, 158, 159–60
Bird, Elizabeth 180
Bisha, Robin 93
Bloch, Marc 39
Bourdieu, Pierre 189
Brewer, Carolyn 177–8
British monarchy 65–6
Brown, Callum 22, 74, 206n
Browne, Henriette 137
Buddhism: co-dependence concept 156; and Japan 77; and kami 76–7; and neo-Confucianism 67; on Self, concept of 12, 45, 156, 162; *see also* Zen
Bulbeck, Chilla 149
bushi (shogunal) rule, Japan 76

ROUTLEDGE HISTORY

Historics

Martin L. Davies

From an author at the forefront of research in this area comes this provocative and seminal work that presents a unique and fresh new look at history and theory.

Taking a broadly European view, the book draws on works of French and German philosophy, some of which are unknown to the English-speaking world, and Martin L. Davies spells out what it is like to live in a historicized world, where any event is presented as historical as, or even before, it happens.

Challenging basic assumptions made by historians, Davies focuses on historical ideas and thought about the past instead of examining history as a discipline. The value of history in and for contemporary culture is explained not only in terms of cultural and institutional practices but in forms of writing and representation of historical issues too.

Historics stimulates thinking about the behaviours and practice that constitute history, and introduces complex ideas in a clear and approachable style. This important text is recommended not only for a wide student audience, but for the more discerning general reader as well.

ISBN10: 0–415–26165–1 (hbk)
ISBN10: 0–415–26166–X (pbk)

ISBN13: 978–0–415–26165–4 (hbk)
ISBN13: 978–0–415–26166–1 (pbk)

Available at all good bookshops
For ordering and further information please visit:
www.routledge.com

ROUTLEDGE HISTORY

Rethinking History

Keith Jenkins

'A startlingly clear and thought-provoking
introduction to current central debates in history
and historiography.'

Robert Eaglestone, Royal Holloway,
University of London

History means many things to many people. But
finding an answer to the question 'what is history?' is
a take few feel equipped to answer. Yet, at the same
time, history has never been more popular. In
understanding our present it seems we cannot escape
the past. In this Routledge Classic Keith Jenkins
guides the reader through the controversies and
debates that currently surround historical thinking
and offers readers the means to make their own
discoveries.

ISBN10: 0–415–30443–1 (pbk)

ISBN13: 978–0–415–30443–6 (pbk)

ROUTLEDGE HISTORY

What is History For?

Beverley Southgate

'An essential read . . . this is an informed scholarly and lucidly written text on the purposes of history which also confronts the inadequate shibboleths of today's dominant 'history culture'.
Professor Keith Jenkins, University College, Chichester

'Beverly Southgate has an elegant and open style that is an excellent vehicle for getting complex ideas across'
Professor Alun Munslow, University of Staffordshire

What is History For? is a timely publication that examines the purpose and point of historical studies. Recent debates on the role of the humanities and the ongoing impact of post-structuralist thought on the very nature of historical enquiry, have rendered the question of what history is for of utmost importance.

Charting the development of historical studies, Beverley Southgate examines the various uses to which history has been put. While history has often supposedly been studies 'for its own sake', Southgate argues that this seemingly innocent approach masks an inherent conservatism and exposes the ways in which history has, sometimes deliberately, sometimes inadvertently, been used for socio-political purposes. This fascinating historicisation of the study of history is unique in its focus on the future of the subject as well as its past and provides compulsive reading for students and the general reader alike.

ISBN10: 0-415-35098-0 (hbk)   ISBN13: 978-0-415-35098-3 (hbk)
ISBN10: 0-415-35099-9 (pbk)   ISBN13: 978-0-415-35099-0 (pbk)

Available at all good bookshops
For ordering and further information please visit:
www.routledge.com

ROUTLEDGE HISTORY

Making History

An Introduction to the History and Practices of a Discipline

EDITED BY

Peter Lambert
and Philipp Schofield

Making History offers a fresh perspective on the study of history. It is a detailed exploration of the practice of history, of historical traditions and of the theories that surround them. Discussing the development and growth of history as a discipline and of the profession of the historian, the book encompasses a huge diversity of influences to examine the professionalisation of the discipline, significant movements in the study of history, e.g. the Annales school, and amateur historical practices, this volume offers a coherent and carefully considered set of chapters to support students and scholars interested in how historical processes have shaped the discipline of history.

ISBN10: 0–415–24254–1 (hbk)
ISBN10: 0–415–24255–X (pbk)

ISBN13: 978–0–415–24254–7 (hbk)
ISBN13: 978–0–415–24255–4 (pbk)

Available at all good bookshops
For ordering and further information please visit:
www.routledge.com

The Routledge Companion to

Historical Studies

SECOND EDITION

Alun Munslow

The Routledge Companion to Historical Studies provides a much-needed critical introduction to the major historians and philosophers together with the central issues, ideas and theories which have prompted the rethinking of history that has gathered pace since the 1990s.

With twenty-nine new entries, and many that have been substantially updated, key concepts for the new history are examined through the ideas of leading thinkers such as Kant, Nietzsche, Croce, Collingwood, White, Foucault and Derrida, and subjects range over class, empiricism, hermeneutics, inference, relativism and technology.

With a revised introduction setting out the state of the discipline of history today, as well as an extended and updated bibliography, this is the essential reference work for all students of history.

ISBN10: 0–415–38576–8 (hbk)
ISBN10: 0–415–38577–6 (pbk)

ISBN13: 978–0–415–38576–3 (hbk)
ISBN13: 978–0–415–38577–0 (pbk)

ROUTLEDGE HISTORY

Deconstructing History

SECOND EDITION

Alun Munslow

Surveying the latest research, this welcome second edition of Alun Munslow's successful *Deconstructing History* provides an excellent introduction to the debates and issues of post-modernist history.

This new edition has been updated and revised and, along with the original discussion material and topics, now:

- assesses the claims of history as a form of 'truthful' explanation
- discusses the limits of conventional historical thinking and practice, and the responses of the 'new empiricists' to the book's central arguments
- examines the arrival of 'experimental history' and its implications
- clarifies the utility of addressing Michael Foucault and Hayden White, and strengthens the analysis of Frank R. Ankersmit's recent work.

Along with an updated glossary, and a revised bibliography, this second edition will not only live up to its predecessor's reputation, but will surpass it as the most essential student resource for studying history and its practice.

ISBN10: 0–415–39143–1 (hbk)
ISBN10: 0–415–39144–X (pbk)
ISBN13: 978–0–415–39143–6 (hbk)
ISBN13: 978–0–415–39144–3 (pbk)

Available at all good bookshops
For ordering and further information please visit:
www.routledge.com